Yale Russian and East European Studies, 14

Structure, Sign, and Function

Selected Essays by Jan Mukařovský

translated and edited by

John Burbank and Peter Steiner

New Haven and London   Yale University Press   1978

Published with assistance from the
Louis Stern Memorial Fund.

Designed by John O. C. McCrillis
and set in Baskerville type.
Printed in the United States of America by
The Vail-Ballou Press, Inc., Binghamton, New York.

Published in Great Britain, Europe, Africa, and Asia
(except Japan) by Yale University Press, Ltd., London.
Distributed in Latin America by Kaiman & Polon, Inc.,
New York City; in Australia and New Zealand by Book
& Film Services, Artarmon, N.S.W., Australia; and in
Japan by Harper & Row, Publishers, Tokyo Office.

Library of Congress Cataloging in Publication Data

Mukařovský, Jan.
    Structure, sign, and function.
    (Yale Russian and East European studies, 14)
    "Selected bibliography of Jan Mukařovský's writings":
p.
    Includes index.
    1. Aesthetics—Addresses, essays, lectures.
2. Arts—Addresses, essays, lectures. 3. Mukařovský,
Jan—Addresses, essays, lectures. I. Title.
II. Series.
BH39.M8175 1978   111.8'5   77-76310
ISBN 0-300-02108-9

Contents

Preface

Structure, Sign, and Function is the second half of a project begun more than five years ago to make available to the English reader a substantial selection of Jan Mukařovský's critical writings. The first volume, *The Word and Verbal Art* (New Haven, 1977), comprised essays devoted to literature. The present volume contains sixteen of Mukařovský's essays on aesthetics and arts other than literature.

The title of this volume draws attention to three terms—structure, sign, and function—which are crucial for Mukařovský's structuralism. His dialectic definition of *structure,* by which he means only a collection of elements whose intrinsic organization is contradictory, causing the permanent movement of the whole, differs significantly from other conceptions of wholeness (for example, German holism). The hierarchy, the mutual subordination and superordination of elements, is in constant motion, and the units which come to the fore at a particular moment constitute the meaning of the aesthetic structure. The work of art is also a *sign* which mediates communication between an artist and his audience. Unlike other signs, however, the artistic sign does not refer exclusively to a particular *denotatum* but rather binds the perceiver's attention to the process of the genesis of meaning. And finally *function* differentiates a work of art from other conscious human creations. The work of art is a tangle of various possible functions, but the only necessary function is the aesthetic, that is, the one not aimed at any particular purpose. In Mukařovský's axiological system the concept of function is closely connected with the notions of norm and value.

Translating Mukařovský's work necessarily entails certain problems. First, since Czech is a highly inflected language, long sentences are not only frequent in writing but typical. The length and complexity of the sentences, moreover, cause the paragraph to play a relatively insignificant role, so that extremely long, loosely constructed paragraphs are quite common in scholarly Czech prose. Therefore, part of translating consisted in dividing excessively long sentences into shorter ones and in some instances in reparagraphing the text.

Secondly, Mukařovský indulged in certain stylistic idiosyncrasies as a reflection of his theoretical outlook. For example, he conceived of structures as processes—dynamic wholes whose elements are charged with energy and interlocked in an ongoing struggle for domination. This point of view accounts for the unusual animation of his descriptions of artistic structures, often created by the use of animate verbs with inanimate subjects. We have been forced at times to tone down this stylistic trait, as it sometimes leads to rather ludicrous English formulations.

Finally, since several of Mukařovský's essays were originally lectures or rough drafts, they lack full documentation. Whenever possible, we have rectified this difficulty, although in a few instances we have been unable to obtain the books or periodicals referred to or even to establish the source altogether. In addition to bibliographical footnotes we have provided some essays with editorial notes where further clarification seemed advisable. Originally we intended to append a brief glossary of the Czech writers whose names appear in Mukařovský's essays, for the convenience of those not familiar with Czech literature. However, Arne Novák's comprehensive volume, *Czech Literature* (Ann Arbor, 1976), has now appeared, which in every respect does more justice to these writers than our short glossary could possibly have done.

We wish to acknowledge with much gratitude the assistance of many people in this project: Professors Peter Demetz, Victor Erlich, Jaroslav Pelikan, René Wellek, and Thomas Winner; F. W. Galan; our editors Whitney Blake, Ellen Graham, and Lynn Walterick; Wendy Steiner; Michelle Burbank; Professor Vadim Liapunov; and Dr. Bedřich Steiner.

March 1977   JOHN BURBANK
                                                                      PETER STEINER

Jan Mukařovský's Structural Aesthetics

"Aesthetics has never fared well. A late arrival in the world as a younger sister of logic, it has been treated with contempt from the start. Whether as the doctrine of an inferior knowledge or as the science of the sensuous veiling of the Absolute, it has always remained something subordinate and incidental. Perhaps on this account and perhaps because of an obscurity in the subject itself, aesthetics has never been able to claim either a sharply defined field or a reliable method."

With these gloomy words, the prominent twentieth-century aesthetician Max Dessoir began the first chapter of his trail-blazing book, *Ästhetik und allgemeine Kunstwissenschaft.*[1] In it he laid out a comprehensive survey of the significant aesthetic theories of his time, dividing them into two broad categories: aesthetic objectivism and aesthetic subjectivism. Under the objectivistic heading he included "all those theories which find the distinguishing feature of aesthetics in the constitution of the object, not in the attitude of the subject who enjoys it" (p. 35), whereas the subjectivistic for him were all those theories which understood aesthetics "as a science of a certain kind of attitude, of inner experience, or the science of a psychic echo" (p. 48). Even though, as Dessoir indicated, not every aesthetician of his day subscribed to such a radical dualism, neglecting one or the other component of the aesthetic interaction, their epistemological outlooks coincided in one important respect. They viewed the aesthetic interaction as involving only two elements—the object of aesthetic experience and the experiencing subject.

The structuralist aesthetics formulated by Jan Mukařovský in the late twenties departed radically from this tradition. It had become clear to Mukařovský that this two-term aesthetics left out a crucial factor. Between the subject and the object, he claimed, lay the paradigm of socially existing aesthetic norms which condition and determine any subject-object interaction which is to be considered aesthetic. Mukařovský succinctly expressed his position on this issue in an encyclopedia entry on "Beauty" in 1934. "Beauty," he

Terms imposed by contract required that this introduction be approved by the Czech copyright holder before publication. It has been slightly edited in consequence.

1. *Aesthetics and Theory of Art,* trans. S. A. Emery (Detroit, 1970).

wrote, "is neither a metaphysical idea shining through empirical reality, nor is it a real attribute of things. The proof of this is the variability in aesthetic evaluations of the same phenomena caused by a change in time or social milieu. This, however, should not lead us to aesthetic subjectivism. Aesthetic norms exist objectively (i.e., independently of the subjective will and of the subjective dispositions of the individual) in the awareness of collectivities. . . . The set of these norms, the aesthetic canon, is changeable above all because it develops. . . . In a particular developmental stage, however, and in a particular collectivity, the aesthetic canon is fixed and obligatory (the ruling taste)."[2]

The contrast we have drawn so far between pre-structuralist and structuralist aesthetics needs some modification at this point, as it is both overly simplified and static. The danger of such sweeping generalities cannot be overemphasized in dealing with structuralism, since for Mukařovský it was neither a theory nor a method, neither "a fixed body of knowledge . . . [nor] an equally unified and unchangeable set of working rules," but an "epistemological stance, from which particular methodological rules and particular knowledge follow, but which exists independently of them and is therefore capable of development in both these directions."[3] Mukařovský's structuralist aesthetics must therefore be seen as a process, a way of posing questions rather than a closed system.

Mukařovský himself stressed many times the fact that his theories were in a constant process of development. "The work does not come to the man in the way he would wish but as a problem evolves from another problem," he observed in an interview for a popular journal in 1942. "For the scholar, almost every study is a further step from which he can see a wider horizon than he could from the previous one." He went on to outline the sequence of central concerns in his development as a theorist: (1) the work of art as an object; (2) development in art; (3) the sign and meaning; (4) the relationship between the creating individual and his work.[4] Twenty-four years later, commenting on the essays from the years

2. "Krása," Ottův slovník naučný nové doby, vol. 3, pt. 2 (Prague, 1934), p. 825.
3. "Strukturalismus v estetice a ve vědě o literatuře" [Structuralism in aesthetics and the study of literature], Kapitoly z české poetiky [Chapters in Czech poetics], 2d ed., vol. 1 (Prague, 1948), p. 13.
4. "Strukturalismus pro každého" [Structuralism for everyone], Čteme 4 (1942), no. 5: 57–58.

1931–1947 collected in *Studie z estetiky* (Studies in Aesthetics), he again contrasted the epistemological unity of his aesthetics to its developmental transformations.

> This book is the result of work determined from stage to stage by a consistent epistemological orientation. But because we are dealing with a *process* of cognition, with the posing of questions which at the time when the individual essays came about were not usually posed in the study of art, its path is not unequivocally straight. Not everything could have been un-ambiguous from the very beginning. One does not ask about things which are clear *in advance*. This book is, however, a cluster of questions. But to believe that the path of theoretical knowledge must be a straight and smooth road is to know nothing about the essence and conditions of scholarly thought.[5]

It is the development of Mukařovský's structuralist aesthetics, therefore, that forms the topic of this introduction to the second volume of his essays to appear in English.

Mukařovský's structuralist period lasted about twenty years, roughly from 1928 to 1948. Within these twenty years we can discern three stages, each with a distinct aesthetic and theoretical orientation. However, as I pointed out above, an underlying epistemological stance unifies all these stages. Moreover, Mukařov-ský's theoretical shifts did not entail the abandonment of previous achievements, but rather a broadening of horizons, a new perspec-tive on the subject matter. This continuity of theoretical approach was a prime concern for Mukařovský, who always insisted that "scholarship is not country-fair magic and new ideas are not pulled out of an empty hat."[6] Thus, most of the topics which became prominent in the later stages of his structuralist aesthetics can be found in some form in the earlier stages as well.

The three stages of his aesthetic theory reflect a different stress on each of the three basic components of the aesthetic interaction with which we began. In the first stage, Mukařovský paid most at-tention to the object itself—the internal organization of the work of art. By 1934, however, he saw such an approach as insufficient and began to investigate what he termed social awareness or con-

5. "Autorův dovětek" [Author's afterword], *Studie z estetiky* (Prague, 1966), p. 337.
    6. "Vztah mezi sovětskou a československou literární vědou" [The relation between Soviet and Czech literary theory], *Země sovětů* 4 (1935–36): 13.

sciousness[7]—the set of norms valid for a particular collectivity, which every work of art implements. Coinciding roughly with the onset of World War II, the third period turned from the previous emphasis on supra-individual codes to the role which the subject plays in the aesthetic process. The subject was no longer conceived of as a mere passive vehicle of supra-individual structures but as an acting force interacting with these structures and changing them in the course of this interaction.

Mukařovský's early emphasis on the aesthetic object is not surprising. As he observed several times himself, upon entering this field his ideas were very close to formalism—the objectivistic approach par excellence.[8] Mukařovský's acquaintance with Russian Formalism was quite thorough, as we can see from his lecture "On Contemporary Poetics" of 1929.[9] But not all of the theories of this heterogeneous trend had the same impact on his thought. The most important for him were Roman Jakobson's phonological studies of metrics (elaborated in Prague, where Jakobson had resided since 1920), which actually transcended the formalist approach to literature in important ways. And Jurij Tynjanov's dialectic concept of artistic form as a struggle for dominance among the components of the art work was echoed in Mukařovský's first discussions of aesthetic structure.

The term *formalism*, of course, does not refer exclusively to the Russian school, but to Herbartian Formalism as well. In contrast to Romantic aesthetics, which emphasized the content of the work of art, the Herbartians proclaimed the form—the relations of elements—to be the source of all beauty. The tradition of Herbartian Formalism was especially strong at Charles University in Prague, where Robert Zimmermann (1824-98) had elaborated Herbart's scattered observations about aesthetics into a coherent system, and where the Czechs, Josef Durdík (1837-1902) and Otakar Hostinský (1847-1910), had further expanded its basic tenets. Though by the beginning of the century Herbartian Formalism had lost its impetus and become obsolete, we can detect its echoes in

7. The terms "awareness" and "consciousness" are etymologically close in Czech (*povědomí* and *vědomí*), and Mukařovský uses them interchangeably.

8. Cf., e.g., his "Předmluva k prvnímu vydání" [Introduction to the first edition], *Kapitoly*, vol. 1, p. 9.

9. "O současné poetice," *Cestami poetiky a estetiky* [On the track of poetics and aesthetics] (Prague, 1971), pp. 99-115.

the aesthetic theories which followed. For example, the leading Czech figure in psychologically oriented aesthetics, Otakar Zich (1879-1934), paid close attention to the material substratum of art which is the basis of aesthetic perception. In his famous study "On Poetic Types" (1917), Zich's analyses of the sound organization of verbal art closely parallel the discoveries of the Russian Formalists written at about the same time. This local formalist tradition made Mukařovský very receptive to the theoretical impulses coming from Russia. But it also enabled him to judge the achievements of the Russians in a broader context. The formalists in Russia were interested in poetics alone and programatically refused to transgress the boundaries of literature. For Mukařovský, poetics was merely a part of the larger field of aesthetics which encompassed not only all the arts but—as Mukařovský realized in the subsequent stage of his development—all aesthetic phenomena, even the extra-artistic.

In the period from 1928 to 1934, Mukařovský's concepts of aesthetics and structural analysis clearly reflected his emphasis on the material aspect of the work. In a short study, "A Note on the Aesthetics of Film," Mukařovský defined aesthetics as the epistemology of art, a discipline which would investigate the "basic possibilities provided by the character of the [artistic] material and the way in which the given art masters it."[10]

Since aesthetics was to investigate the most general rules governing the material of art, structural analysis would determine how these rules organize the material of specific works of art. For example, in Mukařovský's most detailed analysis of a poetic text of this period, *Mácha's May: An Aesthetic Study* (1928), he describes his lengthy analysis of sound patterns as structural because "its purpose was to discover the skeleton which provided the changeable stream of sounds with a firm outline."[11] In a similar manner, he terms his technical paper, "The Connection between the Phonic Line and Word Order in Czech Verse" (1929), not phonetic but structural, "its goal being to determine the link between the phonic line and the other components of a poem."[12] And in a lecture from the same year called "On Contemporary Poetics," Mukařovský described the purpose of structural analysis

10. "K estetice filmu," *Studie*, p. 172.
11. *Máchův Máj: Estetická studie* in *Kapitoly*, vol. 3, p. 87.
12. "Souvislost fonické linie se slovosledem v českých verších," *Kapitoly*, vol. 1, p. 205.

as "discovering in the work those features which cause its aesthetic efficacy."[13]

There might seem to be a certain discrepancy between the first two and the third definitions above. Whereas the former dwell on the particular interrelations of elements within the work, the latter deals with the aesthetic efficacy of the work. However, since for Mukařovský it was precisely the organization of the material which rendered an object aesthetically effective, the three definitions are mutually consistent.

The concept Mukařovský first used as an explanation of the aesthetic efficacy of art was "deautomatization." It was an elaboration of the Russian Formalist notion of "making strange," and referred to the peculiar hierarchical organization within a work of art in which one element (or one group of elements) becomes dominant and subordinates all the others to its own needs. As a result, the work is separated from the automatized context of everyday life and rendered unusual. According to Mukařovsky, every aesthetic deautomatization has two features: consistency and a systematic nature. "The work is consistent in that its deautomatized element is transformed throughout the work in a fixed manner. . . . The systematic character of deautomatization on the other hand rests in the hierarchy of interrelations among its elements; i.e., the elements are subordinated and superordinated to each other. The element which stands the highest in this hierarchy is the dominant. All the other elements and their relations, whether deautomatized or automatized, are evaluated from the standpoint of this dominant."[14]

In contrast to the Russian Formalists, who consciously limited the field of their inquiry to literature, Mukařovský attempted to test the principle of deautomatization on other arts as well. The most remarkable study along these lines is a short paper on Chaplin's acting (1931),[15] probably stimulated by Otakar Zich's *Aesthetics of Dramatic Art* which appeared in the same year. Mukařovský's analysis of Chaplin followed a distinction introduced

13. "O současné poetice," p. 114.

14. "Jazyk spisovný a jazyk básnický" [Standard literary language and poetic language], ibid., p. 120.

15. "Chaplin ve Světlech velkoměst: Pokus o strukturní rozbor hereckého zjevu" [Chaplin in *City Lights:* An attempt at a structural analysis of a dramatic figure], *Studie,* pp. 184–87.

by Zich between the actor, the dramatic figure, and the dramatic character. The first term applies to the artist himself, the actor. The other two refer to what might appear at first a single phenomenon—the role enacted by the actor. For Zich, however, the dramatic figure is the sensorily perceptible substratum (material vehicle) while the dramatic character is the immaterial referent of this vehicle, a *dramatis persona* of a given play.[16] In accord with the overall tenor of his early structuralism, Mukařovsky pays most attention to the material aspect of acting, the dramatic figure. He convincingly argues that gestures, usually a subordinate element in the structure of the dramatic figure, are the dominant of Chaplin's acting. Their deautomatization is so great that it deforms not only all the other elements of the dramatic figure, but the dramatic action of the entire film.

Even though Mukařovský's essay on Chaplin is extremely perceptive, it highlights the limitations of his early structuralist aesthetics. An exclusive concentration on the material vehicle of art necessarily yields limited results because no work of art is reducible to its sensorily perceptible substratum. There are even arts whose material cannot be reduced in this way, for example, literature, whose material, language, was defined by the structuralist linguists as a system of signs. It was the category of the sign, with its bond of the material and immaterial, which opened the path for Mukařovský out of a one-sided orientation to the material aspect of art. The treatment of the work of art as a sign would not deny the necessity of studying the organization of its vehicle, but the description of this organization ceased to be an end in itself. Instead, it was the meaning of the organization that became prominent in the second phase of Mukařovský's aesthetics.

But the equation of the work of art with the sign was not the real departure of this second period. After all, in his early analyses of arts whose material was semiotic—literature, film—Mukařovský had included meaning among the other structural elements. The

16. Zich himself does not use a semiotic frame of reference; instead he employs psychological terms, distinguishing the material basis of perception (the dramatic figure) from the image which is the result of this perception (the dramatic character); cf. his *Estetika dramatického umění: Teoretická dramaturgie* (Prague, 1931), p. 54. For a more detailed discussion of the relation between Zich's theories and their adaptation by the structuralists, see J. Veltruský, "Contribution to the Semiotics of Acting," *Sound, Sign and Meaning: Quinquagenary of the Prague Linguistic Circle,* ed. L. Matějka (Ann Arbor, 1976), pp. 555–57.

real change came in his conception of the aesthetic sign. His observations on this subject appeared in 1931 in an attack against
vulgar psychologism in literary studies. "There are some theoreticians of art who believe that the theory of art is synonymous
with the psychology of art and who in a peculiar methodological
twist deal with the psychology of the work of art instead of the
(absolutely justifiable) psychology of the artist and his creativity.
This is a contradiction in terms, for the work once finished ceases
to be a mere expression of its author's psychic state and becomes a
sign, i.e., a *sui generis* social fact which serves supra-individual communication, severed from the subjective psychology of its author."[17]

It is the treatment of the artistic sign as communicative that
marks the decisive turn in Mukařovský's structuralism. Now he
clearly realized the inadequacy of his previous study of the
aesthetic object alone. For just as a structuralist linguist cannot
adequately analyze the linguistic sign without taking into account
the code which makes it understandable to the members of a given
collectivity, the structuralist aesthetician cannot study the work of
art in separation from the code which makes it what Mukařovský
called a social fact. Moreover, just as the key to the meaning of a
word does not rest in its sensory aspect but in the relation of this
aspect to the code, the key to the understanding of the work of art
must be sought not in its internal organization but in the relation
of this organization to the underlying code. From this point of
view, the organization of the work has only a relative permanence.
It is the aesthetic code, the immediate aesthetic tradition against
whose background the work is perceived, which determines its
actual appearance. "On the basis of a single work," Mukařovský
argued in an interview in 1932, "several different structures with
different dominants and hierarchies of components can be gradually realized in different periods (or milieux). The work therefore is
not an unambiguous structure. It becomes unambiguous only if it
is perceived against the background of a particular immediate
tradition from which the work deviates and against which it is
reflected."[18] Here we are at the theoretical crux of the second

17. "Umělcova osobnost v zrcadle díla: Několik kritických poznámek k uměnovědné
teorii i praxi [The artist's personality in the mirror of the work: Some critical remarks
on the theory and practice of the study of art], *Cestami,* p. 145.

18. B. Novák, "Rozhovor s Janem Mukařovským" [An interview with Jan Mukařov-
ský], *Rozpravy Aventina* 7 (1931–32): 226.

stage of Mukařovský's aesthetic structuralism. The study of the organization of individual works gives place to the study of the aesthetic code underlying these works. To use the parallel to structuralist linguistics, Mukařovský had progressed from the study of *parole* (individual utterances) to the study of *langue* (the paradigmatic system of language).

If in the first stage art was distinguished from non-art on the basis of the organization of the object, in the second stage the criterion was art's relation to the aesthetic code. This in turn raised the question of the relation between the aesthetic code and the other codes mediating between man and reality. To Mukařovský human culture appeared as an intricate net of codes—art, science, religion, etc. This gamut of intangible codes is reality, but reality of a different type from the empirical reality favored by the positivists. It is phenomenological reality, which Mukařovský defined as "the set of functions organizing atomized empirical reality."[19] Thus, a code is differentiated according to its dominant function which groups together objects (atomized empirical reality)—the implementations of this code.

The advantage Mukařovský saw in the functional definition of aesthetic phenomena was the possibility of bringing together the realms of art and non-art which had been radically separated by some of his predecessors, most notably the Russian Formalists. The functional view meant that works of art were no longer grouped exclusively with other "beautiful" objects but were put on an equal footing with all artifacts. By proclaiming the essential polyfunctionality of all human activities and their products, Mukařovský further facilitated the bridging of the gulf between art and non-art. Art was no longer demarcated from other fields because it was the only one in which the aesthetic function existed, but because it was the only one in which the aesthetic function predominated. The aesthetic function was seen as present in all activities pursuing practical goals, and practical functions were present in those pursuing aesthetic goals. Thus, art is not hermetically sealed from non-art; the two always interpenetrate and overlap, so that the scholar is often unable to identify every object as unequivocally artistic or non-artistic.

The inseparability of art and non-art becomes clear if we consider their relationship from a developmental point of view. All the

19. Ibid., p. 225.

functional codes are only relatively independent, since in reality they always coexist and together comprise the ultimate structure of the culture of a given society. As the society evolves there is further interaction among these codes. In the course of development they become interlocked in an ongoing struggle for domination, at the same time influencing each other and being influenced. Thus, their relations, internal structures, and even the realms of empirical reality which they govern are in constant flux. A history of art written from an immanent standpoint, taking into account only the impetus for change coming from the aesthetic code, would therefore be necessarily limited. It would disregard all the impulses from other spheres of culture which affect art, an only relatively autonomous part of culture.

The sources from which Mukařovský drew inspiration in the second stage of his structuralism are numerous. Certainly a primary influence was structuralist linguistics as outlined by Ferdinand de Saussure and redefined and developed by Mukařovský's colleagues from the Prague Linguistic Circle. The most important stimulus in the field of contemporary aesthetics was the work of Max Dessoir and Emil Utitz (from 1934 on, a professor at the Prague University in the position vacated by von Ehrenfels). They propounded the view that the spheres of the aesthetic and artistic are not identical, the aesthetic exceeding the scope of art and art resisting any reduction to aesthetics. Another important source, Broder Christiansen's *Philosophie der Kunst* (1909), elaborates the distinction between the sensorily perceptible work of art and the immaterial aesthetic object, the latter a result of the subject's synthesizing activity. Christiansen goes on to argue that the aesthetic object is not merely a product of the immediate subject-object relation but is affected by the existing artistic canon, so that in different periods the same work of art can correspond to very different aesthetic objects.

Mukařovský's concept of aesthetics in this period is perhaps best summarized in his 1940 encyclopedia entry, "Structuralist Aesthetics." Here he wrote, "For structuralist aesthetics, everything within the work of art and in its relation to the external context appears as a sign and meaning. In this respect it might be considered a part of the general science of signs, *semiotics*. . . . Its [structuralist aesthetics'] essence and destiny are to elaborate the system and method of the *comparative semiotics of art*. However, we must add that the comparative orientation of structuralist aesthetics is not exhausted by art alone, for the aesthetic . . . is potentially present in every human act and potentially contained in every human product. This means that structuralist aesthetics pays attention to the constant interplay of three phenomenal spheres: the artistic, the aesthetic, and the extra-artistic and extra-aesthetic, and to the tension among them which affects the development of each."[20]

The opportunity for Mukařovský to present his semiotics of art before an international audience arose in September 1934 when the Eighth International Congress of Philosophy convened in Prague. Mukařovský's contribution, "L'art comme fait sémiologique," is, at least to my knowledge, the first attempt in the history of aesthetics at a systematic semiotics of art. Since this essay appears in the present volume I shall describe it only briefly. As a sign, the work of art consists of three components: a material vehicle (the "work-thing"), a meaning (the "aesthetic object" lodged in the collective consciousness), and a relation to the thing signified. It is the mode of referring of the aesthetic sign that differentiates it from all other signs. Mukařovský used the term "autonomous" to describe it, a choice which was rather unfelicitous. For he was not trying to imply that the aesthetic sign refers to nothing but itself. He meant that this type of sign signifies not particulars but the total context of social phenomena. Even in cases when the work of art aims at a particular (the portrait is perhaps the best but certainly not the only example), the aesthetic sign does not lose its autonomous character because the relation between it and its referent is devoid of any existential value.

Another important paper by Mukařovský from the year 1934 was "Polák's *Sublimity of Nature:* An Attempt at an Analysis and Developmental Classification of a Poetic Structure."[21] Directed specifically to the domestic audience, it dealt with the most important work of a rather neglected Czech poet, Milota Zdirad Polák (1788–1856). The study addressed a problem in literary history: how to bring together the internal development of literature and the external influences affecting the structure of a

20. "Strukturální estetika," *Ottův slovník naučný nové doby,* vol. 6, pt. 1 (Prague, 1939–40), p. 454.

21. "Polákova Vznešenost přírody: Pokus o rozbor a vývojové zařadění básnické struktury," *Kapitoly,* vol. 2.

particular poetic text. A vivid discussion followed its publication
in which critics of all ideological camps participated. In fact, it was
this discussion which established structuralism as a canonized term
among Czech theoreticians of art.

In his analysis Mukařovský paid especially close attention to
versification, for *The Sublimity of Nature* had appeared at a crucial
moment in the development of Czech metrics. The poetic school
prior to Polák—the Puchmajerians—had introduced syllabotonic
versification into modern Czech poetry. Like many pioneers, they
adhered strictly to the rules which they had advanced, trying to
keep the rhythm of their poems as close as possible to meter. Thus,
the beginning of each foot coincided with the beginning of a word
(the word boundary being the phonological basis of Czech meter).
The result was a monotonous, usually trochaic verse composed
largely of disyllabic words with few variations in metrical impulse.
Unimaginative and restrictive, this system could not long survive.
The radical path of revolt led to a totally different system of
versification, the quantitative system (Palacký, Šafařík), while the
more moderate one changed the syllabotonic system from within
by introducing variety into it. It was Polák who took the initiative
in this "adaptation of Puchmajerian verse" (p. 145), breaking its
rhythmical monotony by freeing the foot boundaries from their
"obligatory" coincidence with word boundaries. In *The Sublimity
of Nature* words often exceed the foot, and foot boundaries often
fall within a word. Polák achieved this diversity very simply; he
used a great number of polysyllabic (mostly tetrasyllabic) words
as the verbal material of his poem.

Statistics regarding the number of syllables per word and the
stress distribution in Polák's poem show the deautomatizing effect
of tetrasyllabic words on the previous metrical tradition. A semantic analysis of these words also reveals important facts. Mukařovský shows that the most common derivational suffixes of tetrasyllabic words (e.g., *-ní* [English *-ing*] in verbal nouns, *-ost* [English
-ness] in adjectival nouns, etc.) are closely related to the
periphrastic descriptions permeating Polák's poem. The suffix *-ost*,
for example, renders a quality a thing; Polák thus replaces the usual
name of an object with an adjectival noun referring to the essential
quality of the designated object. Such periphrasis was a reflection
of the descriptive theme, in turn a part of the canon of nature
poetry to which Polák's poem belongs.

Thus, the organization of *The Sublimity of Nature*, from sound level to theme, is directly related to the immanent history of Czech literature. But this discovery was merely the first aim of Mukařovský's project. His ultimate goal was to establish the link between the structure of the poem and extra-literary phenomena. At this point he recurred to the idea of the integral character of culture mentioned above. "It would be wrong," he argued, "to place poetry in a vacuum under the pretext of its specific function. We should not forget that the developmental series of the individual structures changing in time (e.g., political, economic, ideological, literary) do not run parallel to each other without any contact. On the contrary, they are the elements of the structure of a higher order and this structure of structures has its hierarchy and its dominant element (the prevailing series)" (p. 166).

Thus, Mukařovský states that when *The Sublimity of Nature* was written, during the early years of the Czech National Revival, nationalism was clearly the dominant cultural structure. The literature of this time was thus subordinated to nationalistic ends. Mukařovský argues that the primary target of the nationalists in these early years was the educated stratum of society for whom Czech literature had as yet nothing to offer. Polák's choice of the genre of descriptive poetry therefore had a social motivation. He "attempted a 'high,' exclusive poetry which was to gain for the nationalistic idea the 'higher' strata of society" (p. 172). Thus, Mukařovský shows how the immanent development of art is affected by its place in the hierarchy of cultural structures. And one can now proceed from the opposite direction as before, seeing the link between genre and theme, theme and word choice, etc. From his analysis Mukařovský concludes that there is a dual motivation behind every developmental change: "The poetic structure under study is carried on the one hand by the immanent development of the national literature, and on the other by the tendencies stemming from societal development. Within this chain of interrelations linking immanent development and external intervention, the issue of a unilateral determination of one element by another becomes meaningless [pp. 172–73]."

These two essays of 1934, "Art as a Semiotic Fact" and "Polák's *Sublimity of Nature*," mark the beginning of Mukařovský's second phase of structuralist aesthetics. The culmination of this phase was the axiological study, *Aesthetic Function, Norm, and Value as*

Social Facts, which tackled the classical themes of aesthetics from a structuralist standpoint. Its first two chapters dealing with the concepts of function and norm appeared in a sociological revue in 1935. The definitive version with two new chapters came out as a book in 1936.

As the title indicates, the three notions of function, norm, and value comprise the conceptual frame of Mukařovský's aesthetic axiology. The way these factors interact is suggested in Mukařovský's university lecture, "Problems of Aesthetic Value" (1935–36): "By function we understand an active relation between an object and the goal for which this object is used. The value then is the utility of this object for such a goal. The norm is the rule or set of rules which regulate the sphere of a particular kind or category of values."[22]

Mukařovský goes on to place certain restrictions on this broad scheme. The most important concerns the concept of function, the factor which differentiates cultural codes. Because of his stress on the social, Mukařovský does not consider every teleological relation functional. "The notion of function means that we commonly use the object which is its vehicle for such and such a purpose. Custom, repeated usage, is a necessary precondition of a function. This term is not appropriate for a single and unique use of a thing. But not even the subjective customariness of a certain usage of a given object, a customariness limited to an individual, comprises a function in the proper sense of the word. Furthermore, there must be a social consensus about the purpose which the object serves. A particular mode of using a given object must be spontaneously comprehensible to every member of a given collectivity."[23] And as he adds in several other essays, not only the usage of a functional object but the goal to be achieved by means of this object must transcend the individual, must be generally acknowledged and fixed by the given collectivity.[24]

What has been said so far pertains to all functions without exception. But Mukařovský went on to provide the differentia of the aesthetic function. In all "practical" functions, the telos lies outside of the object which is the vehicle of the function, either in

22. "Problémy estetické hodnoty," *Cestami,* p. 17.
23. "K problému funkcí v architektuře" [On the problem of functions in architecture], *Studie,* p. 196.
24. Cf., e.g., "Problémy estetické hodnoty," p. 17, and *Estetická funkce, norma a hodnota jako sociální fakty* in *Studie,* p. 27.

the subject whose particular need is to be satisfied or in the surrounding context which is to be changed. In contrast to this, the
telos of an object dominated by the aesthetic function lies in the
object itself. "Is it possible," asks Mukařovský, "for an object to
function only vis-à-vis itself, to be its own goal?" We can explain
this in the following manner: the aesthetic function is the necessary dialectic negation of function in general. Usually an object
functions vis-à-vis something external to it. However, as soon as
the aesthetic function takes over the object, this normal state of
affairs is disrupted and the object functions only vis-à-vis itself."[25]
In other words, the difference between the practical and aesthetic
functions is that the former are allotelic whereas the latter is
autotelic.

In the sphere in which the aesthetic function predominates—art—
this inverted quality leads, moreover, to the reversal of the usual
relationship between norm and value. "Whereas outside of art
value is subordinated to norms, here [in art] the norm is subordinated to value. Outside of art the fulfilment of the norm is
synonymous with value. In art the norm is often violated and only
sometimes fulfilled, but even in this case the fulfilment is just a
means, not the goal."[26] This fact had escaped previous schools of
normativistic aesthetics, which conceived of the relationship between aesthetic norms and value in terms of practical functions
and ascribed aesthetic value to the fulfilment of whichever aesthetic norms they had formulated.

The ontological status of the aesthetic norm reflects its subordination to aesthetic value. In contrast to the norms of other functional spheres (e.g., law, language, etc.) aesthetic norms seem the
least codifiable, the least monopolistic (i.e., the least tending toward an exclusive dominance by a single system of norms) and the
least stable. For this reason Mukařovský refuses to regard the
aesthetic norm as an a priori rule but instead sees it as a regulatory
principle which is constantly violated, but which, like all norms,
"demonstrates its effectiveness and thus also its existence precisely
when it is violated."[27]

Mukařovský presented yet another reason for the subordination
of the aesthetic norm to aesthetic value: the difference in the

25. "Problémy estetické hodnoty," p. 17.
26. *Estetická funkce*, p. 40.
27. "Estetická norma" [The aesthetic norm], ibid., p. 76.

scope of their efficacy in art. "The application of an aesthetic norm subjects a specific case to a general rule and pertains merely to a single aspect of the object—its aesthetic function—which [outside of art] does not even have to be dominant. Aesthetic evaluation, on the other hand, judges a phenomenon in its overall complexity, for all the extra-aesthetic functions and values are involved here as components of aesthetic value. For this very reason aesthetic evaluation conceives of the work of art as a closed whole (totality) and is an individualizing act. In art, aesthetic value appears as unique and unrepeatable."[28]

This complex notion of aesthetic value returns us to Mukařovský's premise of the essential polyfunctionality of every human activity. As we saw above, he claimed that art differs from non-art because of its subordination of extra-aesthetic functions to the aesthetic function. But since the allotelic practical functions and the autotelic aesthetic function are direct opposites of each other, the question arises as to how they can coexist in a single whole, especially since the dominant aesthetic function in the work of art blocks the realization of any practical functions. Mukařovský argues that it is precisely this "zero utility" of an object dominated by the aesthetic function which lifts it from the context of everyday life and renders it art. Though unrealized, the practical functions do not vanish from the work. They remain there in all their potentiality.

Mukařovský's belief in the social habit as the foundation of all functions links function to the sign, since the sign is also rooted in a social consensus. "The object," Mukařovský observes, "not only performs but also signifies its function."[29] And since the dominant aesthetic function prevents the actualization of the ends of extra-aesthetic functions, their corresponding values are switched from the empirical to the semantic plane. Extra-aesthetic values become meanings which contribute to the total semantic structure of the work.

The question remains, then, of what happens to the dominant aesthetic value. Mukařovský's answer to this is crucial for an understanding of the second period of his structuralism. "From the most abstract point of view, the work of art is nothing but a

28. *Estetická funkce*, pp. 40–41.
29. "K problému funkcí," p. 196.

particular set of extra-aesthetic values. The material components of the artistic artifact and the way they are exploited as formal devices are mere conductors of energies represented by extra-aesthetic values. If, at this point, we ask ourselves where aesthetic value is, we find that it has dissolved into the individual extra-aesthetic values and is nothing but a general designation for the dynamic totality of their interrelations."[30]

Thus, the second stage of Mukařovský's structuralism encompassed several important achievements. Above all it succeeded in incorporating art into the larger whole of human culture and demonstrated the inseparability of the two. Further, during this phase, Mukařovský elaborated a semiotic frame of reference which enabled him to conceive of culture as an intricate network of signs —an interpenetration of codes and their material implementations—facilitating communication among the individuals belonging to this culture.

Still, there are problems as well as successes in the aesthetic theories of this period. The emphasis on the social codes mediating every subject-object interaction leads to an overt relativism. Since everything social is also historical, it is subject to change. Thus, to conceive of every aesthetic interaction merely in terms of the particular historical moment (a unique cultural configuration) has as its ultimate consequence the destruction of the epistemological basis of aesthetics. Even if we accept the fact that what is aesthetic or extra-aesthetic at this or that moment depends upon the aesthetic code valid for a particular collectivity, as aestheticians we must rely on some common denominator to transcend fleeting states of social consciousness and conceive the aesthetic codes of different times and milieux as indeed aesthetic. And this common denominator can be seen not only as the historical invariant of an actual aesthetic process, but also, genetically, as one of its preconditions.

During the late thirties Mukařovský became keenly aware of this problem and began to revise his structuralism. The postulation of supra-social invariants within the aesthetic process is one aspect of this change. To extend the parallel between structuralist linguistics and aesthetics I drew above: in the final stage of his structuralism Mukařovský progressed from the study of *langue* to the study of

30. *Estetická funkce*, p. 51.

langage, which he understood as "several laws of language in general, namely, the human faculty to communicate by means of linguistic signs."[31] In other words, around the beginning of World War II, Mukařovský switched from the study of the cultural codes mediating every aesthetic interaction to the study of the universals which make such an interaction possible.

The second flaw in the middle stage of Mukařovský's structuralism had been a programmatic neglect of the subject's role in the aesthetic process. During this stage Mukařovský regarded the subject—whether author or perceiver—as a member of a particular collectivity whose framework of consciousness "is constituted, even in its innermost layers, by contents belonging to the social consciousness."[32] The subject defined in this way was a peripheral component of aesthetic interaction. As an author he was a mere vehicle of impersonal impulses coming from the previous artistic tradition and the extra-artistic context. As a perceiver he only complemented the social core of meaning of the work by his subjective, and hence irrelevant, private associations.

The fallacy of this approach is patent. Aesthetics—the humanistic study par excellence—was leaving man outside of its purview. But further, man's relationship to the supra-individual structures was perceived in a lopsided way. He became the product of these structures instead of the other way around. The initiative belonged to the structures and man filled in as a passive actor whose role was prescribed regardless of his will. This inadequacy was remedied only in the final stage of Mukařovský's structuralism when he shifted his attention from impersonal and self-regulating cultural codes to man—the subject and ultimate source of every aesthetic interaction.

It is important to note that an emphasis on the subject does not necessarily imply subjectivism. This would be inconceivable for Mukařovský, especially if we consider the universalistic tendency of his late structuralism. It was this very universalism, in fact, that required the inclusion of the subject in the theory of aesthetic interaction, because without him such a theory would be neces-

---

31. "Může míti estetická hodnota v umění platnost všeobecnou?" [Can there be a universal value in art?], *Studie,* p. 83.

32. "Umění jako semiologický fakt" [Art as a semiotic fact], *Studie,* p. 83.

sarily incomplete. Moreover, Mukařovský's conception of the subject precluded any subjectivism. He was seen as: (1) an intersubjective creator and perceiver participating in the aesthetic process; (2) a member of the species *Homo sapiens* with the predispositions determined by his unchangeable biological and anthropological constants; (3) an embodiment of the principle of individuality— the pole of accidentality which stands in opposition to the determinism of cultural systems.

The third stage of Mukařovský's structuralism is further characterized by its connection to phenomenological philosophy. Of course, I am not implying that there were no previous links between the two; on the contrary, the close contacts between members of the Circle and leading European phenomenologists (including Husserl) throughout the thirties are well known.[33] Mukařovský's embracing of phenomenology, however, occurred somewhat later (for the most part during the war) when the international contacts of the Circle were severed.

Mukařovský described his concept of aesthetics in this period as "the study of the aesthetic function, its manifestations and its vehicles."[34] Though this statement reflects little change from those of previous years, the third phase represents a profound change in the notion of function in general and the aesthetic function in particular. Originally function had been treated from the standpoint of the object or the cultural codes regulating the relationship between object and goal; now it was the subject whose perspective was adopted. Thus, in the fall of 1942, in "The Place of the Aesthetic Function among the Other Functions," Mukařovský defined function as "the mode of a subject's self-realization vis-à-vis the external world."[35]

Seeing the subject as the source of all functionality further enhanced Mukařovský's thesis concerning the polyfunctionality of all artifacts. For if functions are situated in the object, there is

33. Cf., e.g., L. Landgrebe, "Erinnerungen eines Phänomenologen an den *Cercle Linguistique de Prague,*" *Sound, Sign and Meaning,* pp. 40–42, or E. Holenstein, *Roman Jakobson's Approach to Language: Phenomenological Structuralism* (Bloomington, 1976).

34. "Význam estetiky" [The significance of aesthetics], *Studie,* p. 55.

35. "Místo estetické funkce mezi ostatními" [The place of the aesthetic function among the other functions], *Studie,* p. 69.

always the danger of neglecting all functions except the one for which the object was originally produced. Situating function in cultural codes, especially in our modern society, does lead to a precise differentiation of objects according to their purpose, "but as soon as we look at functions from a subject's point of view, we shall immediately see that every act by which man orients himself toward reality in order to affect it in one way or another corresponds simultaneously and jointly to several purposes which sometimes not even the individual who originates the act is able to differentiate. Hence the uncertainty about the motivation of actions. Social coexistence, of course, compels man constantly to limit his functional heterogeneity, but it never succeeds in making him a biologically monofunctional creature such as a bee or an ant. As long as man is man, various functions will necessarily contend with one another, will be arranged hierarchically, will intersect and interpenetrate in each of his acts [p. 68]."

However, since the subject conceived as an individual introduces his free will, and hence accidentality, into the functional process, he cannot serve as the basis for a universal typology of functions—the goal Mukařovský had set forth in his lecture. One alternative, therefore, was to treat the subject as an anthropological constant and deduce the basic functions from his internal organization as a human being. Mukařovský actually suggested this solution in his 1937 article concerned with functions in architecture and subsequently applied it in his theoretical search for the essence of norm and value. In the early forties, however, he deemed it inadequate and opted for a conception of the subject as an intersubjective agent interacting with the surrounding material world. It was the phenomenological *Wesensschau*—the deduction from the subject-object relation itself—which Mukařovský chose as his method for constructing his universal typology of functions.

All possible subject-object interactions, according to Mukařovský, can be subsumed under four main functions: the practical, theoretical, symbolic, and aesthetic. There are two co-ordinates which classify them. The first relates to the type of subject-object relation, i.e., whether it is direct and "immediate," or, on the other hand, mediated, "semiotic." The second co-ordinate relates to the hierarchy of subject and object in the functional interaction. Either the subject dominates this interrelation or the object toward which the function is oriented does so. This typology can be visualized as follows:

type of function domi- nant component	IMMEDIATE	SEMIOTIC
OBJECT	Practical functions	Symbolic function
SUBJECT	Theoretical function	Aesthetic function

In the practical and symbolic functions, the object dominates the interaction with the subject, and the functional thrust is toward affecting reality, either directly or through the mediation of signs which are in an effective relationship to this reality. In the theoretical function, on the other hand, man strives to grasp the object cognitively without actually affecting it; therefore it is the cognizing subject who dominates the interaction. In the aesthetic function, "the semiotic function foregrounds the subject." This formulation appears to re-introduce subjectivism, which the social thrust of the second period had resisted so strongly. Thus, even though Mukařovský pointed out correctly that to speak of the subject does not necessarily imply subjectivism, it is not entirely clear why the reflection of reality as a whole in the aesthetic sign should be organized "according to the image of the subject's organization" (p. 70). To grasp what Mukařovský means we must first discuss how he conceived of the aesthetic sign in the last stage of his structuralism. And before we can do that we must describe at least in brief the final transformation of his two other crucial concepts—norm and value.

Of all the aesthetic categories, the first to turn Mukařovský's attention to the problem of universals was the aesthetic norm. And interestingly it was this norm that had triggered his early interest in cultural codes. As we have noted, Mukařovský considered the aesthetic norm the weakest of all norms, constantly being violated and revealing its existence only through this violation. However, the fluidity of the aesthetic norm should not be overstated. Every norm, even a mere regulatory principle, must be endowed with some authority in order to be a norm. The validity of a norm cannot be derived solely from its invalidation of the previous norm, or we would not know when the aesthetic norm was being violated.

By his second phase, Mukařovský himself was aware that his concept of the aesthetic norm had a distinctly relativistic coloration which undermined its theoretical value. To rescue it he decided to link the aesthetic norm to man's atemporal anthropological constants. "Let us proceed from the fact that the ultimate source of aesthetic norms—and of all norms alike—is man's attitude toward the world. And man, despite all his historical and social changeability, is by his physical and partially also by his mental organization an anthropological constant. Well then, are there some principles related to aesthetic norms which could constitute a permanent basis for them? Yes, there are; one such principle is the rhythm given by the physiological processes in the human body; another anthropological constant is the symmetry furnished by the structure of the human body and by its practical consequences for the physical and mental behavior of man."[36] In other essays Mukařovský added to his list a few other such principles (e.g., the complementary distribution of colors). However, he did not elaborate this issue any further.

For him these anthropological constants were neither "ideal" aesthetic norms in the metaphysical sense nor actual aesthetic norms. 'The absolutely regular rhythm of running machines puts us to sleep, the perfect symmetry of an isosceles triangle is aesthetically indifferent."[37] Instead, these constants relate to actual aesthetic norms as their constitutive principles. They provide a fixed point in the permanent flux of aesthetic norms. It is only against their background that we perceive particular violations as more or less "normal."

A year after propounding this thesis about the link between aesthetic norms and anthropological constants, Mukařovský rejected any connection between anthropological constants and "objective (i.e., independent and permanent)" aesthetic value. For "the work of art as a whole is by its very essence a *sign* directed to man as a member of an organized collectivity, not as an anthropological constant."[38] This move would appear to reduce aesthetic value to a relativistic category, since value is denied a basis in the anthropological constant and placed, instead, in the sign, a constantly

36. "Problémy estetické normy" [Problems of the aesthetic norm], *Cestami*, pp. 44–45.
37. "Estetická norma," p. 77.
38. *Estetická funkce*, p. 44.

shifting entity. However, one component of the sign does not change through time—its material vehicle—and thus Mukařovský locates "objective" aesthetic value in the sensorily perceptible substratum of the work. "We can conclude that the greater the bundle of extra-aesthetic values an artistic artifact attracts and the more dynamic it renders their interplay, the greater the independent value of the artifact will be. All of this is independent of the historical changes in the quality of these values."[39]

This answer, however, did not completely satisfy Mukařovský. Its vagueness is immediately obvious: even if we accept the idea that an artifact capable of attracting a greater number of extra-aesthetic values throughout time and space carries more "objective" aesthetic value than an artifact lacking this quality, the nature of the artifact's organization remains a mystery. Therefore it is not surprising that Mukařovský returned to this problem in the final stage of his structuralism when he reassessed the role of the subject in the value-creating process. At that point he made a change in his terminology. Since every value, aesthetic included, cannot exist independently of man, Mukařovský speaks not of "objective" but of "universal" aesthetic value.

The universalistic thrust of Mukařovský's late axiology is not, however, merely a matter of nomenclature. It affects the whole hierarchy of his theoretical priorities. Whereas earlier he had studied mainly the social mechanism behind changes in aesthetic value, now he became increasingly intrigued by natural objects (crystals, precious stones) and artifacts (some children's books) which enjoy aesthetic status regardless of cultural barriers. What is it that makes these phenomena universal objects of aesthetic experience? Mukařovský decided that it was the close affinity between their organization and the constitutive principles stemming from man's anthropological constants. Once this connection is established it becomes obvious that the basis for universal aesthetic value must be sought in the anthropological constitution of man. But, as with the aesthetic norm, Mukařovský is cautious not to confuse this basis with an "ideal" aesthetic value. "Man's anthropological constitution in itself does not contain anything aesthetic, so that there is an ontological tension between it and its aesthetic realization, and every realization reveals a new aspect of man's

39. Ibid., p. 52.

basic organization. For this reason it is also possible that universal aesthetic value based on the general organization of man can stimulate turns and changes in the development of art despite the stability of its substrate."[40]

With this in mind, we may now turn to Mukařovský's mature notion of the sign, which, as we stated above, is essential to an understanding of the aesthetic function. His original semiotic model had been quite simple. The aesthetic sign consisted of a material vehicle, meaning, and reference. Consistent with the orientation of this middle phase, the role of the subject in aesthetic semiosis was suppressed. Meaning was defined as the social core common to all private meanings, lodged in the collective consciousness. The distinctiveness of the aesthetic sign rested in the general mode of its signification; the work of art did not refer to particulars, but to the total context of social phenomena.

The inadequacies of this notion were soon apparent. First of all, it was erroneous to regard the meaning of an aesthetic sign solely as a component of the social consciousness. The source of confusion here appears to be too close an adherence to the linguistic model, in particular, to the notion of lexical meaning. A simple sign like a word operates differently from a complex sign, a work of art. The meaning of a complex sign neither exists a priori as a unit of a code nor is present all at once. Instead, it arises in a process in which the perceiving subject brings together all the partial meanings within the work. Moreover, in art, it is not this result which is important but the process itself.

Mukařovský first discussed the process nature of the artistic work in connection with aesthetic value. But since he believed that values in art function as meanings, the notion of process also has a direct bearing on the semiotics of art. "Whereas all other values primarily emphasize the *result* of evaluation, aesthetic value foregrounds the *act* of evaluation. The perception of the work of art, which is substantially the same as the act of evaluation (whether conscious or unconscious), in reality occupies a considerable time span, and it is for this act and not its result that the individual approaches the work."[41] If the process of perception is the crucial aspect of the aesthetic interaction, then the subject's role in art

40. "Může míti estetická hodnota v umění platnost všeobecnou?" p. 84.
41. "Problémy estetické normy," p. 38.

must be redefined. He can no longer be seen as an irrelevant individual who merely superimposes his private associations upon a socially shared meaning, but as an active force indispensable to the genesis of meaning.

The second component of the aesthetic sign—reference—did not undergo significant transformation in the last period of Mukařovský's thought; that is, the work of art was seen as referring to generalities and its relation to its referent was considered unverifiable. The notion of the aesthetic sign, however, did change. The 1934 definition, according to which the aesthetic referent is the "total context of social phenomena" was too vague. Does the work refer to the social context of its origin or to that of any of its perceptions, or to the social context which it might represent by its theme?

Mukařovský decided that all the references which the aesthetic sign contains are merely potential. To become actual they must pass through the medium of a perceiver and be refracted through many facets of his consciousness. Only the subject has the power to transform "non-semiotic" reality into the referent of an aesthetic sign. To use more unequivocal language, the only reality to which the aesthetic sign refers is the reality of its perceiver.

Mukařovský aired this for the first time in 1936 in his contribution to the International Linguistic Congress, entitled "Poetic Designation and the Aesthetic Function of Language." Here he propounded the thesis that the work of art refers to the "total set of the subject's existential experiences." As an example, he pointed to the reading of Dostoevsky's novel, *Crime and Punishment*.

> It is highly probable that the majority of those who have read or will read this novel have never committed and will never commit murder. It is equally certain that no crime today could be committed in a social, ideological, etc., situation identical to the one which gave birth to Raskolnikov's crime. Nevertheless, those who read Dostoevsky's novel react to their reading with the most intimate of their experiences; every reader feels that *sua res agitur*. The psychological associations and the semantic combinations set into motion by reading will, of course, differ from individual to individual. It is also probable that they will have very little in common with the author's personal experiences which gave rise to the work. The

existential experiences with which an individual will react to
a poetic work will only be symptoms of his own reaction to
the poet's attitude toward reality. The stronger this reaction
is, the greater the set of experiences it will be able to set into
motion, and the stronger will be the influence exerted by the
work on the reader's conception of the world.[42]

These observations which Mukařovský had made during the
second period of his structuralism paved the way for a thorough
revision of his semiotics of art in the third period. The shift in
focus from social codes to the subject which marked the transition
from the second to the third phase was reflected in Mukařovský's
semiotic theory by an emphasis on the perceiver of the aesthetic
sign, who became the crucial factor in aesthetic semiosis.

The most systematic presentation of his new semiotic of art was
the lecture "Intentionality and Unintentionality in Art" delivered
at the Circle on May 26, 1943. It is included in the present volume, so we shall limit ourselves to a brief discussion. The theoretical thrust of this lecture was to describe art in relation to its perceiver. Thus, Mukařovský differentiated three types of phenomena
which create three kinds of attitudes on the subject's part. First of
all there is the sphere of natural events and objects to which we
relate in a spontaneous and direct fashion. We are aware that they
are not the products of someone else's design and therefore we are
free to attribute to them meanings which directly correspond to
our immediate existential experience. The second group of
phenomena are manmade. These are preconceived and intentional
and we must take this fact into account in our perception of them.
This sphere can be further subdivided into the practical and the
artistic. In the perception of the former we take into account their
external context. We ascribe a meaning to them which corresponds
to what we see as the intent of their author or as the goal they
serve to achieve. In contrast to this, works of art are severed from
the practical context. Their intentionality cannot be deduced from
what is external to them but only from their internal organization.
Intentionality in art is a semantic energy which binds together all
the heterogeneous elements of the work into a semantic unity, a
sign. A special attitude in the perceiver corresponds to it. As long
as he assumes this aesthetic attitude, he strives to discern within

42. "Básnické pojmenování a estetická funkce jazyka," *Kapitoly,* vol. 1, p. 162.

the work an organization which will enable him to perceive it as a whole. The meaning of the work of art is thus derived from its own internal organization.

If we return now to our previous discussion of the aesthetic function, it is much clearer why the subject dominates this function. The subject's attitude is instrumental in transforming any phenomenon—even a natural or practical one—into a self-centered aesthetic sign. The objection might be raised that in genuine works of art the subject does not dominate, since these artifacts are semantically unified from within. But according to Mukařovský, even here the perceiver's initiative is necessary because such a unification is never absolute. The organization of a work of art suggests a possible unification of meaning but does not automatically establish it—thus the motivation for the term "semantic gesture" as Mukařovský's name for this semantic energy. He argues that even the semantic unification of the work in our perception is a mere tendency which is never fully achieved if the work is to have any artistic efficacy for us. But since the semantic unification is what renders a work of art an intentional artifact, an ununified work would appear similar to an unintentional natural phenomenon whose meaning is determined by the perceiver's immediate existential experience. It is precisely this transformation which explains why we often react toward art with our innermost emotions. Such a reaction would be peculiar, to say the least, toward an intentional sign only obliquely related to its author and referent. The tendency to perceive the work of art as a natural phenomenon must, however, remain only a tendency if art is to differ from nature.

The specificity of the perception of art lies in bringing together the two tendencies mentioned above. "The work of art demands attention precisely because it is simultaneously a thing and a sign. The internal unification provided by intentionality evokes a *particular* relation to the object and creates a fixed axis around which associated images and feelings can accumulate. On the other hand, since a semantically unregulated thing (which the work is, because of its unintentionality) acquires the capacity to attract to itself the most varied images and feelings, which need not have anything in common with its own semantic charge, the work thus becomes capable of being closely connected to entirely personal experiences, images, and feelings of any perceiver, of affecting not only his conscious mental life but even setting into motion forces governing his subconscious."[43] Mukařovský's concept of the double-tiered perception of art is not relevant for semiotics alone. It also bridges the gulf between the two opposing views of art perception in nineteenth- and early twentieth-century aesthetics—that of disinterested pleasure and that of empathy.

The perceiver, however, is not the only subject participating in art. There is yet another, the author. As Mukařovský pointed out several times, the difference between the creating and the perceiving subject is not absolute. The perceiver always directly or indirectly influences the creation of the work (e.g., as a patron who orders a specific work of art or as the artist's image of the audience for which he creates), and the author adopts from time to time the standpoint of a perceiver (in relation to the works of others or even to his own works during the process of creation). For this reason Mukařovský argued that "in all its modifications art has much in common with a continuous dialogue in which both those who gradually create works, and those who perceive them, participate."[44] Even though the dividing line between the author and the perceiver cannot be drawn with any precision, there is, nevertheless, an important difference between them. The perceiver can be anyone, any individual who approaches the work from an aesthetic point of view. The artist, in contrast, is a specific personality who produces the unique configuration of the work.

The distinctiveness of the creating subject introduced a new category into Mukařovský's structuralist aesthetics—individuality. From our discussion, it is clear that the artist's individuality is of a different order from the perceiver's, which is merely a question of intersubjectivity, i.e., someone else's perception of the work. In the case of the author, however, there is no someone else. His is a unique and therefore to some degree unpredictable personality. But to accept individuality in these absolute terms means to admit accidentality and indeterminism into art and in turn to deny the basic epistemological premise of structuralism: that the aesthetic process has its intrinsic regularity which is the subject matter of aesthetics. To accommodate the theoretical tenets of structuralism to the uniqueness of the artist's individuality Mukařovský relativized the category of individuality.

43. "Záměrnost a nezáměrnost v umění," *Studie*, p. 98.
44. "Individuum v umění" [The individual in art], *Studie*, p. 223.

The relativity of individuality pertains first of all to the artist's personality itself. For Mukařovský, the artist's personality can be seen abstractly as composed of two sets of elements—inherent biogenic features and acquired social characteristics. The uniqueness of an individual, however, does not rest in either. Both the biogenic dispositions and social factors have their own regularities. The uniqueness of the artist's personality comes as the result of their interplay. "Uniqueness," Mukařovský states, "does not rest in the biological sphere, independent of social influences. It occurs only when a particular biological type emerging at birth encounters social influences. Thus, uniqueness lies at the *point of intersection* of biological dispositions and individual social influences and the more factors there are that intersect in the given individual the more pronounced his uniqueness will be."[45]

How relative the individuality of the author is becomes especially palpable when we view him solely in his capacity as a creator of works of art. Here he becomes enmeshed in a very specific regularity, the previous tradition of a particular art. In his reaction (positive or negative) against the works of the past he sets an example (again positive or negative) for future works, and thus inevitably appears as part of a historical process. Within this process the individuality of the artist may be completely submerged, especially if the historian sees his main objective as studying the regularity of this developmental process. In the second state of his structuralism Mukařovský had propounded just such a deterministic concept of history. The creating subject was seen only through the prism of developmental regularity, as a mere embodiment of forces which transcend him and prescribe his role in the historical process.

But however relative the artist's individuality may be, it cannot be eliminated from the development of art. Mukařovský accommodated it in the last period of his structuralism through a radically revised notion of historical process. He abandoned the idea of "self-movement" (*Selbstbewegung*) as the source of developmental change. The motor of history was not the contradictions within a single developmental series or the tensions stemming from the interaction of various series, but the creative subject himself. In "The Individual and Literary Development," a lecture de-

---

45. "Problémy individua v umění" [Problems of the individual in art], *Cestami*, p. 66.

livered at the Circle probably on January 15, 1943,[46] Mukařovský outlined the following model of literary development. The literary series is static and tends toward the preservation of the status quo, so that the impulse for change must come from outside. The only channel through which external impulses can penetrate literature is the individual, since he is the only external factor in immediate contact with literature. The individual's activity is his unique selection and organization of these influences, which he thrusts into the literary series. Therefore, the fundamental antinomy of literary history is the contradiction between the literary series and individuality.

Toward the end of "The Individual and Literary Development" Mukařovský affirmed his new position in unambiguous terms:

> Only by including the individual as a developmental factor in the theoretical study of literature can we definitively eliminate a causal conception of development. As long as we consider only the immanent development [of art] with the other series intervening at just the time and in just the way that their intervention is needed, there is always the danger that the word "regularity," even if the scholar himself understands it teleologically, will contain some latent mechanistic causality, will incline toward a scheme of causes and results necessarily and unequivocally following from them. But as soon as we accept that accidentality, represented by the individual (the individual as genus), constantly and continuously operates behind this regularity as its latent aspect, the notion of regularity is divested of the last traces of causality. Accident and law cease to exclude one another and conjoin in a genuine, always dynamic and dynamicizing dialectic opposition.[47]

The concept of the individual brings us to the end of what I hope is a reasonably extensive picture of Mukařovský's structuralist aesthetics in all its historical complexity. Although Mukařovský

---

46. Though it is not proven, it seems likely that the essay "The Individual and Literary Development" corresponds to the lecture "The Concept of the Development of Art" delivered at the Circle on this date. This is suggested by Felix Vodička in his introduction to *Studies in Aesthetics*, p. 12. For the lectures delivered at the Circle, see B. Kochis, "List of Lectures Given in the Prague Linguistic Circle (1926–1948)," *Sound, Sign and Meaning*, pp. 607–22.

47. "Individuum a literární vývoj," *Studie*, p. 234.

did not solve or even touch upon all the questions that have plagued aesthetics throughout two and one-half millennia, his work has without any doubt opened new perspectives into these questions and suggested new approaches for answering them. To return to Dessoir's gloomy assessment of the state of aesthetics with which we began, we might ask whether Mukařovský succeeded in bringing the subject of aesthetics out of its obscurity, whether he defined the field sharply and provided it with a reliable method. These questions stand open to argument, and now that most of Mukařovský's major theorizing is available in English, one hopes that they will indeed be argued.

PETER STEINER

Aesthetics and General Theory of Art

1

On Structuralism

I would like to attempt a rather cursory survey of the current state of the Czechoslovakian theory of art. I shall not concern myself with either bibliographical or personal data or even with a view of this theory in its entire breadth. In the short exposition that follows it will be most useful, I think, to examine in somewhat more detail a concept which seems characteristic of the current state of this theory of art: the concept of structure. This concept has given its name to structuralism, a methodological movement responding to local evolutionary preconditions and simultaneously, of course, to the stimuli of contemporary world philosophy, linguistics, and the theory of art. In using the word *structuralism,* we are not forgetting that analogous (though not always identical) movements exist in other disciplines. The structuralist theory of art is most closely tied to linguistics, as that science is understood in the Prague Linguistic Circle. The development of phonology in linguistics has opened up to literary theory a way of probing the sound level in the verbal work of art; analysis of linguistic functions has given the study of the stylistics of poetic language new possibilities; and, finally, emphasis on the semiotic character of language has made possible the understanding of the work of art as a sign.

First, of course, we must say what our theory of art means by structure. Structure is usually defined as a whole, the parts of which acquire a special character by entering it. It is usually said that a whole is more than the sum of the parts of which it is composed. From the standpoint of the concept of structure, however, this definition is too broad, for it includes not only structures in the literal sense of the word but also, for example, configurations (*Gestalten*), with which Gestalt psychology is concerned. Thus with the concept of artistic structure we stress a sign more special than the mere correlation of a whole and its parts. We designate

"O strukturalismu," a lecture at the Institut des études slaves in Paris, 1946; published in *Studie z estetiky* (Prague, 1966).

interrelations among the components—relations dynamic in their very essence—as the specific property of structure in art. According to our conception we can consider as a structure only such a set of elements, the internal equilibrium of which is constantly disturbed and restored anew and the unity of which thus appears to us as a set of dialectic contradictions. That which endures is only the identity of a structure in the course of time, whereas its internal composition—the correlation of its components—changes continuously. In their interrelations individual components constantly strive to dominate one another; each of them makes an effort to assert itself to the detriment of the others. In other words, the hierarchy—the mutual subordination and superordination of components (which is only the expression of the internal unity of a work)—is in a state of constant regrouping. In this process those components which temporarily come to the fore have a decisive significance for the total meaning of the artistic structure, which constantly changes as a result of their regrouping.

But what in art appears to us as a structure? A structure is first of all each individual work of art in itself. If an individual work of art is to be understood as a structure, however, it must be perceived—and have been created—against the background of certain artistic conventions (formulae) provided by the artistic tradition that is lodged in the consciousness of both the artist and the perceiver. Otherwise it would not be perceived as an *artistic* creation. And precisely because of its involuntary confrontation with artistic conquests of the past, which have already become common property and have therefore become arrested, immutable, the work of art, in contradistinction to them, can appear as an unstable equilibrium of constantly shifting forces, hence as a structure. Partly by conforming to the artistic conventions of the past and partly by clashing with them, the structure of the work prevents the artist from being in conflict with the most current reality and with the current state of both the social consciousness and his own consciousness. The connection of a work with the artistic conventions of the past prevents it from becoming unintelligible to the perceiver. Even the dialectic relations among the components and their counterbalancing become palpable within the work as a result of its clashes with tradition.

A structure is not, however, only a single, isolated work of art. We have already determined that a reference to what has preceded it in art—and, let us add, to what will follow—inheres in its very essence. The fact that the structure of a given work palpably differs from tradition—and every original work of art differs from it—always means that at the same time an appeal is directed to future creation. Every work of art, even the most "original," thus becomes part of a continuous stream passing through time. There is no work of art that is not part of this stream, even if some works seem quite unexpected in relation to it (e.g., Mácha's *Máj* in Czech literature).

The structure of a work of art, which appears as an event even when we look at a single work, appears even more as motion if we look at the contexts of which the work is a part. First of all, a particular work of art is not usually its author's only work. Almost always it is only one link in a whole chain of creations. In the course of time, the author's attitude toward reality and his creative method change, and thus the structure of his works varies. Of course, this change is not independent of changes in the national literature as a whole, which, in turn, is liable to changes due to the development of the social consciousness. The evolution of the individual structure of the author's work in the course of time is not, however, such that the structure changes in sudden leaps; its continuity is not broken even by the most radical changes. The tension between what changes and what remains always endures. The author is confined within the limits of his artistic individuality, which, to be sure, he constantly redefines; but precisely because of this he cannot overstep its limits.

What is valid for an individual's work is also valid for the development of any art as a whole. Here, too, the components constantly regroup; their hierarchy—the gradation of their revelance for one another—constantly changes. This regrouping does not, however, occur in the artistic production of a particular moment either to the same degree or in the same direction. Each contemporary generation of artists represents by its creation a different structure which is often substantially unlike the others, and these structures affect one another. For example, not only do the predecessors influence the newcomers, but frequently the structure of the younger artists' creation has an effect upon their predecessors who are still creating. The internal dialectic of a particular art, as it manifests itself in a whole, includes personalities, generations, movements, as well as individual artistic genres, as partial artistic structures. On the other hand, in the culture of a given nation none of the arts, understood as a series of artistic expressions, is isolated: painting and sculpture stand next to literature, music stands next to them, and so on.

Each of the individual arts is necessarily related to the others, and these relations are full of tension. For example, within a given national culture the individual arts converge (they strive to attain by specific means, peculiar to each of them, mastery of the tasks belonging to another art), or, again, they disperse. In this process what changes most often is the hierarchy of the individual arts. For example, music and the visual arts are distinctly in the foreground in the Czech Baroque period; literature and theater occupy this place at the time of the Czech National Revival; and literature, visual arts, and music attain equal importance in the generation of the National Theater.

The picture of the evolution of art hence appears as a very complex process, if we look at it from the standpoint of art itself, its internal structure. Finally, we must not neglect the interrelations among the arts of different nations, for instance, the relations among individual national literatures. Traditional comparative literature used to consider these relations as essentially one-sided. With an almost a prioristic certainty it attributed to some literatures the ability to exert an influence, whereas it considered others condemned to passive acceptance of foreign influences. Historians of individual national literatures, such as those of Czech literature, have shared this approach. This view is, however, fundamentally incorrect, even when, as it often happens, influences in concrete historical situations are one-sided. In such cases it is not a question of a fundamental one-sidedness of influence in the sense that the literature accepting the influence (or influences) is a passive partner; rather, it may happen that a literature confronts several influences simultaneously and then proceeds to choose among them, gradate them hierarchically, and allow one to prevail over the others; in so doing, it gives meaning to this entire set of influences. In other words, influences do not function in the environment which they penetrate without a precondition: they collide with the tradition of the local literature, to the conditions and needs of which they are subordinated. The local artistic and ideological tradition can create dialectic tensions among the influences. Thus in some periods and in some writers of nineteenth-

and twentieth-century Czech literature there is a dialectic relation between the influences of Russian and other Slavic literatures (especially Polish) on the one hand and Western influences on the other. As soon as Russian and Slavic influences in general have become more strongly felt, they have always strengthened the national specificity of Czech literature, its individuality in contrast to others, which, despite all their beneficence, have weakened this individuality. The effect of Slavic influences is especially apparent in Havlíček, Hálek, Mrštík, Šrámek, and the like. This is how influences appear, if we proceed from dialectic and, thereby, structural relations among literatures.

In sum, we can say that the relation of each national literature to others, viewed from its own standpoint, appears as a structure of individual relations (influences), where the single parts are arranged hierarchically and change their places in this hierarchy during development. If those scholars who proceed from the opposing premise that influences are fundamentally one-sided carry their argument to its logical conclusion, they necessarily arrive at a picture of an utterly inactive literature whose development is governed by accidental collisions of influences penetrating now from this side, now from that side. As we have indicated, such a conception was not alien to some historians of Czech literature (especially those who yielded to the "small nation" complex); indeed, even the historians of Czech visual arts were close to this conception. Thus, it is particularly worthy of note that Antonín Matějček and his pupils demonstrated through an explication of Czech Gothic painting an example of a national art which was distinctly individual, coherent, and active, even though it was touched by several simultaneous influences.

In the foregoing paragraphs we have perhaps succeeded in demonstrating—at least by implication—that not only the individual work of art or the evolution of each art as a whole but also the interrelations among the arts have the character of structures. And if we view all of these as structures (i.e., as a labile equilibrium of relations), we do not find ourselves in conflict with reality; nor do we impoverish the variety of investigative possibilities, but, on the contrary, we point to their richness.

At this point, we shall take the opportunity to examine another important property of the work of art, its nature as a *sign*. Like any sign, the work of art is supposed to mediate (in its special

way) between two parties; here the artist is the originator of the
sign, the perceiver is the party receiving the sign. The work of art
is, however, a very complex sign: each of its components and each
of its parts is a vehicle of partial meaning. These partial meanings
comprise the total meaning of the work. And only when the total
meaning of a work is closed does the work of art become a testimony of the originator's attitude toward reality and an appeal to
the perceiver that he adopt the artist's attitude—cognitive, emotional, and volitional—toward reality. But before the perceiver
reaches the total meaning, he must have experienced the process
of the creation of the total meaning. This process is particularly
important in the work of art. From the history of art it is known
that in some periods the work tends toward openness of meaning,
but this does not detract from its artistic efficacy. In such cases,
openness of meaning is a component of the artist's intention. The
ability to have manifold meanings—again without detracting from
its effectiveness—is a characteristic of the work of art as a sign.
In some periods the capacity to have more than one meaning is
stressed (e.g., in the Symbolist period); at other times, on the
other hand, it is only indicated and turns into concealed semantic
energy. Essentially, however, such a capacity is always present.

Hence the work of art, unlike other kinds of signs, for example,
linguistic ones, places primary emphasis not on a resultant, unequivocal relation to reality but on the process by which this
relation originates. One could, of course, object that every process necessarily occurs in time and that therefore the above statement is valid only for arts whose perception occurs in temporal
succession (e.g., literature, music, theater, film). However, even
works of spatial art, such as painting, sculpture, and architecture,
appear to the perceiver as a semantic process. For instance, it
requires time in painting for even a very basic orientation in the
total semantic organization of the pictorial plane, let alone for the
careful perception induced by an effort to penetrate deeply into
the most intrinsic sense of the painted creation. Even in painting,
therefore, single, partial meanings comprise the total meaning
through a meaning-creating process occurring in time.

Every work of art therefore appears to the perceiver as a
semantic continuity, as a contexture. Every new partial sign which
the perceiver apprehends during the process of perception (i.e.,
every component and every part of a work when entering the

meaning-creating process of contexture) not only attaches itself to those which have penetrated previously into the perceiver's consciousness but also changes to a greater or lesser extent the meaning of everything that has preceded. And, conversely, everything that has preceded affects the meaning of each newly apprehended partial sign. In the "temporal" arts, succession in the perception of the individual parts of the work is left to the discretion of the perceiver, but in a way in which the author has predetermined. Even the "spatial" arts, however, are not different. For example, a painter guides the perceiver's attention from that point on the plane which he wants to be the starting point to the remaining part of the plane and to the partial meanings which these sections carry. He does this by manipulating the quality and lightness of the color-patches, by shaping and placing contours and volumes, and so on. In every work of art, the emphasis rests first of all on the very method and process which create the semantic contexture whose purpose is to help the perceiver construct his own attitude toward reality. We need only add that our use of the word *own* does not imply an unconditional emphasis on individual uniqueness, for in using this word, we do not lose sight of the dialectic relation between individual consciousness and social consciousness.

We now must determine which components of a work of art are capable of being vehicles of the meanings which, together, create its total meaning. This is not a superfluous question because the idea has not yet been completely discredited that the components of "content" (in conventional terminology), in contrast to the "formal" components, are the only vehicles of the meaning of an artistic work. However, all components without exception are vehicles of meaning (as we have presupposed from the beginning of this semantic section of our study) and are thereby the factors which, together, create the total meaning of a work. All the components participate in the semantic process which we have called contexture. For example, in a poetic work, single words, sound components, grammatical forms, syntactic components (the sentence structure), and phraseology participate in the same way as the thematic components. In a painting, line as well as color, contour as well as volume, the organization of the pictorial plane as well as the subject are equally instrumental in the creation of the contexture.

The methods by which the components are used in a work of

art (the artistic devices) also have meaning-creating value. Furthermore, so do the interrelations among the components. For instance, in a poetic work, the relation between the structure of the
speech sounds (euphony) and the meaning of the words in the
euphony can evoke semantic relations among words which lack an
immediate semantic connection in the text and can emphasize
words important for the total meaning of the poem by virtue of
the fact that a speech-sound group characteristic of such a word
occurs many times in the text, while the word itself is not repeated. Components, which are, at first glance, semantically indifferent, can effectively intervene in the semantic structure of a
work. For example, in poetry, meter does this by dividing the
text—sometimes in agreement with, sometimes in contradiction to
the syntactic articulation—through its pauses, and, of course, in
many other ways. Here is another example from painting: Color is
an optical phenomenon without any intrinsic semiotic character
(if we disregard its symbolic use); nevertheless, as the component
of a painting, even an athematic one, it becomes a sign. Thus if a
patch of azure is placed in the upper part of the plane of an
abstract painting, it will very easily become the vehicle of the
meaning *sky;* in the lower part of the pictorial plane it can take on
the meaning *body of water.* In both cases, of course, these are not
concrete meanings but rather allusions to particular realities. The
partial overlapping of contours, even those lacking any objectivity
whatsoever, can, in an abstract picture, indicate the depth of a
space filled with some, albeit unnameable, objects.

In a work of art all components which are traditionally called
formal are therefore vehicles of meanings, partial signs. And, conversely, components which are usually assigned to "content"
(thematic components) are by their nature mere signs which acquire full meaning only in the contexture of the work of art. Let
us take as an example a character from an epic or dramatic work.
In realistic art, the artist will strive to arouse in the reader (or the
spectator) the impression that he is concerned with a particular
individual who existed somewhere and at some time. Simultaneously, however, he necessarily strives to make the character seem
as universally valid as possible, to give the reader (spectator) the
impression that something of this character is in every man and
even in himself. The inseparable connection of concreteness and
generality is a characteristic of every art. However, the connection

is possible only because the work of art signifies reality *after* it has become a sum of all its components and parts (among which are its individual characters), at the same time referring to reality as to a whole. And thus every individual character of an epic work is fully understandable only in relation to the other characters, the plot, the artistic devices which have been employed in the work, and so on. Only the great characters of world literature are permitted to step out of the contexture of the work of art and enter into direct contact with reality. Even they, however, do not lose the dual nature of an artistic sign: to appear simultaneously as universal and individual.

The relation of art to reality, precisely because of this specificity of its semiotic character, is not unequivocal and immutable but rather dialectic and therefore historically changeable. Art has many of the most varied possibilities to signify reality as a whole. We can observe the variation of these possibilities in the course of its history. Here the span is great—from the striving for an utterly faithful picture of all the heteromorphism of reality (and also of all the accidentality contained in this heteromorphism) to the seemingly complete rupture between art and reality. Even the most distanced relation to reality does not cease to be an indispensable factor of the structure of a work, making possible the internal variety, the constant renewal, and the vital import of a work of art, both for the perceiver as an individual and for the society as a whole.

The last phenomenon that should be discussed, if we wish to characterize the current state of the Czechoslovakian theory of art, is the concept of *function*. This concept (which the theory of art shares with linguistics and also with the study of folklore and with architecture in the sphere of art) concerns the relation of the work of art to the perceiver and to society. The concept of function acquires full objectivity only if it means the variety of purposes which art serves in society. Some works of art are, from their very origin, unequivocally designated for a particular kind of social activity. This designation manifests itself in their structures by, for example, the assimilation of the canon of that artistic genre which serves this need; it also reveals itself in other ways. But a work is capable of fulfilling several functions simultaneously. It can also alter its functions in the course of time. Most often, such a shift in function has the appearance of a shift in the dominant of the system of possible functions; a change in the dominant function necessarily manifests itself in a shift in the total meaning of the work.

The functions of art are many and varied; because of their capacity for combination, it is not easy to present their full enumeration and classification. Among them, however, there is one which is specific for art and without which the work of art would cease to be a work of art. This is the aesthetic function. Yet it is clear that the aesthetic function is by no means limited to art but penetrates all the works of man and all the activities of his life. It is one of the most important factors creating man's attitude toward reality; it has the capacity, as will be shown in more detail, to prevent a single function from gaining a one-sided supremacy over the others. In spheres outside the limits of art it affects a much greater number of individuals, and its activity there is more extensive; in art, on the other hand, it is more intensive.

How does the aesthetic function manifest itself in art? First of all, we must realize that, unlike all other functions (e.g., cognitive, political, educational, etc.), the aesthetic function does not have any concrete aim; it does not tend toward the fulfillment of any practical task. The aesthetic function sets a thing or an activity aside from practical associations, rather than incorporating it into some of these. This is especially true of art. If the thesis about the special property of the aesthetic function is accepted, it is usually concluded—sometimes positively, sometimes negatively—that emphasizing the aesthetic function necessarily results in the severance of art from life. This is a mistake, however. If the aesthetic function does not tend toward any practical aim, this does not mean that it will obstruct the contact of art with the vital interests of man. Precisely because it lacks unequivocal "content," the aesthetic function becomes "transparent" and does not act inimically to the other functions but helps them. If other "practical" functions compete with one another when they are juxtaposed and strive to dominate one another, exhibiting a tendency toward functional specialization (toward monofunctionality, which culminates in the machine), then it is precisely because of the aesthetic function that art tends toward as rich and as many-sided a polyfunctionality as possible, without, at the same time, preventing the work of art from having a social effect. By manifesting itself in art as a specific function, the aesthetic function helps man overcome the one-

sidedness of specialization which impoverishes not only his attitude toward reality but also the possibility of his conduct toward
it. The aesthetic function does not obstruct man's creative initiative but helps to develop it. It is no accident that a sophisticated
interest in art is often a characteristic feature of the biographies of
great scholars, inventors, and explorers.

Up to this point we have looked at the functions of art only
from the standpoint of society. Now, however, let us look at them
from the standpoint of the individual, whether the creating or the
perceiving individual. Even when the artist adapts the structure of
a work to a certain function, he does not exclude a priori any of
the others. Otherwise he could not enter into live contact with
reality through his work. If he forcibly simplified the functional
richness of the work, he would also impoverish his own approach
to reality and its stimulative capacity. Thus, only if we look at the
functions of art from the individual's viewpoint do the functions
of a work appear as a set of live energies which are in constant
tension and conflict with one another. Only then do we also fully
grasp that the functions of a work are not separate compartments
but motion, which constantly changes the appearance of a work
from perceiver to perceiver, from nation to nation, from period to
period. This will be especially evident to us if we look at a work
through its perceiver's eyes rather than its author's.

Not only the individual perceiver but also entire social formations, such as different milieux and strata, appear as the individualizing factor from the standpoint, of course, of the functions of
the work of art. These social formations in particular determine
how the shifts in the total structure of the functions occur.

We must, however, note, at least in passing, the role which the
subject plays in the determination of the artistic value of a particular phenomenon. As long as we have in mind only the artist's
subject, it is a simple matter. One way in which the artist introduces his subjectivity into the work is by adapting its structure to
a specific predetermined function. The perceiver also determines
to a certain extent whether a particular object is to function as a
work of art (thus, above all, aesthetically). The Surrealists intentionally exploited such a possibility in the choice and creation of
"objects" which in themselves would appear remote from any
functionality whatsoever, even aesthetic. A higher demand is made
on the perceiver's subjectivity in this process than in intentionally

created works of art. Even in the case of Surrealist objects, however, the aesthetic function is objectified in the perceiver's consciousness because he evaluates the object on the basis of a confrontation with specific artistic conventions, partly observed, partly violated. The acceptance of a Surrealist object as a work of art is, however, only an extreme exaggeration of a quite common phenomenon: the feeling of freedom in the determination of the functionality of a work of art, a feeling which is a necessary factor of its efficacy.

We have examined several basic concepts of the structuralist theory of art. It has turned out that as soon as we begin to look at art as a labile, constantly tense, constantly regrouping equilibrium of forces, traditional problems appear in a new light and questions which have not been posed emerge. Many prospects which open up are direct challenges demanding an immediate answer. Let me mention only one example: the comparative theory of arts. The question is not new. Lessing posed it for the first time with ingenious clairvoyance in his *Laocoön,* and a number of other scholars did so after him. However, in understanding the individual arts as structures bound together by historically changeable, dialectic tensions, structuralism sees not only their delimitation according to the properties of their materials and other conditions (as Lessing recognized) but also the possibilities for their approximation to one another since in specific evolutionary situations they strive for reconciliation, penetration, and even substitution. This conception of the interrelation of the arts is especially fruitful for the history of art. Even a cursory glance at the fates of some national cultures often convinces us of its methodological relevance. For instance, we can observe some shifts in the hierarchy of arts in Czech culture of the nineteenth century. In the period of the National Revival at the beginning of the century, literature and the theater stand prominently in the foreground; in the seventies (when Smetana and Neruda are creating side by side in music and in literature, respectively), music and literature are the leading arts; in the eighties and nineties, during the time of the construction of the National Theater, literature, music, visual arts, and the theater reach a collaboration based on equal rights. (In literature the generations of the Májovians and Lumírians are simultaneously active; in music Smetana and Dvořák; in visual arts Aleš, Hynais, Myslbek, and others; in theater J. J. Kolár at the head of a large acting school.) These are, of course, only suggestions for a study which would have to be developed on the basis of extensive material and a profound knowledge of the history of the individual Czech arts. The problems are, however, clearly apparent in outline and are urgent precisely today, when we realize more clearly than ever before that things are universally interconnected.

As regards the history of individual arts we must mention in addition that the structuralist method also throws new light on the question of so-called *influences* and their significance for the histories of these arts. Again it is a very complex question, and the current possibilities for its solution can be indicated only in the roughest outline. The traditional conception understands influence one-sidedly, opposes the influencing party and the influenced party to each other in permanent contradiction without taking into account that an influence, if it is to be accepted, must be prepared for by local conditions which determine what meaning it will acquire and in which direction it will operate. In no case will an influence operate so that it annuls the local developmental situation, which is the result not only of the previous evolution of art but also of the previous development of social consciousness and its contemporary state. In the study of influences, therefore, we must take into account that individual national arts associate with one another on the basis of mutual equality (not on the basis of an essential subordination of the influenced to the influencing). Moreover, one art form of a certain nation, for example, literature, is only exceptionally influenced by a single foreign national art. As a rule there is a whole series of foreign influences, and there is not only the relation of each of them to a given art being influenced but also interrelations among the influences themselves.

For example, in the course of the nineteenth and twentieth centuries, Czech literature was related to a whole series of foreign literatures—German, Russian, French, Polish—and, of course, Slovak literature. These relations touched Czech literature not only successively but often simultaneously. From the standpoint of the influencing literatures the majority of these relations was one-sided, inasmuch as Czech literature did not participate actively in world literary events (because after the period of decline during the Counter-Reformation Czech literature had to work up to the level of modern European literatures). Yet these influences in no way prevented the intrinsic development of Czech literature. There was a whole multitude of influences; so they counterbalanced one another, their relative importance changed in the course of time, and Czech literature sometimes inclined one way, sometimes another, thus creating a mutually fruitful dialectic tension between the influences and itself and also among the influences themselves. Hence influences are not, let it be recalled once more, a manifestation of a basic superordination and subordination of individual national cultures; their basic form is reciprocity, springing from the mutual equality of nations and the equisignificance of their cultures. From the standpoint of each national culture (and hence of each national art) relations to the cultures (and hence to the arts) of other nations create a structure bound by internal, dialectic relations which constantly regroup because of the impulses coming from social evolution.

We are at the end of our consideration of structuralism in the study of art but far from the end of the enumeration of the prospects which structuralism opens up to a theoretical and historical study of art. We have not been concerned with completeness but only with characterizing structuralism with respect to several basic questions more concretely than we could have done in a general consideration. Structuralism was born and lives in an immediate connection with artistic creation and, at that, with contemporary creation. It does not relinquish its relation to contemporary creation even when it attempts—in light of current artistic sensibility—to elucidate the art of the past, to show how that art solved its problems of creation. The connection between contemporary art and structuralism in the study of art is reciprocal. That is, artists and theoreticians are in agreement that our time obliges both of them to think out consistently and boldly the regularities of artistic creation in relation to the revolutionary changes of man's situation in the world.

2

The Significance of Aesthetics

It is not so long ago that the question "What is aesthetics?" used to elicit the stereotyped response "The science of beauty." Consequently many people conceived—and perhaps still do—the aesthetician as someone who presumes to determine what others should consider beautiful or even how artists themselves should create the beautiful. Certainly aesthetics has been aware for quite some time that in prescribing rules for the beautiful, it does nothing more than adopt a particular artistic convention and generally, in fact fatally, a respectably obsolete convention. Modern aesthetics, however, does not dare to prescribe either rules of the beautiful or even rules of taste. If the image of a dry pedant peevishly tutoring artists and the public is appalling enough, the image of the "aesthete" at the beginning of this century, the aesthete who at times camouflaged his mental emptiness by means of an aesthetic hyperaesthesia, is even more appalling. All of this (and many other things) aesthetics is not. It now remains for us to agree upon what aesthetics is. But if we have realized only that aesthetics is a perfectly respectable and sober discipline, we have not said enough for our present purpose. Well then, if I am to try to define aesthetics, I will not find a better solution than the following: it is the study of the aesthetic function, its manifestation, and its vehicle. Now, however, we must clarify what we mean by the somewhat vague term "aesthetic function." We shall proceed from a tried and true narrative method—from Adam. At first we shall say nothing at all about the aesthetic function; this concept will reappear only later. We shall begin with an observation on the attitudes that man adopts toward reality.

Man adopts various attitudes toward reality, the world that surrounds him. He adopts one attitude toward reality, for example, when he is acting practically, another when he conceives it theoretically or scientifically, another when he apprehends it religiously.

"Význam estetiky," a lecture delivered in 1942; published in *Studie z estetiky* (Prague, 1966).

Each of these attitudes takes hold of his entire person, of all his abilities, and orients them in a particular direction. Although, as we shall see, it is not impossible for these separate attitudes to interpenetrate, to accompany one another, and so forth, they also frequently exclude one another, obstruct one another, interfere with one another precisely because each of them demands a different regulation of all the abilities, of the entire personality at a given moment. Each of these attitudes is directed at a certain goal which is, however, defined by the attitude itself only very generally and which acquires specificity only with the concrete task that is to be fulfilled within the limits of this attitude at a given moment. The result is a rich differentiation, especially in the practical attitude. The artisan is oriented practically in his work, that is, toward an activity, in the same way, for instance, as the merchant in selling and the diplomat in political dealings. As we can see from these cases, there is a very rich gradation of means, mental sets, and so on, here. The attainment of the goal requires an activity and certain implements. We say that the implements and the activity suitable for the attainment of a certain goal are capable of functioning with respect to this goal, that they are the vehicles of this or that function. The implement of an activity is often a permanent thing that exists even when it is not precisely in action. In this case as well, however, the implement suited for a certain activity, for the attainment of a certain goal, bears traces of this capability in its organization. A function thus appears not only as an accidental mode of using certain things but also as a permanent property of its vehicle.

Let us now tackle the aesthetic function. This function also has its source and directive in one of the basic attitudes which man adopts toward reality, the aesthetic attitude. What is the nature of this attitude? How does it differ from the other attitudes? Let us attempt to compare it with them. If we adopt a practical attitude toward reality, we are concerned with an immediate effect upon it. When we act practically, we wish to alter reality in some way by means of our intervention, and only with respect to this anticipated result do we take an action and choose its implements. In the choice of implements we value only those of their properties which are suitable for the attainment of the expected result of the activity; the remaining properties of these implements are indifferent for us; in fact, they do not even exist for us. It is well known—and this has been exploited in humorous literature quite often—that people of different occupations who work with the same material do not view it in the same way. For the woodsman the forest is flora; for the cabinetmaker, cooper, and wheelwright a source of wood; for the hunter a hiding place of game; and finally, if you like, for children a place where raspberries and strawberries grow. A philosopher has shrewdly remarked about the practical attitude: "Man must live, and life requires that we perceive things according to the relation which they have to our needs. Life depends on action. To live means to receive only useful impressions from things and to respond to them with appropriate reactions; the other impressions must be obscured or be projected to us only vaguely. I see and hear of the outer world only what my senses select from it for the purpose of guiding my behavior. . . . My senses and my consciousness provide me only with a practically simplified image of reality."

So much for the practical attitude. Let us now take the theoretical, cognitive attitude. If we approach reality with the intention of cognizing it, then reality—this time the material of cognition—appears to us only from the aspect from which we wish to cognize it. Not even in this case is it a thing which we make the object of cognition, a goal in itself. On the basis of an agreement of certain of its properties with other things, reality is subordinated to a particular concept and becomes a member of a general context. The assertion of general regularities is the goal of cognitive activity. The cognitive attitude, just like the practical attitude, is therefore directed somewhere *beyond* the reality which is at hand and in sight at a given moment.

Let us now proceed to the religious attitude, or rather the magico-religious, if we want to grasp the full extent of its range. Here we are already on different ground than we were with the practical and theoretical attitudes. Every reality which enters the range of the magico-religious attitude becomes a sign of a special kind, and it does so immediately upon its entry. The theoretical attitude, of course, is also characterized by the fact that it converts reality into a sign, namely a concept; here, however, we confront precisely a conversion which is not self-evident, given in advance, but which requires a cognitive effort. In the magico-religious attitude, realities are not converted into signs but are simply signs intrinsically. This is why they are also capable of functioning as what they represent (an amulet and the like). They are sign-symbols.

Finally, there is the *aesthetic* attitude. The reality entering its range also requires a semiotic nature. Let us mention only a concrete case: physical exercise. Insofar as physical exercise is conceived in its practical function (strengthening of the body, training in dexterity, etc.), the action that the body performs is considered only with regard to these results, as a means to their attainment. Let us suppose, however, that an aesthetic consideration becomes concomitant or even predominant. Immediately the action performed in the exercise will acquire value in itself, and attention will be directed to all the stages and details of its course and continuation.

How can we explain this change? Here, too, the reality entering the range of the aesthetic attitude becomes a sign and, of course, a sign of a special kind, distinct from the magico-religious sign. With the magico-religious sign, as we saw, consideration was directed not to the sign itself but to what stood behind it, to what it represented—a mysterious force or a deity.[1] Conversely, with the aesthetic sign, attention is concentrated on the very reality which becomes a sign. The entire wealth of its properties a, pears before our eyes, and so do the entire wealth and complexity of the act by which we perceive it. The thing that becomes an aesthetic sign reveals and allows man to perceive the relationship between reality and itself. Any reality, even the whole universe, can be perceived and experienced according to the way in which man perceives and experiences a certain given reality toward which he has just adopted the aesthetic attitude. *For this reason* the phenomenon toward which we adopt the aesthetic attitude becomes a sign, and a sign *sui generis,* for to refer to something beside itself is precisely the property of a sign.

An aesthetic sign refers to all the realities which man has experienced and can still experience, the whole universe of things and actions. The manner in which the object that the aesthetic attitude has seized is organized and the object which has become the vehicle of the aesthetic function provide a certain direction to

---

1. The doctrine of transubstantiation is characteristic of this attitude and of the nature of the magico-religious sign. The properties of the bread and the wine remain, but the *essence* changes: The bread and the wine *become* in their essence Christ's body and blood.

our view of reality in general. This applies to a greater degree, of course, to the work of art which has been created specifically for the purpose of evoking the aesthetic attitude in the observer. No matter how minute is the segment of reality which it represents, and even when it does not represent anything at all—as a musical work, for example—the work of art as an aesthetic sign has the capacity to refer to reality as a whole and to express and evoke man's relation to the universe. Art is not, however, the only vehicle of the aesthetic function. Any phenomenon, any action, any product of human activity can become an aesthetic sign for an individual or even for a whole society.

So much for the individual attitudes. We have seen four of them: the *practical,* the *theoretical,* the *magico-religious,* and the *aesthetic.* These are the basic attitudes; others derive from their further differentiation or from their blending and fusion. The practical and theoretical attitudes apply to reality itself: they either directly change it (the practical attitude) or prepare for a more effective possibility of intervening in it by contributing to our knowledge of it (the theoretical attitude). The magico-religious and aesthetic attitudes convert the essence of reality into a sign by their very contact with it. These two attitudes and the functions belonging to them are therefore closer to one another than either one of them is to the other two. They can be grouped together under the common designation of the semiotic functions.

But even so, the aesthetic attitude and the aesthetic function in a certain sense stand alone opposed to all the others. None of the other attitudes and functions is concentrated upon a sign, for all of them primarily direct attention to what the sign signifies, to what it refers. For the practical function the sign, insofar as it uses one (e.g., a linguistic sign—a word), is merely an implement of more complicated actions; for the theoretical (cognitive) function the sign (a concept and a word expressing it) is again a means for mastering reality. For the magico-religious function the real importance does not lie in the symbol but in that invisible power which it embodies. Only in the case of the aesthetic function does the major emphasis lie in the sign itself, in that sensorily perceptible thing which acquires the task of signifying something, of referring to something. Only thus is it possible for the aesthetic sign to detach itself to a considerable extent from direct contact with the thing or event that it represents (the plot of a novel, the theme of

a painting as realities directly represented by the work) and transcend it in some definite way to signify man's general relation to
the universe which is not bound to any concrete reality. The
aesthetic function thus appears as a certain counterbalance, a
certain antithesis, of the other functions. For all these others, the
things which they seize for their purposes, which they make their
vehicles, are *implements,* valuable only insofar as they are suited
for the purpose, the attainment of which they serve. Only for the
aesthetic function is the vehicle of the function a value in itself—
a value because of the way in which it is created and organized.

Why have we expounded all of this when we wish to speak about
the significance of aesthetics for life? So that we shall be aware of
the position and range of the aesthetic, the subject of aesthetics,
in everyday life. We see that the aesthetic function constitutes a
certain counterbalance to all the other functions, of which especially the practical is directly and unconditionally necessary for
the preservation of bare human life. Let us add, however, that the
aesthetic function is a necessary counterbalance even to this function. We have already quoted a philosopher's statement that a
practical mental set, if left alone, impoverishes, makes one-sided,
and inordinately simplifies man's relation to reality. And practical
life itself, as well as man's existential struggle with the reality surrounding him, would eventually suffer from this impoverishment.
If man has to do battle with reality again and again, he must keep
approaching it from new directions, keep discovering previously
unexploited aspects and possibilities. An absolute restriction to the
practical attitude, of course, would unmistakably lead eventually
to total automatization, to a restriction of attention to already
obtained and exploited aspects. Only the aesthetic function can
preserve for man vis-à-vis the universe the position of a foreigner
who keeps coming to unknown regions with fresh and keen attention, who is constantly aware of himself because he is projecting
himself into the surrounding reality and is constantly aware of the
surrounding reality because he measures it with himself.

And so it is with the aesthetic attitude and the aesthetic function
as well as with the other attitudes and functions. There is no
human act and no thing from which the aesthetic function is
excluded, even if these acts and things serve other functions. From
the realm of the practical function let us cite, as telling examples,
artisans' activities and their products (not only typography or

even goldsmithing but also the tailor's and shoemaker's trades have their aesthetic aspect). Whenever the aesthetic aspect is accentuated in any of the trades, this emphasis results in a perfection of the technical aspect. As further examples of the aesthetic function in the realm of the practical attitude let us take physical exercises, physical culture, which we have already mentioned, or social behavior, rules and customs of social interaction. The importance of an aesthetic orientation as the aid and attendant of the practical function is particularly evident in forms of social interaction. Relieving tensions, gaining sympathy, maintaining personal dignity, and other similar requirements of social interaction find valuable support in that special kind of disinterested and calm pleasure which accompanies the aesthetic attitude.

Let us go further and take the theoretical function. It might seem that the very strictly defined and exclusive realm of cognition would exclude any foreign elements. Well, the affinity of scientific and artistic fantasies has already been emphasized and demonstrated by the psychology of creation on more than one occasion. The presence of aesthetic elements in the course of scientific creation is also directly evident from the numerous facts disclosed in this study. The case of the chemist Kekulé von Stradonitz is often cited: the graphic likeness of a long-sought chemical formula first emerged from his subconscious in the form of an ornamental figure, a coiled snake biting its own body. But even the result of scientific work, a scientific solution, sometimes bears traces of the aesthetic function. The simple and elegant solution of a mathematical problem can produce (besides its cognitive value) an aesthetically satisfying impression. Finally, the aesthetic function becomes a direct part of the scholarly method itself in some disciplines. It has frequently been said, as we know, that history lies on the very dividing line between art and science.

Let us now take up the relationship between the aesthetic and magico-religious functions. This relationship is particularly close because of the affinity of the two functions mentioned above (both turn the reality that they seize into a sign immediately, at the same moment). Often we cannot distinguish one from the other. They coalesce in primitive ornamentation, for example. Let us also recall the close union of many cults with visual arts and the religious roots of the theater. Indeed, it even happens that the two functions compete and that the aesthetic function attempts to substitute for the religious function. Hence the extreme reactions, such as Savonarola's, against art in the church; compare as well the aesthetically motivated religious feeling of Romantics like Chateau-briand.

We have already used the word *art* several times in the last paragraphs, even though we have been concerned with showing to what extent the aesthetic attitude penetrates all of man's activities, even his extra-artistic ones. Art constitutes a group in itself. Here we are no longer dealing with phenomena which acquire an aesthetic function only as a concomitant to the main function, and which sometimes acquire it accidentally, but with products created with the intention that aesthetic effect be their main task. It would, however, be wrong to believe that art therefore does not belong in this chapter on the aesthetic and life, that art is something like a quiet oasis of aesthetic contemplation beside the real events of life. It would require a special essay to account for all the ties of art to life, all the interventions of art in the currents and the development of extra-aesthetic functions and interests in the development of art. A few examples will therefore have to suffice. After all, each of the arts eventually enters the realm of the practical functions in some way, and the practical functions are the most typical manifestations of what we call *life,* or *everyday life.*

The situation of architecture is characteristic in this respect. Everything—every building from a barn to a cathedral—is an architectural work. The argument about where in this extensive scale art begins and a predominantly practical creation ends will remain unresolved forever. We could even claim that the continuous oscillation of these poles in the ongoing argument is one of the strongest developmental mainsprings of architecture. As we know, the theory and practice of architecture recently passed through a period—in fact, a period that is not yet entirely over—during which the aesthetic function was purged from architectural works once and for all and the practical purpose proclaimed as the sole decisive criterion of the perfection of an architectural work. It soon turned out in architectural practice, however, that the apparent purpose sometimes concealed the originator's unconscious efforts at aesthetic perfection. Occasionally it even happened that a finished building already in use exhibited certain defects that on closer inspection appeared as an exaggeration of the apparent purpose to the advantage of its aesthetic effect. Soon architectural theorists began to point out that although the individual using a building has material needs (e.g., sufficient space and the possibility of unrestrained movement within it), he also has equally important "psychic" needs and requirements and that one of them is indisputably the need for aesthetic satisfaction. And in the most recent period we are witnesses to the fact that the most competent arbiters, the architect-artists, are themselves beginning to think about the practical need and practical justification for the ornament, the most obvious aesthetic element of architecture.

This case, which we have examined in somewhat more detail because of its representativeness, shows us clearly that not even art, or creation, the characteristic feature of which is the dominance of the aesthetic function over the others, stands outside the realm of practical life. In just the same way we could show to what extent the theater, for example, is a part of the business of life. It is enough to remember the Czech theater during the first half of the nineteenth century—the striving for an independent Czech theater, the attempt at the first grand Czech stage—for it to become clear what a rich blend of practical considerations (e.g., a consideration for the National Revival, a consideration for national education, etc.) functioned in addition to the aesthetic consideration, and even predominated over it. And literature? Let me limit myself to an anecdotal allusion to Petr Bezruč who complains very aggressively, for instance in the poem "Čtenáři veršů" [The readers of verse], about those who want to understand his poems as aesthetic creations and ignore the practically conceived protest which these poems express.

Not even when art remains restricted to its essential definition—the aesthetic function—is it excluded from the context of life. If there are periods which emphasize the exclusion of art from everyday life, we must understand their protest against the connection of art with everyday life as a developmental reaction against the opposite extreme, the dissolution of art into extra-aesthetic activities and interests. There is, of course, a constant tension, or rather a never ending clash, between art and everyday life. But it is precisely this tension which makes art a perpetual ferment of human life.

We have thus seen that the aesthetic, the aesthetic attitude, and the aesthetic function pervade life continuously and that there is no place in the context of life where the aesthetic function cannot penetrate. Consequently the aesthetic is not merely froth, merely a decoration of life, but an important component of all of life's activities. Why have we expounded all of this when we are supposed to be talking about aesthetics and not about the aesthetic? Because we had to outline the basis on which aesthetics, the study of the aesthetic attitude and the aesthetic function, can be applied in life. Precisely because the aesthetic manifests itself so widely and so heteromorphously—and we can say that it has begun to manifest itself much more visibly in modern life, which emphasizes aesthetic culture, than it did not long ago—it requires theoretical support. We have already said that modern aesthetics is not a normative discipline which seeks to determine what is beautiful and what is ugly, what is tasteful and what is not tasteful, what is aesthetically appropriate and what is not. Let us add that in viewing its domain without bias, modern aesthetics has even come to the conclusion that supreme aesthetic expressions sometimes have their roots in areas of so-called bad taste or untrained—often only seemingly untrained—taste. Aesthetics enlightened by history is aware that the boundaries between good taste and bad taste are at times dictated only by a contemporary convention. Folk art, which Romanticism exalted and which has since appeared as such a fertile source of artistic creation, was considered to be a wilderness unworthy of serious attention before Romanticism. And other, even more scorned domains of the aesthetic such as the broadside song or the art of signboards then followed folk art out of obscurity. If we stand before Henri Rousseau's paintings, we may have reasonable doubts about what comes to his work from primitive folk creation and what from the monumental intention of the great masters of European painting.

Today is therefore less than any other time a period when aesthetics would seek and be able to sit in judgment, thereby transgressing its most essential purpose as a discipline which ascertains, states, and reveals the regularity of aesthetic activity. Modern aesthetics is also aware of the fact that discoveries in the realm of the aesthetic can have their source only in an aesthetically conceived creative activity, whether artistic or extra-artistic. And it conclusively rejects the idea—at times implied, at times fully and unashamedly expressed—that it should accept the task of purveying recipes for poems or dramas. After so many negations it is, of course, desirable to make an affirmation. Knowledge, it must be admitted, does not outdistance development and does not pass judgment when it contents itself with its own task which is precisely to be knowledge, the effort toward a theoretical mastery of reality; but at the same time it constantly intervenes, though at times involuntarily, in practice. Let us take, for example, endeavors toward an aesthetic culture which grow increasingly urgent in a period that tends toward the broadest possible social bases of the entire cultural effort: the culture of language, the culture of habitation, the culture of artistic perception, and so on. Like every form of education, this requires a solid theoretical basis. It is futile to preach to someone that he should be interested in expressing himself eloquently if you do not make it possible for him to see the subtle and complex structures of language, if you do not instruct him how the aesthetic function is present in their individual components and how this aesthetic function increases not only the aesthetic perfection but also the practical usefulness of an utterance.

There are, however, still other ways in which aesthetics penetrates aesthetic practice. Let us take, for example, its very relation to artistic creation. It is, of course, true, as we have said, that the creating artist will hardly want someone to meddle with his work. But there is yet another possibility of contact between the theory of art and artistic practice which was once—and not too long ago—formulated by an artist himself approximately as follows: As soon as the principles which subconsciously guided the artist in his creative activity have been rationally elucidated, the artist feels an urgent need to go higher, to go beyond what will henceforth be accessible to every epigone. Hence the negative contact between art and aesthetics, which is nevertheless an intense contact; it could even be said to be the ideal case of possible interaction. Indeed, we have heard quite recently the complaint of the younger generation of poets—I do not know, of course, whether it is too courageous and self-conscious a complaint—that they lack contemporary theoreticians.

Naturally, aesthetics shares these contacts with art and with the theories of the individual arts. There is no fixed boundary here; the theory of literature is often spoken of as the aesthetics of literature. Aesthetics itself, as the general philosophy of the aesthetic, serves the function of a connecting link, and, as we have seen, its interest goes far beyond the realm of art itself. Neverthe-

less, it cannot disclaim an intimate relation to live material. Instances of aesthetic systems being founded on the premises of a
particular art, though they include the whole range of the aesthetic, will always recur. There are aesthetic systems such as
Durdík's clearly founded upon literature; others such as Hostinský's are in the final analysis based upon music.

Thus aesthetics stands on a great many boundary lines: it relates
to various aspects of practical life, to art and artistic creation, and
to the concrete studies of the individual arts. Let us add yet other
relations, active and passive, to many disciplines, the proper
material of which is not the aesthetic, such as psychology, sociology, and linguistics. These relations are sometimes—in various
periods—so close that more than once they have even threatened
the very specificity of aesthetics. At one time it appeared that
aesthetics would be absorbed by psychology and disappear; at another time it was about to dissolve into sociology; at another time,
in Croce, it was identified—at least in anticipation—with linguistics.
But each time it escaped from this seeming stranglehold, renewed
and confirmed in its autonomy.

Today, when after further development, dating from about the
beginning of this century, aesthetics is based on the notions of the
aesthetic function and the sign, it stands more steadfastly in its
specificity than ever before and not only borrows from neighbor-
ing disciplines but also makes contributions itself. It meets psychology by demonstrating the difference between an authentic document and an aesthetically intentional expression which, before it
can be used by psychology, must be analyzed aesthetically to
clarify to what extent it is a document and to what extent an
aesthetically intentional deformation of reality. That even today
studies are often written which consider artistic expressions as
authentic material (e.g., for psychiatric studies) is not the fault of
modern aesthetics but rather of whoever is ignorant of its present
state. The contribution of aesthetics to sociology consists not only
in the fact that together with sociology, but from a slightly different standpoint, it deliberates questions of the relationship between art and society but also in the fact that aesthetics has
indicated that art, just like society, is divided into strata; indeed,
the whole realm of the aesthetic is divided into separate "layers"
("low" and "high" art, then a further stratification in each of
these spheres), and this stratification has a certain but by no

means direct relation to social stratification. This knowledge has revealed a large set of problems which have not been entirely worked out and resolved today. Modern aesthetics lends linguistics a hand in questions of the linguistic aesthetic and of poetic language. To those who are willing to look, it is more and more evident that aesthetics, which regards language from the standpoint of the aesthetic function, can distinctly see the very dynamics of the linguistic system because the linguistic aesthetic constantly reorganizes—precisely for the purpose of renewing aesthetic effect —the structure of the linguistic system, foregrounding this or that component and thus letting us see many phenomena and many linguistic processes that in the practical usage of the language are overshadowed by the communicative task of the linguistic sign.

Finally, let us not forget the paramount relationship between aesthetics and that area of theoretical thought from which it arose and to which it always returns, namely, philosophy. It was recently pointed out that the aesthetic function constitutes an integral part of the process of philosophical thinking, and it was concretely demonstrated (by C. Lalo) that many properties of philosophical systems and many connections interlinking the components of their complex structure have much more of an aesthetic than a logical character. So much for the "formal" aspect of the structure of philosophical systems. That the aesthetic also plays a significant thematic role in philosophical systems as a subject of thought is demonstrated by Schopenhauer's system in which the aesthetic is one of the basic metaphysical principles. Here the aesthetic appears as the antithesis of will which according to Schopenhauer forms the essence of the universe. But what is the relationship between aesthetics and philosophy from the standpoint of today when all-embracing philosophical systems are in low supply? If there are no systems, then certain actual, sometimes pressing, problems that provide for both the specific development of philosophy itself and the general events of the period come to the surface the more distinctly. And aesthetics has something to say about many of these problems from its own perspective and on the basis of its own material. For example, it is by no means accidental that in recent years the problems of the aesthetic norm and aesthetic value, the questions of universality and supratemporality or of the changeability of aesthetic value, and so on, have come to the attention of aesthetics with great urgency. In the same period the

very same problems have arisen independently, but just as urgent-
ly, in other areas of philosophical thought: in philosophy in the
narrower sense of the word, in the philosophy of language, in the
philosophy of law, and so forth. Such, therefore, is the participation of aesthetics in philosophical thought, and such are the
possibilities of its active intervention in the development of this
thought.

3

The Place of the Aesthetic Function among the Other Functions

The problem of the place of the aesthetic function among the other functions—its situation in the overall structure of functions—is, in fact, the problem of the aesthetic as it exists outside of art. As long as we regard the aesthetic from the standpoint of art (art as we understand it today, of course), the position of the aesthetic function is not a problem. Here the aesthetic function tends toward dominance. (There is, of course, the question of what kind of dominance this is, but this problem does not interest us at the present.) But as soon as we go beyond the realm of art, difficulties arise. On the one hand, we continually find ourselves attempting to consider the aesthetic function as something secondary which may exist but is not necessary; on the other hand, the aesthetic function compels our attention outside of art so frequently, turns up in so many of the most varied manifestations of life, and even appears as an essential component of habitation, dress, social intercourse, and so forth, that we must think about its role in the overall organization of the world.

A quick look at the history of aesthetics instructs us that philosophy began to consider beauty (hence the aesthetic) as a metaphysical principle, and a factor in the order of the universe, much earlier than it began to consider the aesthetic in art. Plato saw the aesthetic outside of art and art itself separated from one another to such an extent that he considered the aesthetic outside of art as one of the three supreme principles of the world order, whereas he almost banished art from his ideal state, or at least subjected it to strict control in the interests of state order. In modern times when the aesthetic has been acknowledged as an essential component in art, the problem of the aesthetic outside of art nevertheless retains its metaphysical importance, for example, in Herder's concept of natural beauty. Even Ruskin placed natural beauty above artistic beauty in a radical fashion. With the decline of

"Místo estetické funkce mezi ostatními," lecture at the Prague Linguistic Circle on November 30, 1942; published in *Studie z estetiky* (Prague, 1966).

metaphysical thought, the problem of natural beauty degenerates into a secondary question which usually elicits the answer that natural beauty is subordinate to artistic beauty (as a projection of contemporary artistic convention into the perception of natural phenomena). Here, of course, the problem reaches a dead end.

The question of the aesthetic outside of art, however, does not disappear; on the contrary, it has acquired a new immediacy in the present. The recent development of art and its consequences have contributed to this fact above all. In recent times we have witnessed an exclusive emphasis on the aesthetic function in art, and we have seen the aesthetic almost identified with art in theory as well. The aesthetic thus liberated has come to a sovereign, self-oriented game connected with everyday life only through latent, almost subterranean passageways. At the same time, however, life outside of art has become very strongly aestheticized. As examples, let us mention business advertising of all kinds, illuminated advertising in particular, the culture of habitation, and the aestheticization of physical culture (training in rhythm and the like). Art soon felt the exclusive supremacy of the aesthetic function as the cause of its isolation, and it has been trying for several years to overcome this isolation in various ways, without at the same time giving up the conquests of the preceding period. The aesthetic outside of art has, then, become conscious of itself, and it is demanding normalization and regulation. And thus the question of the position of the aesthetic function among the others—and naturally the question of the aesthetic outside of art as well—has come up again with renewed urgency. Today's lecture is a contribution to the solution of these two problems, or rather a cursory suggestion for their solution (for it is just an outline). We shall proceed from the aesthetic outside of art.

Today we are not interested in the metaphysical aspects of this question. We are not concerned with whether beauty exists or does not exist independently of man (and therefore suprahistorically) in the universe as a whole, but with how the aesthetic manifests itself in human activity and its creations. Let us keep in mind the shift which has thus occurred. Today we are not interested in studying whether the aesthetic clings to things, but in discovering to what extent it is present in human nature itself. We are not concerned with the aesthetic as a static property of things, but with the aesthetic as an energetic component of human activity.

For this reason we are not interested in the relation of the aesthetic to other metaphysical principles, such as the true and the good, but in its relation to other motives and goals of human activity and creation.

All of this, of course, entails a considerable shift in the methods and material of thought. The notion of function replaces the notion of beauty as the basic methodological premise; the acts of which human behavior consists and the results of these acts—human creations—replace natural phenomena as material. There is a sharp, rarely passable dividing line between nature and human creation, and especially between nature and art. Therefore, as long as the problem of the aesthetic outside of art was viewed *sub specie* of natural beauty, it might have seemed that they were two separate worlds. If these worlds were to be connected in some way, it was necessary to subordinate one to the other: either art to nature as, for example, with Plato, or nature to art, indications of which we already see in Neo-Platonism. Art subordinated to nature is ultimately always an imitation of nature by art (and the imitation is always less perfect than the original). If, on the other hand, nature is subordinated to art, it always occurs ultimately on the basis of the premise that art gives nature its final shape, that it perfects nature.

Still a third starting point is possible: to understand the two, nature and art, as independent and unconnected. Attempts at this have been made in the modern period beginning with Symbolism in literature and its theory and with Impressionism in painting (for which a natural theme is a mere pretext). Karásek ze Lvovic's statement expresses this belief in clear terms: "It cannot be forgotten that the truth of art and the truth of life are two quite different things. It can almost be said that where art is right, life almost never is right and that it is not the real world but merely our dreams which tell us about the meaning of things."[1] Compare Liebermann's statement about painting: "A bunch of asparagus, a bouquet of roses, an ugly girl or a beautiful girl, an Apollo or a deformed dwarf is enough for a masterpiece: it is possible to create a masterpiece from everything, of course with a sufficient amount of fantasy . . . . the value of a painting is absolutely independent of its subject."[2] Accordingly it is said that "beauty" does not lie in

1. J. Karásek ze Lvovic, *Sodoma* (Prague, 1921), p. 6.
2. M. Liebermann, *Die Phantasie in der Malerei* (Berlin, 1916), pp. 24–25.

the reality represented but is an autonomous matter of the work itself. These three solutions—the subordination of art to nature, or the subordination of nature to art, or, finally, their independence and alienation from one another—are possible if we consider the aesthetic outside of art from the standpoint of "beauty" as a property of things.

If we look at the aesthetic outside of art from the viewpoint of functions, however, the situation appears completely different. Whereas in the preceding case the two spheres (i.e., the aesthetic outside of art and art) seemed to be separated by a chasm that had to be crossed, now the interrelation of the aesthetic outside of art and the aesthetic within art will appear so close that the two domains will merge at countless points, and the difficulty will be to distinguish them rather than to seek a connection between them. For no longer will we be considering the relationship between nature and art, but interrelations of various kinds or, in some cases, just aspects of one and the same activity.

Such are the differences, then, between the way in which traditional aesthetics has approached the problem of the aesthetic outside of art and the way in which we prefer to conceive this problem today from a functional perspective. This change in perspective does not, of course, lack theoretical premises. I refer mainly to Guyau to whom aesthetics is indebted for the suggestion that there is not an insurmountable difference between practically and aesthetically oriented activities. Guyau says that "in exterior objects . . . utility always constitutes a certain beauty. This beauty at one time resolves itself into a satisfaction of the *intellect,* which finds the thing well adopted to the purpose, at another into the satisfaction of *sensibility,* which finds this purpose agreeable and enjoys it."[3] We must also mention Dessoir and his school. In his general work Dessoir divided the philosophy of the aesthetic into two equal parts: aesthetics and the general theory of art. His statement that an aesthetics could be written without the word "art" even being used is often cited. Such, then, are the historical premises for the attention that we are devoting to the aesthetic outside of art—the aesthetic as a constituent of human behavior and its creations. As concerns the notion of function itself, its antecedents are well enough known: functional

3. J. M. Guyau, *Problems of Contemporary Aesthetics,* trans. H. L. Mathews (Los Angeles, 1947), p. 19.

architecture and functional linguistics. We shall soon see, however, that the very notion of function will have to be revised before we can use it safely. Finally, if I were permitted to include my own works among the antecedents, I would mention especially the book *Aesthetic Function, Norm and Value as Social Facts*[4] and the study "On the Problem of Functions in Architecture,"[5] as well as the study "The Esthetics of Language."[6]

Now let us take up the actual question of the aesthetic function outside of art. How should we begin? Should we first attempt to enumerate all the instances in which the aesthetic function occurs outside of art? As soon as we attempted such an enumeration, we would immediately recognize its difficulty. Let us take language, for example. Where are the limits of the aesthetic here? Are there some linguistic forms in which the aesthetic participates and others in which it does not? Only an affirmative answer to this question would permit a limitation and enumeration. But we can see even in passing that aside from poetic language no form of speech is obligatorily accompanied by the aesthetic function; on the contrary, and even more importantly, none, not even the most ordinary colloquial speech, is in principle devoid of the aesthetic function. And so it is with all other human activities. Let us take crafts, for example. It is obvious that the aesthetic function is more visible in the goldsmith's craft than in the baker's or butcher's crafts; the goldsmith's craft is even mentioned in the history of art. But can we therefore say that the other two crafts are essentially devoid of the aesthetic function? That would mean forgetting about the shapes of a baker's products. Even their color and smell add aesthetic elements, and the same holds true, albeit to a somewhat different extent, for the butcher's craft. In brief, we shall find no sphere in which the aesthetic function is essentially absent; potentially it is always present; it can arise at any time. It has no limitation, therefore, and we cannot say that some domains of human activity are in principle devoid of it, while it belongs to others in principle.

4. *Estetická funkce, norma a hodnota jako sociální fakty* (Prague, 1936); English translation by M. E. Suino (Ann Arbor, 1970).

5. See part two of this anthology.

6. "Estetika jazyka," *Slovo a slovesnost* 6 (1940): 1–27; English translation by P. L. Garvin in his anthology *A Prague School Reader on Esthetics, Literary Structure, and Style* (Washington, D.C., 1964), pp. 31–69.

Furthermore, there are cultural forms (we are using "cultural" in the broad sense meaning not only material culture but also civilization and intellectual culture) in which functions—among them, of course, the aesthetic—are almost indistinguishable from one another, in which they appear with every act as a compact bundle, at most changeable only in its aspects. Such, for example, is the domain of folklore culture where we cannot distinguish and delimit even art itself—an activity with a predominant aesthetic function—from other activities. But if we cannot distinguish activities to which the aesthetic function pertains from those which essentially lack it in extra-artistic spheres, the opposite is also true. We cannot deny the presence and participation of extra-aesthetic functions in art where the aesthetic function dominates in principle. This has already been considered more than once. Dessoir's entire *Kunstwissenschaft* is based upon this knowledge, and thus I cite one of Guyau's statements more for historical reasons than as proof: "The keenest aesthetic emotion, the one least mingled with sadness, is met with in those cases where it converts itself immediately into action, and in this way it satisfies itself. The Spartans felt more intimately all the beautiful verses of Tyrtaeus, the Germans, those of Koerner or of Uhland, when these verses led them in combat. The volunteers in the Revolution were probably never so moved by the Marseillaise as the day when it inspired them with its song on the hills of Jemmapes. So, two lovers bending over some love poems like the heroes of Dante and living that which they read will experience deeper enjoyment, even from the aesthetic point of view."[7] Guyau's examples, we must admit, are very simple—many other, more complicated examples could be found; nevertheless, they illustrate well the correlation and interpenetration of the other functions with the aesthetic function in art.

If we say, then, that the aesthetic function is omnipresent, this is not panaestheticism, for the other functions are equally omnipresent, existing as a group not only in opposition to the aesthetic function but also in opposition to each other. There are no segments of human activity which are irrevocably and essentially reserved for this or that function alone. Any function, not just the one which the acting subject ascribes to his act or creation, can al-

7. *Problems of Contemporary Aesthetics,* pp. 32–33.

ways be evoked. As a rule, several functions are not only potential-ly but actually present in an act or creation, and among them there may be some which the agent or creator did not think of or did not even desire. No sphere of human action or human creation is limited to a single function. There is always a greater number of functions, and there are tensions, variances, and balancing among them. The functions of a permanent creation can change in the course of time. We began, then, with a consideration of the aes-thetic function outside of art, and we have quickly reached a conclusion pertaining to functions in general. It can be formulated as the basic polyfunctionality of human activity and the basic omnipresence of functions.

Here we find ourselves at the point where we disagree, especially as regards the theory, with original functionalism, whose principles were expressed with crystal clarity in architectural functionalism. Architectural functionalism proceeds from the premise that a building has a single, precisely delimited function given by the purpose for which it is built. Hence Corbusier's well-known com-parison of a building to a machine, a typically unambiguous prod-uct from a functional point of view. Functionalism was thus an unusually fruitful notion as a developmental stage of architecture, and it was also theoretically justified as a polemic against the pre-ceding historicizing period which delighted in assuming a purpose other than the one for which a building had been constructed. Nevertheless, its weakness soon became apparent. A building, especially a residence, cannot be limited to a single function, because it is a setting for human life, and human life is hetero-morphous. The function of a residential building and of each room in it is simultaneously manifold, not because the building has to serve several different purposes (although such a case is not, of course, impossible) but because even when it serves a single purpose, a building or a room must be made to suit those of man's needs which are not specifically included in its purpose but are essential to the one who uses the premises, precisely because he is a complete, many-sided human being. Thus even architects have realized that the functional concept of a building does not involve a single logical deduction from the purpose of the building but a complex consideration which inductively accounts for the in-habitant's concrete and multiple needs.

And what is valid for functions in architecture is also valid for

functions in general. Functions must not be one-sidedly projected
into an object but must be considered primarily with a subject as
their live source. As long as we project them into an object, we
shall always be tempted to see a single function, for an object, a
human creation, will always bear more distinct traces of its adaptation to that single purpose for which it was produced. But as soon
as we look at functions from a subject's point of view, we shall
immediately see that every act by which man orients himself toward reality in order to affect it in one way or another corresponds
simultaneously and jointly to several purposes which sometimes
not even the individual who originates the act is able to differentiate. Hence the uncertainty about the motivation of actions.
Social coexistence, of course, compels man constantly to limit his
functional many-sidedness, but it never succeeds in making him
a biologically monofunctional creature such as a bee or an ant. As
long as man is man, various functions will necessarily contend
with one another, will be arranged hierarchically, will intersect,
and will interpenetrate in each of his acts.

What is the consequence for the aesthetic function of this manner of conceiving functions? That we stop viewing the aesthetic
function as something accidental and additional, as it appears to
those who look at functions from the standpoint of an object,
insofar as this object is not a work of art. From the standpoint of
a subject and the totality of his attitude toward the external
world, it is indisputably clear that the aesthetic function, like any
other, constitutes a necessary part of his overall reaction to the
world around him. From the standpoint of a subject, the necessity
of the aesthetic function is not determined by whether or not it
tends toward some purpose exceeding the given action or creation
but by the fact that it adds a facet to the acting individual's functional diversity in some way. (We shall attempt to define this more
precisely later.)

But as soon as we connect functions with a subject and see their
correlation, the problem which interests us—the problem of the
place of the aesthetic function among the others, its relation to the
others—begins to appear not only as a question of the aesthetic
function itself but as a question of functions in general, their fundamental interrelation. We cannot, of course, conceive this relationship as a hierarchy whereby one function fundamentally dominates the others and the others are subordinated to it. Subordina-

tion and superordination of functions occur only in concrete
cases, during particular acts, in particular creations. There are, of
course, more permanent hierarchies of functions—periodic hierarchies—but these are also changeable and hence not essential. Precisely the fact that all functions are potentially omnipresent—that
every act is accompanied by a whole cluster of functions—leads us
to conclude that the question of the fundamental interrelation of
functions is not one of a hierarchy but of a typology which assigns
a place to each function with respect to the others—not under or
over them but with respect to them.

It is now a matter of how we arrive at such a typology, of
whether we do so by induction or deduction. Induction would,
of course, presuppose as complete as possible an enumeration of
concrete functions according to which man can view and affect
reality. It is evident beforehand that such an undertaking would
be a Sisyphian task under the present conditions of research on
functions, and it is questionable whether such an enumeration is
at all possible without crudely violating the continuity of the real
state of affairs. Perhaps, then, deduction could lead to our goal.
But from what are we to deduce? We have said that the source of
functions is man, their subject. We would accordingly have to
deduce their typology from the constitution of man—man in
general, not the individual; for only man in general belongs to the
suprahistorical design which interests us here. But is the constitution of man in general so definite a notion that unambiguous
conclusions could be drawn from it? We are therefore left with a
single path, the phenomenological *Wesensschau,* also essentially
deductive but deducing from the thing itself, not from something
outside of it, hence in the given instance deducing from the essence of a function.

Thus our first question is: What is a function viewed from the
perspective of a subject? We add the words "viewed from the
perspective of a subject" as an essential feature on the basis of the
preceding considerations which showed us that only from this
standpoint do functions appear to us undeformed in their entirety.
As long as we define a function in terms of an *object,* it appears
bound to a specific goal which has to be reached by an act or
creation. Hence our perpetual tendency to conceive functions
monofunctionally. Only if we conceive functions as modes of a
subject's self-realization vis-à-vis the external world do we see them

undeformed, do we think polyfunctionally in accordance with the real state of affairs. What, then, is a function from the perspective of a subject? I have already used the words "a subject's self-realization"; let me add the word *mode* (perhaps we could also say *way* or *method*). The definition will then read: "A function is the mode of a subject's self-realization vis-à-vis the external world." I say advisedly "a subject's self-realization" and not *effect upon reality* because not every function must tend toward an immediate modification of reality—viz., the theoretical function.

Proceeding from this definition, we ask further—of course, taking into account, as is natural in a phenomenological analysis, personal, I would say *introspective* experience—whether it is possible somehow to differentiate "man's modes of self-realization" vis-à-vis reality without leaving something out. Such a differentiation is possible: man can realize himself vis-à-vis reality either directly or by means of another reality. Here is an example to make things clear. A man realizes himself directly vis-à-vis reality when he reorganizes it with his own hands so that he can immediately use this reorganization to his own advantage. (He breaks branches in order to start a fire by rubbing them together.) Even if he uses an implement in this reorganization, his self-realization vis-à-vis reality need not become indirect. (In the above example the broken branches have already become an implement.) But if, for example, a man stabs a picture of his enemy in expectation of injuring the person whom it represents, or if before going hunting he shoots at a picture of an animal in the conviction that he is actually hitting the animal before he has seen it and shot it, he is acting indirectly vis-à-vis reality through the mediation of another reality. The reality which serves as the intermediary (the picture) is not an implement but a sign, in fact not a sign-implement but an individual sign equivalent to the reality that it represents. We shall discuss this individuality later. For the present it is enough for us to state that man's self-realization vis-à-vis reality can proceed in two fundamental ways. There is no third way: in other words, the basic articulation of functions divides them into *immediate* and *semiotic* functions.

Is there yet another necessary division of these two groups? Yes, for it is provided by the pair subject–object: self-realization proceeds from a subject and aims at an object. If we apply this pair to the group of immediate functions, its further division into the subgroups of practical and theoretical functions will be apparent. In *practical functions* the object is in the foreground, because the subject's self-realization is directed at a reorganization of the object, that is, reality. In the *theoretical function,* on the other hand, the subject is in the foreground, because its general and ultimate goal is the projection of a reality into the subject's consciousness in an image organized according to the organization of the subject (understand a supra-individual, universal subject) and according to the basic make-up of human attention which is capable of focusing on only a single point. The reality itself, the object of the function, remains untouched by the theoretical function; in fact, the purer the theoretical attitude, the more meticulous the effort to exclude from the cognitive process the very least possibility of intervention in the cognized reality—viz., the guarantees of the purity of an experiment.

Let us now turn to the semiotic functions. These also divide spontaneously for us if we apply to them the duality of orientation according to subject and object. A function in which the *object* is in the foreground is a *symbolic function.* In this case attention is focused on the effectiveness of the relation between the symbolized thing and the symbolic sign. Either reality is affected by means of the sign, or reality operates by means of the sign; both the sign and the reality represented by it, then, appear as the object. This effectiveness of the relationship between the sign and the thing designated by it is therefore a fundamental and indispensable feature of a symbolic sign. Wherever it is missing, the symbol turns into an allegory. Let us take a sign (of a state, for example). Insofar as there is a causal relation between such a sign and the thing—for example, such that an affront to the sign is an affront to the state, the sign is a symbol. If this property is lost, the sign becomes an allegory such as so-called conventional symbols (heart–love, anchor–hopes). The symbolic function therefore foregrounds the object.

The semiotic function foregrounding the *subject* is the *aesthetic function.* I do not want to comment too extensively on the fact that the aesthetic function changes everything that it touches into a sign; I refer to my paper for the Eighth Philosophical Congress[8]

---

8. "Art as a Semiotic Fact"; see below.

and my paper for the Copenhagen Linguistics Congress.[9] But why do we presuppose that the subject is in the foreground in the case of the aesthetic function? Is there not the danger that we shall stray into the theory of the emotional expressiveness of aesthetics which we have rightly opposed so many times? Well, let us not forget that the subject about whom we are speaking here is not an individual but man in general. Emotional reactions belong—we could say *ex definitione*—to the individual. Second, the reality of which the aesthetic function takes hold is a sign, hence a matter of supra-individual communication. This fact need not, of course, be an obstacle to expressiveness, for as we know precisely from linguistics, even an emotion uses signs for its expression. But in such a case the signs are an instrument which *serves* to express the emotion, and thus the emotional function belongs among the practical functions. An aesthetic sign does not serve, it is not an instrument; but in exactly the same way as a symbolic sign it belongs to the object; indeed, it is the only distinctly visible object, being its own ultimate purpose, whether the aesthetic function has taken hold of it as something completed or whether it creates it. Therefore, insofar as it is perceived as an aesthetic sign and also to the extent that it is so perceived, it cannot be the means for expressing emotion.

The "subjectivity" of an aesthetic sign unlike the "objectivity" of a symbolic sign must be seen in something else. An aesthetic sign does not affect any particular reality as does a symbolic sign, but instead it reflects in itself reality as a whole (hence the so-called *typicality* of the work of art, a notion which means no more than that the work of art, the purest aesthetic sign, demonstrates on the basis of a particular all other particulars as well as their set—reality). Reality reflected as a whole is also organized in an aesthetic sign according to the image of the subject's organization. In this organization of reality, the aesthetic function resembles the theoretical function, although, of course, it differs from it by virtue of the fact that the theoretical function strives for a total and unifying *image* of reality, whereas the aesthetic function establishes a unifying *attitude* toward it. For the theoretical function—just as for the practical—the immediate object is

9. "Poetic Designation and the Aesthetic Function of Language," *The Word and Verbal Art: Selected Essays by Jan Mukařovský,* trans. and ed. John Burbank and Peter Steiner (New Haven, 1977), pp. 65–73.

cognized reality itself, and the sign is only its instrument (just as an instrument that is as functionally unambiguous as possible appears most advantageous for the practical function, the theoretical function also strives for unambiguity of the signs which it uses).

For the aesthetic function, reality is not an immediate object but a mediated one. Its immediate object (hence not an instrument at all) is an aesthetic sign which projects into reality as a general law the subject's attitude realized in the structure of this sign that nevertheless does not lose its independence. The aesthetic sign manifests its independence by always referring to reality as a whole, never to one of its individual segments. Its validity cannot therefore be limited by another sign; it can only be accepted or rejected as a whole. In contrast, a sign serving a theoretical function (a concept) always signifies only a certain segment or partial aspect of reality. In addition, there are always other signs (concepts) which limit its validity. Let us recapitulate: an aesthetic sign—just like a symbolic sign—is a sign-object, but unlike a symbolic sign it does not affect reality; rather it projects itself into reality.

Such, we believe, is the typology of functions: two groups, immediate and semiotic functions, each of which is divided further; the immediate into the practical functions and the theoretical function, the semiotic into the symbolic and the aesthetic functions. One thing in this formulation may strike us. We speak about the practical functions in the plural, whereas we talk about the theoretical, symbolic, and aesthetic functions in the singular. This corresponds to the real state of affairs, however. There are many nuances of the practical function: some of them have conventional names; for others we must occasionally look for a name; and still others, though discernible, perhaps even resist nomenclature. Functions other than the practical lack such a distinct spectrum; we could hardly differentiate the various theoretical or aesthetic functions.

It is clear why precisely the practical function is so richly differentiated internally. Of all the functions it is the closest to reality. Unlike the semiotic function, it is directly oriented toward reality; unlike the theoretical function, it strives to affect reality, to change it. The rich heterogeneity of reality is therefore reflected in the practical function; its nuances correspond to the separate classes and kinds of realities with which it comes into contact. Moreover, its heterogeneity is affected by the fact that it provides the most basic conditions of man's existence. The practical function is therefore to a certain extent the function κατ' ἐξοχήν, the unmarked function; the other functions gather around it, by no means always yielding to it; instead they enter into close relations with it, and some of its nuances originate from its mixing with another function. The magical function, for instance, is an obvious mixture of the practical function with the symbolic. We could, however, also consider to what extent and in what way the practical function participates together with the symbolic function in the composition of the erotic function (cf., erotic symbolism).

Let us make another comment on the typology of functions. The typology which we have attempted is constructed purely phenomenologically and has nothing to do with questions of genesis. However, in reality this typology of functions is a reflection only of very advanced developmental stages of culture and not of the original state of these functions. The fact that the functions appear so distinctly differentiated to our modern consciousness is obviously developmentally parallel with the advancement of machine technology, for only a machine, a very complex machine, provides the model of pure monofunctionality. Therefore it is also true that our typology is thinkable only from the standpoint of contemporary man. For a primitive the severance of the practical function from the symbolic, for example, would be simply unthinkable: for him every practical act and creation has at the same time and with equal importance a symbolic significance.

What follows from our attempt at a typology of functions with respect to genesis is only that none of the functions can be reduced to another one. We cannot, for example, assume, as is sometimes done, that the theoretical function arises from the practical function. Bonds at least equally strong link it to the symbolic function (the symbolism of all original knowledge, the mythological cosmogony as the original science), but it cannot be deduced from the symbolic function either. This is the same in all other cases.

In dealing with the "semiotic" functions, we have named the symbolic and the aesthetic functions, excluding from the domain of the semiotic functions signs which the practical and theoretical functions use as instruments for their purposes. The reason for our apparent splitting apart of the realm of signs was the fact that symbolic and aesthetic signs are objects, whereas signs in the practical and theoretical functions are instruments. Nevertheless, this bifurcation of the realm of signs is only apparent: the properties which unify all signs regardless of their functions are too substantial for a real bifurcation to be possible. We must also assume that signs were noticeably polyfunctional in periods when the differentiation of functions was nonexistent or weak, in which cases a practical sign was at the same time a symbol. In our time children's speech bears traces of such a state (the word as an object: a cloud is called a cloud because it is grey, an umbrella is called an umbrella because someone can jab us with it—Piaget); even in the speech of contemporary adults the link between signs which serve and sign-objects has not disappeared. See above all the close connection of poetic, hence aesthetically oriented, language with non-poetic language; further, the spontaneous (hence not conventional) symbolism which a linguistic sign can acquire if it approximates a fixed idea or if its mastery slips out of the power of the individual who has used the word.

The connection between sign-objects and sign-instruments has an enormous significance for keeping the sign—especially the linguistic sign—alive. If the sign-instrument were left to itself, it would necessarily approximate either absolute unambiguity or, on the other hand, semantic indifference, meaninglessness, and thereby, in both cases, automatization. It would change from a sign into an indicator, which, though strictly unambiguous, was nevertheless fixed and deprived of semantic flexibility (viz., mathematical symbols, logical symbols, etc.); or it would degenerate into a mere *flatus vocis*. Only the constant potential presence of the symbolic and aesthetic functions maintains both the consciousness of the power of referential relation (reference as the operative energy in a symbol) and, on the other hand, the opposite awareness of the independence of the sign from a particular reality (viz., the autonomy and self-orientation of the aesthetic sign). In other words, in order for a word to exist as an instrument, the word must—even with today's functional differentiation—exist as a symbol and as an aesthetic sign. As far as the genesis of language is concerned, we might mention in passing that it seems to follow from our typology that theories deducing the origin of language unilaterally from whatever function, be it the practical (need for communication) or the symbolic, are fallacious. Even in this case it is necessarily true that all the functions are equally important and equally original.

At this point I should perhaps make a brief comment on my dispute with my colleague Professor Kořínek over the self-orientation of theoretical language.[10] After what I have said in this lecture, I believe that my opinion on this matter is clear. The sign is an instrument in the theoretical function, whereas it is part of the object in the aesthetic function. In other words, in the theoretical function attention is focused on a reality which is outside the sign (therefore the sign in the theoretical function is subjected to control with respect to its conformity to this reality); in the aesthetic function attention is directed to the sign itself, which reflects reality as a whole in itself. In this case, control of the sign by reality does not make any sense, because both the sign and reality are objects and confront one another as independent wholes. A sign functioning theoretically acquires the semblance of self-orientation only in juxtaposition with a sign which serves the practical function and strives to *affect* reality. But this is a very relative, only apparent self-orientation: non-intervention in reality does not deprive a theoretically functioning sign of instrumentality.

But I can also see the circumstance that led my colleague Kořínek to confuse aesthetic and theoretical self-orientation and that in itself finds support in the actual state of affairs. I have in mind the similar positions of the theoretical function among the immediate functions and the aesthetic function among the semiotic functions. Both foreground the subject in contrast to the practical and symbolic functions which foreground the object. Even here, of course, there is the difference mentioned above. The theoretical function strives for a unifying image of reality created by means of signs and their meanings which play the role of an *instrument* in this process. The aesthetic function projects into reality as a unifying principle the attitude which the subject adopts toward reality. This attitude can, however, be projected into reality only in such a way that in its course toward reality it passes through *objectification* which it receives in the aesthetic sign. This, I think, has clarified my position on the apparent self-orientation of theoretical language. As concerns Kořínek's identification of the aesthetic and emotional functions, I have already responded in one of the previous paragraphs.

10. *Editors' note.* J. M. Kořínek's views on this subject are found in his article "O jazykovém stylu" [On style in language], *Slovo a slovesnost* 8 (1941): 28–37.

We must now look at the interrelations of the individual functions that follow from our suggested typology. We have already emphasized, and I think repeatedly, that a fundamental typology, valid regardless of time, cannot contain subordinations and superordinations of its individual members. This, after all, follows from the very premises of structuralism which always sees a hierarchy as a dynamic process, as a constant regrouping. But nothing can prevent us from asking whether a typology of functions contains some correlations, hence interrelations, of its members. Such correlations are not, of course, hierarchical, but they can become tracks along which hierarchical shifts occur in development. Well, such correlations are partially provided by the very scheme of our typology. We have shown which properties link together the members of the pair of immediate functions (the practical and the theoretical) and the members of the pair of semiotic functions (the symbolic and the aesthetic). We have also shown that despite the boundaries between these two groups, the functions similar to one another in them are coupled through a particular feature: the practical with the symbolic and the theoretical with the aesthetic.

We must still ask whether the two remaining possible pairings are somehow founded: the practical function with the aesthetic and the theoretical function with the symbolic. There are, in fact, a great many actual links between the members of these pairs. The practical function is frequently coupled with, indeed even blended with, the aesthetic (viz., architecture or theater); likewise the theoretical with the symbolic (viz., the long symbiosis of symbolism and knowledge, last in Baroque mystical philosophy). But phenomenologically the members of these pairs are maximally separated. The practical function leads to a direct affecting of reality, the aesthetic to the self-orientation of the act or thing which it controls. The theoretical function deprives the signs which it uses of any initiative, rendering them as maximally fixed terms or even indicators; conversely, the symbolic sign is the initiative itself, for it is not only an object but an operative object. From where, then, do the actual links between these pairs come? They come from the fact that the functions in question, the practical with the aesthetic and the symbolic with the theoretical, are interconnected precisely because of their antithetical natures. The relationship between the aesthetic and practical functions can furnish proof of this. They are so antithetical that from the standpoint of the aesthetic function, if we wish to juxtapose it to everything outside of it, *all* the remaining functions, the theoretical included, appear to be "practical." And what is the consequence of this "hostility"? It is that wherever the practical function retreats just a step, the aesthetic function immediately follows it as its negation so that frequently these two functions enter into dispute with one another, even simultaneously fighting for the same thing or the same act. There are, therefore, interrelations among all the basic functions, and the scheme of their typology is totally saturated with these relations.

This observation concludes our general discussion. We would have to study on the basis of the concrete development of the structure of functions how these associative potentials of functions encounter one another in evolution or, in some cases, how they contest one another in the constant emergence and dissolution of the structure of functions. This is, however, beyond the scope of our study. Now we should devote ourselves to a more detailed discussion of individual functions; we should especially return to the aesthetic function which was the starting point of our deliberations. By not doing so, we are guilty of disproportion in our overall plan. But I hope that I will be forgiven this disproportion, if you consider that what you have heard is a mere outline and that time does not permit a further extension of my lecture. I therefore conclude, somewhat in the middle, comforting myself with the awareness that I have discussed at least in brief outline what concerned me the most: an attempt at a typology of functions.

4

The Aesthetic Norm

Before we begin an analysis of the aesthetic norm, we should devote at least a few words to the general characterization of norm. The concept of norm is inseparable from the concept of function, the realization of which the norm implements. Because such a realization presupposes an activity tending toward a specific goal, we must admit that the limitation by which this activity is organized has in itself the character of energy as well. One of the great merits of modern linguistics consists in the fact that it has been able to distinguish the norm from the rule which is its codification. It has not escaped the attention of linguists that there are linguistic systems, such as most dialects, which have never undergone grammatical codification and which, nevertheless, have norms that are spontaneously observed by linguistic collectivities; moreover, the compelling force of these norms is no weaker than the force of norms in codified linguistic systems. A second reason which has caused linguistics to differentiate carefully the norm from the formula expressing its codification derives from the existence of norms that resist any form of codification whatsoever. In every linguistic system there are norms which are not expressible in words—for example, some stylistic norms, whose authority is not at all weakened by this inexpressibility. Hence codification is not identical with norm. It can even happen that a codification is false, that is, it is in disagreement with an existing norm.

An uncodified norm, then, appears to us as a primary aspect of norm; it thus provides us with a starting point for our deliberations. At this point, however, a new question arises: the question of codification. For what is a norm if it does not have the nature of a rule? With respect to what has already been said, we prefer to define norm as a regulating energetic principle. To the acting

"La norme esthétique," *Travaux du IXe Congrès international de philosophie,* vol. 12, pt. 3 (Paris, 1937); Czech version: "Estetická norma," *Studie z estetiky* (Prague, 1966).

individual a norm makes its presence felt as a limitation on the freedom of his action. For the evaluating individual the guiding force is his own judgment; however, the individual has the right to decide whether to subordinate his judgment to the constraint of this pressure. Therefore, whether a norm is applied consciously or unconsciously, it is in essence energy rather than a rule. Because of this dynamic nature, a norm is subjected to continuous changes. We can even consider that every concrete application of a norm is at the same time necessarily a change in norm. Not only does the norm influence the organization of the concrete case (e.g., a work of art), but at the same time the concrete case influences the norm. Even the legal norm, the most stable of all, is subjected to changes which derive from the fact that the norm is in use. Evidence of this is the limited legislative authority granted to courts of appeal.

Having made these preliminary remarks, we shall try to determine the specific nature that distinguishes the aesthetic norm from others. First of all, we should recall that the aesthetic norm is in opposition to these others because it does not tend toward a practical goal but rather aims at the object itself which is its vehicle so that this object becomes the only immediate goal of the activity. The result is the individualization of aesthetic value. As soon as we begin to regard an object as purely aesthetic and to evaluate it as such, which is the case of works of art, we start to see it as a unique fact. This uniqueness results in a shift within the inner structure of value. Above all, it does not depend on the *result* of the evaluation; the *act of evaluation* is what comes to the fore. The perception of a work of art, which largely coincides with the act of evaluation, has unlimited possibilities of repetition and is to a great extent the cause of the interest that a work of art arouses in us. Of primary importance is the perception of the work, not the determination of its artistic value, which, on the contrary, comes to the fore when we consider practical values.

But what are the consequences of this individualization of aesthetic value for the norm? At first glance it may appear that the uniqueness of artistic value precludes the possibility of a norm. There are, however, circumstances which save this possibility. Above all, the uniqueness of a work of art is not absolute. Like every other value, artistic value has its immanent development, and single works are only realizations of gradual stages of this development.

But even more important for us is the fact that the application of a general norm is not at the same time an obstacle to the fundamental uniqueness of value, if the positive relation between the norm and the evaluated work is not considered as an absolutely adequate one—in other words, if the perfect fulfillment of the norm is not considered as the only desirable one. We can indeed look to the history of art and confirm that a positive value in art is by no means identical with the perfect correspondence of an artistic work with a norm. On the contrary, it often happens that positive evaluation is a response to a radical violation of the traditional norm. It is entirely possible that our pleasure from the perception of a work which we evaluate highly was based on a rather intense concomitant displeasure. In the histories of all arts, we know numerous cases of works which, when made public, provoked such unqualified and widespread displeasure that violent protests were made. Nevertheless, these works have become undeniable values with the passing of time. Hence, it is characteristic for aesthetic evaluation that not only agreement but also disagreement with the norm can result in a positive evaluation.

In connection with this, we must also mention the coexistence and interpenetration of several systems of aesthetic norms in the evaluation of the same fact. In the art of a specific period, valid for a specific collectivity, we can always distinguish the simultaneous activity of several different systems of norms, which gradually arise in successive periods. Thus if we overlook all the richness of the variety in contemporary painting, it appears to us as a conglomerate of successively applied systems of norms, beginning at least with Impressionism and ending with Surrealism. Within today's art each of these systems has its own sphere of activity determined by the social differentiation of the audience or by the internal differentiation of the given art itself. The isolation of the individual spheres is not, however, hermetic. The work of art can be perceived against the background of a system of norms different from the one which is its own, and in such a case, it can be evaluated as a deformation of this different system. Often, newly created works partly obey and partly contradict traditional rules of art. Frequently, the artist, in order to revive a traditional system of norms, juxtaposes to it, in the very structure of the work, a different system of norms adopted from peripheral art, archaic art, exotic art, and so on. Such a confrontation of heterogeneous norms is, of course, felt as a conflict but as a desirable conflict, which is a part of the intention from which the work arose.

Aesthetic evaluation does not exclude as inadequate any possible relation between the norm and the evaluated work, not even a purely negative relation. Other categories of norms behave in a quite different way. The legal norm, for example, always requires a positive and direct application. The simultaneous application of several irreconcilable norms in the same case is avoided in principle, even to the detriment of the one who is concerned in the case. Sometimes, of course, the application of a linguistic norm fluctuates between the preservation and the violation of the norm; so it is, for instance, in emotive language which has a tendency to violate norms and thus is close to poetic language. But emotive language is not the basis and normal appearance of language; this role belongs to communicative language, of which emotive language is merely a deformation, and communicative language tends toward the upholding of the norm.

To sum up, we can state that the specific character of the aesthetic norm consists in the fact that it tends to be violated rather than to be observed. It has less than any other norm the character of an inviolable law. It is rather a point of orientation serving to make felt the degree of deformation of the artistic tradition by new tendencies. The negative application, which in other categories of the norm functions only as a concomitant, often uninvited, phenomenon in its positive application, becomes the normal case for the aesthetic norm. If we look at a work of art from this point of view, it will appear to us as a complex tangle of norms. Being full of internal harmonies and disharmonies, it represents a dynamic equilibrium of heterogeneous norms applied in part positively, in part negatively. This equilibrium is inimitable in its uniqueness, even though, on the other hand, it participates in the continuous immanent movement of a given art precisely because of its lability.

Which norms can the structure of a work of art include? Are they only aesthetic norms, or can the work also contain other categories of norms? We shall try to answer these questions by means of a complete enumeration of the norms which may obtain in a work of art.

At the very surface we encounter the norms that the material of a given art brings to the work. These norms are visible especially in literature whose material is language, and language by its very nature is a system of norms. Linguistic norms in themselves do not have anything in common with aesthetic norms, but the way in which they are exploited in art gives them the additional value of aesthetic norms. However, in arts whose materials are concrete, and hence completely devoid of a normative nature, such as architecture and sculpture, the natural properties of these materials likewise gain the value of aesthetic norms on account of the mode in which they are used. Thus in the development of architecture there are periods which emphasize the properties of material and others which maximally suppress these properties. In any case, we must acknowledge that the natural properties of materials are capable of fulfilling the function of aesthetic norms.

The next type of norms which we encounter in the work of art are those that can be called "technical norms." By this term we wish to designate certain habits, petrified residues of the long evolution of art, which have already lost the immediate efficacy of live aesthetic norms; their place is, figuratively speaking, at the entrance to the interior of the work of art. Such conventions (e.g., metrical schemes in poetry, traditional musical forms, etc.) are considered as necessary elements of artistic apprenticeship. The necessity of observing these norms seems evident. Nevertheless, these rules evolve, for they are also subjected to deformation through inadequate usage; thus they always gain once more the character of live aesthetic norms. Among such conventions we should also include the regularities of genres (literary, architectural, etc.) and styles.

The third type of norms which obtain in art are practical norms (we choose this term as a contrast to the term "aesthetic norms"): ethical norms, political norms, religious norms, social norms, and so forth. They enter the work through the theme. Even though they are essentially alien to the aesthetic sphere, they nevertheless acquire the range of action of aesthetic norms because of the role which they perform in the structure of the work of art. The structure of a tragedy, for example, can be based on the conflict between two ethical norms or on the struggle between a moral law and its violator.

The fourth type of norms consists of aesthetic traditions, that is, norms, or rather systems of aesthetic norms, which are older in their origin than the work of art but which the artist brings into it as elements of its structure. They also become the instruments for "artistic devices" because their observance as much as their violation can become a part of the intention realized by the work of art. They differ from the preceding type only in that they belong to the aesthetic realm in their very essence. It can happen that several aesthetic traditions, which originated in different periods, in different strata of art, or in different social milieux, meet in a particular work of art and that the planned effect of the work depends precisely on their contradicting one another.

The multiplicity of norms included in a work of art hence suggests very wide possibilities for building the unstable equilibrium which is the structure of a work. We can also consider as proven that the interrelations among all these norms, which function as instruments for artistic devices, are too complex, too differentiated, and too unstable for the positive value of the work to be able to appear as virtually identical with the perfect fulfillment of all norms obtaining in it. The history of art has much more the nature of a perpetual revolt against the norm. There are, of course, periods tending toward maximally attainable harmony and stability; they are usually called periods of classicism. On the other hand, there are periods when art seeks out maximal lability in the structure of artistic works. We are now experiencing one such period.

In light of the preceding statements, the danger arises that our own weapons will be turned against us. If the aesthetic norm exists to be more or less violated almost constantly, would it not be better to reject its existence altogether? First of all, we could reply to such an objection that every norm, even the legal norm, makes felt its activity and hence its existence precisely at the moment when its violation occurs. Moreover, we must mention the enormous sphere in which the aesthetic function plays only a concomitant role and which lies outside the boundaries of art. This sphere is related to the sum of human activities as well as to the whole world of things. Every activity and every object can become—on account of social convention or individual will—a permanent or temporary vehicle of the aesthetic function. In relation to the prevailing practical functions this aesthetic function is only secondary but, nevertheless, effective. And it is precisely here that the aesthetic norm acquires the validity of a law. The system of aesthetic norms called taste has such considerable authority here that its violation can result in individual or even social depreciation of the one who violates the rules of taste. But taste is closely associated with the norms of art. Practical life continuously provides artistic creation with its aesthetic principles; artistic creation returns these principles to it rejuvenated. Hence the aesthetic norm acquires in practical life the authority of which it is then always deprived in art. We should add that there are entire vast areas of art in which the authority of the aesthetic norm is largely acknowledged. Such an area is folk art, in which for lack of a distinct delimitation of functions the predomination of the aesthetic function over the others is not completely unequivocal.

Finally, is an authoritative norm utterly without significance for autonomous art as we understand it today? It is enough to recall the significance of an authoritative norm for artistic training. Nevertheless, living art itself needs clear and distinct norms. The more precise the codification of rules is and the closer it stays within the path of living art, the more effectively it forces art toward new conquests, for it is not possible for art to remain long in regions already explored and easily accessible to anyone who attempts artistic creation.

Despite what has just been said, however, one more question demands elucidation. The aesthetic norm, as we have conceived it, has appeared infinitely changeable. Even though we have tried to save its authoritativeness under these circumstances, we have not completely escaped from relativism, which is dangerous because it threatens the recognition of the very existence of a norm. The fact of immanent development mitigates this danger only partially. Therefore we must find the constant from which the authority of the aesthetic norm can be derived and which can become, because of its stability, the unchangeable nucleus of all its possible historical metamorphoses. We believe that such a constant should be sought in the anthropological organization of man, common to all human beings regardless of differences of time, place, and social position. There are certain aesthetic postulates which have their immediate source in this organization, such as the postulate of rhythm for succession of time, the postulate of symmetry and perpendicularity for positioning in space, and the postulate of the stability of the center of gravity for three-dimensional bodies. Do these postulates deserve to be called basic aesthetic norms? Yes, as long as we do not, of course, identify the concept of basic norm with the concept of ideal norm—if we do not consider the full realization of these postulates as the ideal of artistic perfection. All these "anthropologically" motivated postulates, which we have mentioned as examples, have not only been frequently violated in art, but their perfect realization makes the arousal of aesthetic pleasure impossible. The absolute regular rhythm of running machines puts us to sleep; the perfect symmetry of an isosceles triangle is aesthetically indifferent. Hence anthropological postulates are not ideal norms; but this by no means prevents them from fulfilling their important and necessary task as the essential motivation of concrete aesthetic norms. If we must thus abandon completely the presupposition of absolute aesthetic norms, in no way do we have to reject altogether the very concept of norm for art and thereby drown in inescapable relativism.

SUMMARY

We must distinguish between the norm and its codification: the uncodified norm is a force which governs the realization of the relevant function. This is true of norms of all kinds because many norms which are valid and functioning never reach codification; there are even some norms which are not capable of codification at all. What is valid for all norms is even more valid for aesthetic norms; that is, they are more dynamic than others. If the norm generally exhibits the tendency to effect the postulate which it poses, the application of the norm in art, which is the aesthetic sphere par excellence, is governed by the opposite tendency: to violate the norm. The structure of a work of art has the nature of an unstable equilibrium of different types of norms, aesthetic and others, which obtain in the work and are applied in part positively, in part negatively.

5

Can There Be a Universal Aesthetic
Value in Art

I

The last Congress of Philosophy has proved with sufficient clarity
that the philosophical study of value is in a state of radical reconstruction. Mankind has passed through a period of axiological
relativism, which, of course, is still not over, and is now striving
to reintroduce the idea of a fixed value capable of resisting the
diversity of individual attitudes as well as changes in the collective
mentality in different times and places. There are certain philoso-
phers who are trying to return to an ontological solution. We have
no intention here of presenting a critique of these attempts. We
even believe that a thinker proceeding from a total and original
metaphysical system will probably be capable of discovering unknown aspects of this question if he carries his thinking through to
the end. Our own intention and task, however, will be different,
since our point of departure will be data furnished by the history
of the arts and literatures and our goal will be a contribution to
the methodology of these disciplines. We shall attempt here a
critique of a universally applicable value for the development of
art and its study. Likewise we shall consider the philosophical
question of the source of the universality of aesthetic value from
the standpoint of the history of the arts. As every discipline attempts to remain as independent as possible from any ontology
whatsoever, we shall be obliged to attempt a purely epistemological
solution to the problem.

We must thus answer the following question: Can or even must
the history of art admit as a working hypothesis the existence of a
universal aesthetic value? This question is not insignificant with
respect to the history of the arts, for history must regard its
materials as the results and objects of a constant activity. This is

"La valeur esthétique dans l'art peut-elle être universelle?", *Actualités scientifiques et
industrielles,* vol. 851 (Paris, 1939); Czech version: "Může míti estetická hodnota v
umění platnost všeobecnou?", *Česká mysl,* 35 (1941).

why the history of the arts has reaped such great benefit from the relativist conception of values. Only through this relativism was it able to understand the successive structural changes in works of art as a continuous sequence whose course is determined by an immanent internal regularity. Nevertheless, the problem of a universal value, which might once have appeared definitely outdated, has emerged revitalized and demanding solution by historians of art. The changes in aesthetic value that the historian discerns may seem to be proof of the fundamental relativity of this value, and he may find a justification for any work. However, the task of his research remains to trace the continuous developmental line of art, and at every step along the way he encounters works that exert an active influence long after they have left the artist's workshop. In these works universal aesthetic value thus appears as a powerful factor collaborating in the vicissitudes of art. The historian of the arts accordingly has a great interest in the question of the universality of aesthetic value.

It is true that the majority of created works do not attain this prolonged or renewed resonance, but the act of artistic creation does always seem to be accompanied by the artist's intention to achieve unconditional acceptance.[1] Even though this aspiration appears at first glance as something purely subjective, it has great bearing on the objective development of art since it causes the artist's subjective intentions to result in a work which exceeds the private expression of the subjective state of his mind. But how is it that only a minority of the works that leave the artist's workshop outlive their time? In what way and by what right do those works which survive their time affect the development of art? These questions are still unanswered. This is further proof that the methodology of the histories of the arts and literatures cannot avoid the problem of the universality of aesthetic value. For this reason we are going to approach this problem from a methodological point of view.

At first glance we are likely to discern a lack of universality and

---

1. Even if the artist rejected the general public as incompetent, he would still take into account the experts. And finally, if he foresaw a universal lack of understanding of his work, he would at least take into consideration an ideal, though nonexistent, reader or spectator. We have in mind the statement of a Symbolist poet who declared that he would even be content with "not a single reader." "Not a single reader" is, nevertheless, more than no reader; what is denied is the real existence of such a person, though not its ideal possibility.

stability of value in art. Upon its origin the work is frequently accepted by only a part of the collectivity, even if it is successful. There are works whose significance remains limited for a long time, if not forever, to a single social milieu or even to a narrow group of specialists. In the course of time, the social significance of a work can broaden or, conversely, narrow. In broadening, it can overstep the boundaries of the national collectivity in whose sphere it originated, and in this case its resonance can even become stronger in its new homeland than in its original one. (Such has been the fate of Byron's poetry on the Continent.) In brief, the universality of the value of a work of art appears quite variable in space, even for works which have attained an undeniable success. The same is true of time, for the value of a work almost never remains constant throughout its entire existence: it grows and diminishes, it disappears and reappears. Even works whose value is not contested pass through periods in which they live a mere phantom life, their fame subsisting as an empty convention. It also happens that the official value of a particular work is maintained by school curricula prescribing for students the study of a poem, the analysis of a painting, and so forth. There are works which acquire immense glory and lose it in a short time. On the other hand, works which at their origin went almost unnoticed can be "discovered" quite a long time afterward and gain a late but durable fame.

Furthermore, not only universal value itself but even the conception of it vascillates. There are moments when it is greatly emphasized (in periods of classicism); there are others when the period cares little about it, or at least about certain aspects of it. Sometimes there is disinterest in the stability with which universal aesthetic value resists the flow of time (for example, in Italian Futurism, which in its beginnings proposed the destruction of museums of art); at other times that aspect of value which causes maximal resonance in space and society is rejected so that works destined for specialists arise (Symbolism). Also the practical range of resistance with which the work of art opposes time differs according to the art in question. We could not, for example, understand the development of theater without regard to the constantly renewed interventions of certain great works such as Shakespeare's dramas and Molière's comedies. In film, the art immediately contiguous with theater, the universality of value is, on the contrary, limited to a wide acceptance of value in a single moment without a future. Finally, it is not perhaps without interest for the question of universal aesthetic value that great museums dedicated to preserving "eternal" values nevertheless furnish proof of the instability of these values by constantly changing their exhibits and by rearranging the works and thereby altering the prominence of their positions.

Is it still possible and useful after all these objections to maintain the presupposition of the genuine universality of aesthetic value, or would it be preferable to admit only one more or less rich scale of relative values? In opting for the second of these possibilities, we would—in spite of everything—be in disagreement with the very meaning of artistic development. Though aesthetic value always vascillates, the artistic creation does not deviate from its unswerving search for perfection. Without this feature the development of art would be a current lacking specific direction and meaning. As we have already said, every work of art is necessarily created with the intention of achieving universal success. Proof of this is the resentment so often shown by artists, even those most contemptuous of immortality, toward their colleagues' efforts, even when these are parallel to their own.

Universal value thus exists and operates in a very palpable manner, but it neither merges with maximal resonance in space and time nor irrevocably attaches itself to specific works. It has, on the contrary, the character of live energy which to remain active must of necessity renew itself. With a revelatory and moving beam it illuminates the past of art and thereby discovers, always anew, its previously unknown aspects. Thus arises a fruitful tension between the past and the future of art, and this tension affects present artistic activity. It is as necessary for the development of art to follow tradition as to be guided by the impulse of the moment. Universal value as live energy makes possible the synthesis of these two antithetical necessities. It is precisely the changeability of universal value that directs the artist's attention to those of his predecessors whose works correspond to current tendencies. In this lie the significance and importance of the universality of aesthetic value for the development of art. In order for us to discover this, we need only abandon a static conception of universal value and realize that it also has the character of perpetual live energy.

II

Until now we have been concerned with the methodological significance of universal aesthetic value, and we have left aside the question of a criterion of this value. The moment has come to turn to this, for without a criterion the very notion of universality would remain vague and indefinite. Let us say first that there are several equally valid criteria: (1) value is universal when it attains a maximal extension in space, including a maximal extension across different social milieux; (2) that which successfully resists time; (3) that which is evident. One could even object that these three criteria are really only a single criterion with three correlative aspects, and indeed this would be so if the ideal universality of aesthetic value were really possible. In this case every concrete universal value would be valid everywhere and always and equally evident for any individual. But we have already stated that universal value vascillates, that either its scope or its object is constantly changing. As a result of this lack of stability these criteria frequently diverge. For example, a value which has attained a maximum extension in space need not possess either temporal endurance or evidence, and so forth.

We must therefore examine each criterion of universal aesthetic value separately. The criterion of extension in space and in various social milieux seems the least convincing. In a case where a work which has gained a very broad resonance loses it quickly, we are inclined to credit time over space in saying that the universal value of this work is indeed small or nil. However, this does not mean that extension in physical and social space is without interest for the history of the arts. On the contrary, one of the essential tasks of this discipline is not only the study of the synchronic extension of every single artistic work but also the investigation of the general attitude of every period with respect to the relative circulation of specific works of art. There are epochs in the development of art when it is generally believed that the universality of a work depends upon its being accepted by a certain social class (e.g., French literature in the period of the great literary salons of the seventeenth and eighteenth centuries). At other times an even more restricted but international elite suffices for the success of the work (the "post-war avant-garde" whose participants, the artists, were at the same time their own audience). At other times a general agreement of all classes and social milieux is required as an indication of universality (e.g., certain tendencies of the present period which demand the most generally accessible art). All these attitudes and others which are likewise possible alternate throughout the entire development of art, and they contribute to the characteristics of each of its stages.

As we have already mentioned, temporal resistance seems a more important criterion of the universality of aesthetic value than mere extension in space. Can we submit this instinctive preference for the criterion of time to critical analysis? We believe so, for only time can test the real significance of a work. In judging a work of art, we are not evaluating the material product itself but the "aesthetic object" that is its immaterial equivalent in our consciousness and that is a result of the intersection of impulses arising from the work with the living aesthetic tradition which is collective property. This aesthetic object is, of course, subject to variations, even though it is constantly related to the same material work. The metamorphosis of an aesthetic object occurs when the work penetrates new social strata different from that to which it owes its origin. These synchronic changes of the aesthetic object are, however, almost always insignificant in comparison with the diachronic changes which it undergoes in time. In the course of time a materially identical work can become several aesthetic objects radically different from one another, each corresponding to a different stage in the development of the structure of the given art. Thus the longer a work retains its aesthetic effectiveness, the greater is the certainty that this endurance of value does not lie in a transient aesthetic object but in the way in which the work itself is created in its material appearance. This significance of time for the universality of aesthetic value cannot, however, prevent the evaluation of this criterion itself from oscillating in the course of development. Moments can be found in the history of the arts when very little emphasis is placed upon it. We have already cited the case of Futurism which proposes the destruction of art museums dedicated to preserving works of long-lasting significance.

The third criterion of the universality of aesthetic value is that of evidence, which means that the individual judging a work of art has an immediate certainty that his judgment has not merely an individual range but, in fact, a universal one. He then attempts to impose this certainty upon other people as a postulate. It is this feeling of aesthetic evidence which led Kant to attribute an a priori character to aesthetic judgment. We prefer to avoid this term, for despite its subjective evidence aesthetic judgment does not seem to fit the necessary conditions for an a priori judgment. Such a judgment must be independent of all experience, whereas aesthetic judgment frequently appears to be derived from previous experiences, one's own or borrowed. It is not rare to meet people who consciously base their judgment on authorities. Proof of this is the existence of literary and artistic criticism, one of the tasks of which is to guide the judgment of those who are not capable of evaluating on their own. Certainty in aesthetic evaluation is frequently gained through special education which is based upon acknowledged values. To be a priori, an aesthetic judgment must always be independent of the specific dispositions of the individual who pronounces it. But it is easy to make sure that all of the same person's judgments, no matter how definitive his taste is, comprise a very coherent line determined precisely by his dispositions. The evidence of aesthetic judgment is therefore only subjective; its aspiration for unlimited validity is merely a postulate addressed by the individual to the collectivity.

This is why the historic role of the evidence of aesthetic judgment is subject to change. For example, there have been periods when the evidence of judgment in the affairs of art has been attributed to those who have ordered works of art rather than to the artists themselves. For instance, Chaucer asked a certain nobleman to correct his poems in order to have them conform to the prevailing taste. Michelangelo, on the other hand, revolted against the aesthetic opinions which the Pope wanted to impose upon him. In our times, in certain countries, public authority tries to monopolize the right to the unmotivated evidence of aesthetic judgment. Sometimes the evidence of aesthetic judgment is ascribed to specialists, sometimes to the broad strata of the audience (e.g., Molière who gave his plays to the maid for evaluation). Thus the criterion of evidence is also a historical factor which is under the influence of continuous artistic activity and has, in turn, a constant influence upon it like the other two criteria. Nevertheless, the criterion of evidence has a special, privileged position in relation to the other two.

Both the criterion of time and that of space have only an indirect relation to the development of art. They offer only examples to be followed, whereas the criterion of evidence is an integrating part of the very act of creation and governs the artist's aesthetic attitude in it. Being applied this way in artistic creation, this criterion provides the artist with the subjective certainty that he has attained the only objectively adequate solution. As a result this criterion plays the role of mediator between the artist's subjective intention and the objective developmental tendency of art which manifests itself through the work and is at the same time influenced by the work throughout the course of its development.

It appears, therefore, that all three criteria of the universality of aesthetic value are rooted in development and thus are subject to change; none of them has demonstrated its independence from historical changes in taste. Nevertheless, we have not abandoned the traditional idea of a universal aesthetic value which differs substantially from relative value yet notwithstanding retains all its real changeability, an ideal identity in the course of time. But can a value which constantly remains identical to itself be conceived otherwise than as an ontological value? It must not be forgotten that identity as we conceive it has quite a dynamic character which consists in a mere aspiration, constantly renewed, for universality. To explain this we need not retreat to the assumption of an unchangeable value; instead we must ask about the source of this aspiration for universal validity. This will be the subject of the third part of this paper.

III

We shall take the inherence of universal aesthetic value in the material object (aesthetic value as a characteristic of the material work of art) as a provisional starting point. Admittedly, this supposition has already been rejected many times. It seemed dead once and for all when people realized that aesthetic evaluation does not concern the material work but rather the "aesthetic object" which originates through the interpenetration of impulses arising from the material work and the living aesthetic tradition of the given art. This interpenetration takes place in the consciousness of the evaluating individual. Thus it has appeared impossible to ascribe aesthetic value directly to the material work as if it were its attribute; but this does not mean that the material work does not play a significant role in evaluation through the manner in which it has been made. Otherwise it would be incomprehensible that certain material works can acquire a constantly renewed aesthetic efficacy, despite all the changes in the aesthetic objects corresponding to the same work, in the course of the development of the given art. Aesthetic value is therefore bound to the material work, but this relation is not that of an attribute to its vehicle.

What kind of relation is it? Let us remember first that every material work comes from human hands and is addressed to man. Thus only man can establish a relation between the material work and the value directed at the immaterial aesthetic object. Is this relation established by a human individual? And can this individual be anyone who perceives the work of art or only the one who creates it? Several decades ago the most popular idea was that the value of a work rests in the perfect agreement between the work and its creator, or even in the agreement which exists between the author's specific, individual mental state and the work. It was forgotten that as soon as the material work leaves its author's hands it becomes something public which everyone can understand and interpret in his own way. Not only is the author an individual, but so are the reader and the viewer, which means that not only does the author lend his personality and mental states to the work, but so do the reader and the viewer. There are works that easily permit personality to enter their internal structure; there are others that hardly allow it.

It is very interesting for the theoretician and the historian of the arts to measure the degree of direct expressiveness which a particular work of art allows, but this finding, despite its importance for the characterization of the work, has no significance for its value since the work of art is in its very essence more than a mere expression of its author's personality. It is above all a sign destined to mediate between individuals, including both the creating individual and the individuals comprising the audience. Even though the creating individual is felt to be the party from whom the sign proceeds and the others as the party who simply perceives it, the mutual understanding between the two parties is made possible by the fact that all the individuals concerned are equal members of the same real or ideal, fixed or occasional community. As a sign the work can simultaneously have several meanings, and even very many "meanings" can be ascribed to the same work, simultaneously or successively. Every such meaning corresponds to a specific aesthetic object connected with the given material work. The greater semantic capacity the work demonstrates, the more capable it is of resisting changes in place, social milieu, and time, and the more universal its value is.

Under what conditions can this capacity attain its maximum? As a member of a society, man is under the influence of the attitude which this society adopts toward the work. It is thus very probable that insofar as the author and the audience of the work belong to the same concrete society, the work will not have to display the entire range of its semantic performance, because all those who approach it do so with approximately the same attitude. Let us assume, however, that the society perceiving the work changes completely in time. This will be the case of a literary work read several centuries after its origin in a country entirely different from that in which it originated. If the work retains its semantic range and its aesthetic effectiveness under these conditions, we shall have the right to consider this as a guarantee that the work does not address itself merely to an individual determined by the momentary state of society but to what is universally human in man. Such a work proves that it is connected with man's anthropological essence. And it is precisely here that we find the universal value of the work of art furnished by its formal capacity to function as an aesthetically valuable object in very different social milieux, though value *itself* is qualitatively different in these various environments. After all, universal aesthetic value is not exhausted by the aesthetic effectiveness of the work alone. The work that is its vehicle will also have the capacity to reach the deepest layers and the most various aspects of the mental life of the person who enters into contact with it. We could even ask whether universal aesthetic value in its very essence is not merely an index of a certain balance among various values which are contained in the work.

Now only one question remains: Is it possible to formulate explicitly the conditions which must be met if the work is to affect what is peculiar to man in general? It is certain that there is something belonging to man in general at the root of every human act. For example, modern linguistics has discovered several laws of language in general (*langage*), the human faculty to communicate by means of linguistic signs. It is obvious, of course, that the case of language is essentially different from that of art, for language is destined to be at the active disposal of everyone, whereas art, at least as we understand it today, is actively practiced only by specialists whom we call artists. This permits far more liberty and far less uniformity in art than in the normal usage of speech. Nevertheless, it has been rather frequently stated that there are certain significant similarities among the creations of primitive art of different countries, the products of folk art, and children's art. These similarities seem to attest to a common anthropological base from which these creations of beings less complex than mature modern man spring. In this respect it is also characteristic that certain works of children's literature are much more likely to gain a value independent of the flow of time and changes in space than works of adult literature. It is striking how many works of children's literature have enjoyed popularity throughout entire generations and in many countries and social milieux at the same time (cf. Defoe's *Robinson Crusoe* or Amicis' *Cuore*).

Can we thus hope that one day we shall arrive at prescriptions for the creation of works with universal aesthetic value? It is known that in laying the foundations of experimental aesthetics, Fechner expected to find such absolute rules. Today we have already learned, partially through the further development of experimental aesthetics, that between the general anthropological organization of man and concrete aesthetic evaluation stands man-the-individual as a member and partially a product of the community in which he lives and which itself is subject to development. We also know that despite its anthropological background universal aesthetic value is so changeable that the results once attained through artistic creation decline in value through repetition. In saying this, we do not wish to imply that the detailed study of primitive, folk, and children's art, together with a comparative study of more differentiated forms of art, could not lead to quite a comprehensive knowledge of universal principles of serious import. But these principles will not have the character of prescriptions. In the same way that the aforementioned general laws of language have nothing in common with normative grammar because they cannot be violated, the universal laws of art are not prescriptions.

Art will always continue to reach the anthropological basis through new paths that it has not yet traveled. This does not mean that an intense bond cannot be achieved between the concrete work and the universal anthropological basis; on the contrary, such an unconditional victory is quite frequent in art, and every time that it is achieved we have one more masterpiece. Of course, the number of paths from art to "man in general," as has already been suggested, is infinite, and every one of them corresponds to a certain social structure, or rather existential attitude, which is peculiar to this structure. It depends upon the work of art itself whether it is capable of establishing an active relation with a few or even many existential attitudes. We thus return once more, for the third time, to our starting point.

The two preceding sections led us to the conclusion that universal value is in a state of constant genesis; the third has also. But this section has also shown us that the changeability of this value consists in perpetually renewed returns to a specific constant, the general organization. Have we not reached a conclusion close to that ontological solution to our problem which presupposes universal value as an asymptot toward which the development of art constantly tends but which it never reaches? Yes and no. The similarities between these two points of view are quite obvious, but there are also essential differences.

Above all, ontological aesthetic value is unlimited (which is why all kinds of universal values tend to merge for many thinkers); but precisely because of this it is deprived of all concrete content, whereas the anthropological constitution which we substitute for ontological aesthetic value has a qualitative content which obviously limits it: beauty exists only for man. For this reason ontological aesthetic value which lacks concrete content can never attain an adequate realization. On the other hand, the anthropological constitution is capable of an infinite number of adequate aesthetic realizations corresponding to various qualitative aspects of human organization. In contrast, an individual realization of *ontologically* conceived universal aesthetic value can differ only *quantitatively* as greater or lesser perfection.

The anthropological constitution in itself does not contain anything aesthetic; there is therefore a qualitative tension between it and its aesthetic realization, and every realization reveals a new aspect of the basic organization of man. For this reason it is also possible that universal aesthetic value based on the general human organization of man can stimulate turns and changes in the development of art despite the stability of its substratum.

We have not arrived at the codification of universal aesthetic value such as Fechner wanted. We hope, nevertheless, that we have attained our basic goal of relating the idea of universal value to the idea of the constant development of art. We have attempted a chapter in the general methodology of the history of the arts and literature. What this discipline, or rather group of disciplines, needs is not static precepts but a philosophical directive which allows us to comprehend even universal aesthetic value in its historical aspect as live energy. The concept of universal aesthetic value cannot be nullified without distorting the real state of affairs; but the historian would have his hands tied if the static conception of universal aesthetic value were forced upon him.

In concluding our discussion, we dare to risk one more question. Would it not be possible to apply to other kinds of universal values, of course with the necessary modifications, the dynamic solution of universal aesthetic value whereby this value is conceived as a perpetual live energy which is in constant though historically changeable relation to man's unchanging, generally human organization?

6

The Concept of the Whole in the Theory of Art

Today's lecture has an explicitly ad hoc character; it pertains to the theme which Professor Jan Bělehrádek's lectures made a subject of discussion at the Prague Linguistic Circle.[1] In one of these discussions I suggested that a theme so fruitfully analyzed, namely, the concept of the whole, should be made concrete on the basis of various materials in order to determine to what extent it can vary with different materials. At that time I also pointed out that a possible application of the concept of the whole to a specific material, and hence in a specific field, can have a certain consequence for the conception of the whole in other disciplines as well, for each material can reveal certain facets, certain aspects of the concept, *the whole,* which will be more distinctly visible in the given material than in others but which once discovered can appear significant even where they are not visible at first glance. This remark became, at least personally, an obligation for me. If Professor Bělehrádek as a biologist had in mind biological facts as the primary material, even when he spoke about the concept of the whole in general, it seemed to me that it would not be useless to juxtapose the natural-scientific view of the whole with the view which derives from and is even compelled by the material of the disciplines sometimes called humanistic, sometimes cultural, and recently social. If I choose artistic phenomena as my material, I do so only because they are the most common material for me. I am, however, convinced that there is not a substantial difference between them and the materials of other social sciences insofar as the application of the concept of the whole to these disciplines is concerned.

Let me now return for a moment to the expression "ad hoc lec-

"Pojem celku v teorii umění," a lecture at the Prague Linguistic Circle in 1945; published in *Estetika* (1968), no. 3.

1. *Editors' note.* Mukařovský is referring to Bělehrádek's lectures "Structure and Holism" delivered on October 9, 1945 and "Holism and Linguistics" delivered on October 15. For a brief summary of these papers see *Slovo a slovesnost* 10 (1947–48): 191–92.

ture" I used just a little while ago. I would not want to arouse even the least suspicion that I regard an ad hoc character as a failing. By modifying Goethe's famous statement, we can say in a certain sense that every scholarly study is somewhat ad hoc. But even so, we must admit that not for a long time—and perhaps never systematically—have we focused attention on the position of structuralism with respect to other holistic trends. In particular, we have yet to pose the question of the difference between structuralism and other holistic trends in various disciplines because so far we have been concerned with their similarities rather than with their differences. It is, however, only the differences which in the proper sense of the word situate and determine the disposition of similar trends to one another and thereby establish their relationships on a firm basis. We must be grateful for the stimulus that has come from Professor Bělehrádek's lecture, not for what seemed obvious but precisely for what provoked our objections and—we might say—our self-awareness. By no means do I dare to claim that the following lecture can or even seeks to exhaust the theme which I have just mentioned—the distinctive character of the concept of the whole in the social sciences. First, in these days of feverish activity I lacked sufficient time to prepare my lecture; second, the material of the theory of art may be—with respect to the overall scope and differentiation of the materials of the social sciences— too narrow and hence one-sided. If I am not mistaken, the panel of this meeting has indicated that there will be another lecture on the concept of the whole in linguistics. I would very much like that lecture to be given in the interest—if I may say so—of my lecture today.

Having made this introduction, for the length of which I apologize, let me proceed to my theme. In what way, in what sense (or even in what senses) do we use the concept of the whole in the modern study of art? I intentionally pose the question so broadly and carefully, fearing that the narrower question of what kind of whole an artistic structure represents would lead to the neglect of other aspects of this concept that appear in the theory of art besides the concept of structure. And indeed they do appear. The concept *configuration* plays an especially important role in the theory of art. We must mention in advance that the word *configuration* is often used in the theory of art and especially in art criticism with several different meanings, sometimes even simultaneously. I have in mind that precise meaning in which it is used in psychology: configuration—*Gestalt*. A closed whole, in general sensorily perceptible, that in addition to the properties provided by its parts has a total *Gestaltqualität* which characterizes it precisely as a whole. Such configurations (or, even better, patterns) are melody in music, verse in poetry, and so on.

In particular, verse can provide us with a very graphic illustration. We know that as long as verse was conceived as being composed of its elements—feet, hemistichs, and so on—the mystery of verse rhythm could not be fathomed. I am not even speaking about various kinds of free verse. It is enough to consider very regular verse composed of different feet, let us say dactylo-trochaic verse, as we know it, for example, from Neruda's poetry. What regularity of sequence binds, for instance, the scheme $- v - vv - v - v - v$? The experiment with objective isochronism in which the temporal extent of feet, even heterogeneous ones, would be made equivalent in pronunciation, failed, and the proponents of isochronism had to resort to the presupposition of "a tendency toward isochronism," a factor basically psychological, subjective, and uncontrollable. But as soon as Meillet took the entire line as the basis of verse rhythm and its internal organization merely as a factor contributing to the particularity of this total configuration,[2] the way was open for understanding the rhythm of even the freest verse types.

A more detailed exposition would not be appropriate here; after all, these matters are well known. Our concern, however, is to discover toward which aspect of the whole in a configuration we are oriented. The example of verse provides an unequivocal answer: its closure. It is possible for the internal organization of verse to be realized by a very complex collaboration of different linguistic elements, and it is even possible for it to follow several different tracks. This is the case with the Old Persian verse, *mutaquárib,* for the explanation of which we are indebted to Jan Rytka. In this verse, as he discovered, both a precise quantitative scheme and a tendency toward a regular distribution of stresses operate simultaneously.[3] Each of these two articulations

2. Cf. his path-breaking work *L'Origine indoeuropéenne des mètres grecs* (Paris, 1923).
3. "La Métrique du mutaquárib épique persan," *Travaux du Cercle linguistique de Prague* 6 (Prague, 1936), 206.

has in itself the same purpose: to close the line, to characterize it as a whole. We should now ask a further question: Is it possible to call verse conceived as a pattern a structure? It is clear that it is not. These are two different matters. Why and how they are different we shall say when we discuss structure. In the meantime we shall content ourselves with the assertion that the concept of the whole in the study of art can be viewed from various angles.

We could cite still other examples of patterns from the material of the study of art; among them the concept of the composition of the work of art is especially important. Composition could be defined as "the set of means by which the work of art is characterized as a pattern." Here I shall not undertake a more detailed analysis. I would only like to point out in passing that, particularly in the case of composition, the difference between a pattern and a structure is very pronounced. For it is absolutely clear—though sometimes people are confused in this respect—that a literary work is not characterized as a structure by the most detailed compositional analysis, even when a compositional analysis properly does not compose the work out of its parts but proceeds from the total organization of the parts, from the *Gestaltqualität*. Proportionality, symmetry, concentratedness, and similar compositional features are not structural characteristics, even though the structure of a work exerts a decisive influence upon its composition and even though, on the other hand, the way in which a work is composed can be exploited in a study as one of the symptoms of its structure.

Patterns are not, however, the only kind of wholes that we encounter in the study of art, in addition to structure, of course. There is still another kind of whole that we call *contexture,* most distinctly visible in literature, but also occurring in other arts and even in non-temporal ones. We can even speak about contexture in a painting, especially if we realize that the perception of a painting is a temporal process. The basic formula of contexture is familiar enough both to linguists and to psychologists. It is a sequence of semantic units (e.g., words, sentences), a sequence unalterable without a change in the whole, in which the meaning accumulates successively:

```
a  b  c  d  e  f  g  h
   a  b  c  d  e  f  g
      a  b  c  d  e  f
         a  b  c  d  e
            a  b  c  d
               a  b  c
                  a  b
                     a
```

At the end, the entire sequence, at first given successively, is accumulated simultaneously in reverse order. Only when the contexture has been completed, do the whole and each of the individual partial meanings acquire a definite relation to reality (most obviously in detective stories where the last page can change the meaning of everything that has preceded). As long as the contexture is not completed, its total meaning is always uncertain, but the semantic intention tending toward the wholeness of the contexture accompanies its perception from the first word. Even with a contexture, just as with a configuration, attention is focused on wholeness, but with a difference that is best elucidated by comparing a literary work as a pattern (a compositional whole) with a literary work conceived as a contexture. Compositional parts do not interpenetrate; rather they become factors of composition precisely on the basis of as distinct a delimitation and differentiation as possible (indicated by the terms: compositional division, compositional scheme). On the other hand, the individual semantic units composing the sequence of the contexture, as we have already said, do interpenetrate in two directions: successively and regressively. Hence a contexture is created in a different way than a pattern; but they have in common the fact that in them we are oriented toward wholeness.

Structuralism works with both of these kinds of wholes, but the essence of structuralist thought is not to be found in them. To be on the safe side, let me mention at the end of this section that perhaps a more detailed deliberation on the material of the study of art could reveal still another kind or other kinds of nonstructural wholes. This would not, however, change anything about the essence of the matter.

Let us now proceed to *structure.* Just a moment ago we imagined a certain literary work conceived first as a contexture, then as a compositional whole. Let us imagine the same literary work in a third way, as a structure. What will be different about it from the two preceding conceptions? We shall begin with an illustration. We have in front of us a literary work preserved incompletely as a fragment, a torso, as it were. Is it a compositional whole, hence a pattern? Clearly it is not, for the total proportionality or other correspondences of the parts, for example, remain indefinite. Similarly it is not a closed contexture; we are free to complete it in our minds in the most varied ways. But is it a structure? Yes, and quite obviously. We can undertake a complete structural analysis to ascertain, for instance, the specific relationship between the intonation and the meaning, between the sentence structure and the intonation, between the intonation and the syllabic composition of words; we can determine the relation of a work composed as a whole in such and such a way to what has preceded it in development, and so forth.

Well, what are we faced with this time? There is not the least doubt that we are confronting a whole, but here wholeness does not appear to us as closure, or completeness (as it appeared to us in both of the previous cases), but rather as a certain correlation of components. This correlation of components binds the work into unity at every moment of its course (if it is a work of a temporal art) or in each of its parts (if we are dealing with a spatial art). I am aware of a certain degree of schematism in this assertion as well as in some others which will follow in the further course of my lecture; it is impossible, however, to speak about basic matters without a certain amount of schematism. The only thing that matters is that the very essence of the reality which concerns us has not been deformed, and this I intend to observe. But let us proceed! The correlation of components in a structure is unified to such an extent that it appears to us as their reciprocal subordination and superordination. In this sense we speak about the dominant component of the structure and the hierarchy of its components.

Let us now ask what these interrelations of the components of a structure are based on—how they are created. Some of them are created by the nature of the material; for example, a particular grain of stone used as the material of a sculpture or its relative hardness manifests itself necessarily both in the appearance of the surface of the statue and in its shape. This will appear even

more distinctly in literature, the material of which is language, a
system of signs whose components are permeated with very regular
interrelations before they enter the literary work. A particular way
of organizing intonation, for instance, will necessarily be connected
to a particular kind of sentence structure; the choice of words of a
particular syllabic composition—for example, polysyllabic—will
emphasize particular lexical categories, and so on. But are all the
relations in a structure based on the properties of the material?
If this were the case, the structure of a work of art would be an
automatic consequence of the necessities imposed by the material.
Let us, however, take such a case. We have in front of us a poem,
and one of the components of its structure is the metrical scheme,
the meter. This meter is not only a particular scheme but also, as
has been pointed out many times, a certain meaning. One meter
sounds solemn, another has a nuance of the everyday, the common; one meter is typically epic, another is typically lyric or
dramatic—and these associations are also meanings. Even more
concrete meanings of meters are possible.[4] The meaning which the
meter carries is related to the other semantic components of the
poetic structure; it is either in agreement or at variance with them.
Is this meaning of individual meters also somehow contained *a
priori* in the material? Not at all, rather it is an heir of the past
poetic tradition: a meter has been used in connection with such
and such themes (solemn, etc.) or with such and such a poetic
genre. As a consequence, the meter has acquired a particular
semantic coloring which in some cases can be lost in further
development.

We have thus arrived at an important fact. The interrelations of
the components in an artistic structure are largely determined by
what has preceded—a living artistic tradition. A perspective on the
development of a structure is opening up for us. We shall soon see
what important consequences follow from it. But before we
devote our attention to them, I would still like to take a look at
the structure of a single work of art, such as the one that we had
in front of us before, and pay closer attention to the relations

4. Viz., Roman Jakobson's "K popisu Máchova verše" [Toward a description of
Mácha's verse] in the anthology *Torso a tajemství Máchova díla* [The torso and mystery
of Mácha's works] (Prague, 1938), pp. 207-78. *Editors' note.* An English translation of
this article by P. and W. Steiner will appear in Jakobson's *Selected Writings,* 5 (Mouton
& Co.: The Hague, forthcoming).

connecting its components, this time not with regard to their hierarchy or their appearance but with respect to their quality. Structural relations can be of two kinds: positive and negative; they can appear as agreements or as variances. What we mean here by *variance* is clear. Subjectively it is experienced as incongruity accompanied by a stronger or weaker feeling of unusualness, indeed displeasure. Variances are also a factor in an artistic structure, a differentiating and individualizing factor. The fewer internal variances an artistic structure has, the less individual it will be and the more it will approximate general, impersonal convention. If we ask about the origin of the variances among the individual components of a structure, we again arrive at the point we reached a moment ago, the living artistic tradition. That is, a variance occurs where certain components depart from this living tradition and thus oppose others which remain in its tracks. For example, a variance will occur when a theme which used to be expressed by lofty words is now expressed by everyday or even vulgar words. This variance does not threaten the unity of the structure, but rather it enhances it because it individualizes the structure.

These are, after all, generally known facts. We have been concerned only with the proof necessary for our thought process; the correlation of components on which the unity of an artistic structure is based is not necessarily positive, for both agreements and variances weld a structure into unity. A further consequence of variances in an artistic structure is the following: not only what actually is in the work—its immediate structure—but also what has been—the preceding state of an artistic structure, the living tradition—are always present and operative in it. The interrelation of these two stages is, of course, dynamic. They are in constantly renewed variances which again always seek equilibrium. We can therefore say that even the structure of an individual work is an event, a process, not a static, precisely defined whole.

Let us now, however, turn our attention to the concept of the living tradition. We shall first ask where this living tradition exists. One answer, of course, can be that it exists in prior works of art. But what is the connection between them and a new work? There is no alternative but to admit that the existence proper of a structure, particularly the structure of a new work, does not lie in material works (which are only its external manifestations) but in a consciousness. The correlation of components, their hierarchy, their agreements and variances—all of these constitute a certain reality, but a reality immaterial in essence and only therefore capable of being dynamic. A consciousness is the locus of its existence. But whose consciousness? Someone might answer: the artist's, of course. Whereas such a claim might have a semblance of justification in the case of a work which had just been created or completed, it is not valid if we take into account the living tradition. The artist has the same relation to the living tradition as his contemporaries, as the whole collectivity which perceives works of art—the vehicles of the living tradition.

A living artistic tradition is therefore a social reality, just like language, law, and so on. And this reality which we have provisionally called the "living artistic tradition" constantly changes, develops, and endures without interruption. It is an artistic structure in the proper sense of the word; the structures of individual works of art are only particular, often very negligible, moments in this development. Material works of art are, then, the realizations of these particular moments—realizations which under the influence of the further development of the artistic structure can acquire completely different meanings from those which they originally had. Here we shall not go into the problems of the development of structure in art, for the horizons that would open before us would necessarily exceed the time limit of today's lecture. I did, however, want to indicate emphatically the social character of artistic structure and the consequences that follow from this character for the relationship between an artistic structure and a biological structure.

There is no doubt that many of the features which we have cited as characteristic of the structure of a work of art have their analogues in the structure of an organism. But an artistic structure, since it exceeds the individual work in its duration, changes with time, and exists in the collective consciousness, cannot, I believe, have analogues in biology, even though there is also developmental continuity there. In biology a material reality is the immediate vehicle of the structure. A biological structure (an organism) therefore changes less continuously than an artistic structure. The impulses for changes in the realm of biology affect material reality directly. In this respect it seems characteristic that, unlike the social sciences with their emphasis on the unbroken continuity of a structure, biology tends rather to accept emergence, that is, the sudden emerging of new structures. By saying *struc-ture,* a biologist has in mind an organism just as closed and integral as a configuration, whereas a theoretician of art means a stream of forces passing through *time,* constantly regrouping but uninter-rupted. This notion is, of course, quite removed from the notion of a pattern.

In order to complete the notion of structure in art, as we have outlined it, we must still add, at least in passing, that not even in a single art is structure simple; it does not flow in one stream but in many currents (artistic movements, individual strata of art—e.g., high lyrics, the cabaret and movie hit, the street song, etc.); and each of these currents constitutes a special structure developing in itself. These individual structures then combine into structures of a higher order, for example, the literature of such and such a na-tion. This does not, of course, exhaust its complexity, for there are many arts which differ in material but agree in their principal aim. Each art has its own structure, but these structures develop in contact with one another; they approximate one another and drift apart from one another in the course of development; they inter-penetrate, and so forth. We can therefore speak about the overall structure of art. The structure of art then enters the context of an even higher order with the structures of the other cultural phenom-ena. Thus structuralism, the structural conception, appears in the social sciences not as a partial method of a single discipline but as a very concrete methodology or rather as the epistemology of the social sciences.

Structuralism is, of course, akin to what is called "holistic thought"—they are, after all, contemporaries—but it does not coincide with it. The basic notion of holistic thought is the closed whole, whereas the basic notion of structuralist thought is that of the interplay of forces, agreeing with and opposing one another, and restoring a disturbed equilibrium by a constantly repeated synthesis. Hence the generic kinship of structuralist thought with dialectic logic.

Finally, I would like to point out that the notion of the whole is by no means the only basic concept with which structuralism works. There are two other concepts equally significant for structuralism. The notion of *function* is, of course, originally a biological concept; even though the mathematical concept of function can be used here and there, it by no means has the same importance for the structural theory of art as the concept of biological origin. Even here, however, there is a certain difference in the usage of the concept: in biology one speaks about the function of individual organs with respect to the whole of an organism. Of course, mention of the functions of individual components of a structure with respect to the overall correlation of all the components—intonation functions as a rhythmic factor in this structure, and so on—also occurs occasionally in the works of the structural theory of art. But this is not an indispensable concept; rather it is a mode of expression. We could say the same thing differently: intonation is a rhythmic factor.

The concept of function does become extremely essential if it is applied to the relationship between art and society or, better, between art and the goal which society ascribes to art, the requirements which it imposes upon art. On the one hand, function influences the organization of a work of art and thus finds its objectification in its structure; on the other hand, function roots art in the life of society. Here it would be inappropriate to discuss the complex problems of functions in art, but we should point out that for structuralism the concepts of function and structure are closely connected. The terms *functional linguistics* and *structural linguistics* are used almost synonymously, for a linguistic structure cannot be conceived otherwise than as differentiated according to the goals which linguistic expression serves. This is because language is an instrument of practical use. Since works of art are characterized by the aesthetic function, which at least seemingly frees art from practical interests, the theory of art has been willing to thrust aside functional considerations and has thus pursued purely structural analysis longer than linguistics. But the more elaborately the theory of art pursues its problems, the clearer it becomes that even here the terms *structural theory of art* and *functional theory of art* will in time become synonymous. The connection of the concept of structure with that of function is, after all, such that the function of a certain work of art and the function of a certain art in the course of its development constitute a structure whose components—like the components of every structure—are interrelated positively and negatively, in subordination and superordination, and regroup in the course of development. Here we confront a very important set of problems which will have to be studied. The ethnographer Pëtr Bogatyrëv has provided some clues for such a study—on the basis of folklore material—in several of his works.

We must still say a few words about the concept of the *norm*. The concept of the norm, the awareness of what should be, is almost inseparably bound to the concept of structure in the social sciences. Kant, who of course approached the problem of aesthetics from a completely different perspective from ours, emphasized the postulative character of aesthetic judgment. A linguistic structure quite obviously has a normative character; a legal structure even more obviously. In art as well, in the very origin of a work of art, there is an awareness that it is as it should be, that it can make a claim for general acceptance. The individual relations between its components thus acquire a normative character; and the variances between components are experienced as the violation of a previously valid norm. Then as soon as the feeling of violation is blunted by custom, the new relation becomes a norm. A structure could—from the standpoint of the social sciences—be called a set of norms; norms must not, of course, be understood as static rules but as live forces.

In joining the concept of structure, even in partially merging with it, the concepts of function and norm therefore contribute to a specific characterization of structuralism in the study of art, indeed in the social sciences in general.

Finally, there still remains a question or rather a doubt. The phrase "structural conception" has occurred several times in the course of this lecture. Does it mean that structure is, in fact, only a matter of the scholar's attitude toward his material? Is it something which the scholar brings to the material, whereby he orders and organizes it for his own purposes? Is it only a matter of scholarly (not, of course, the scholar's private) subjectivity? In no way did I intend to express such an opinion, even though I am aware that in order to recognize a structure one must orient one's view in a certain manner. A structure is, as we have already said, a *reality* which is immaterial but manifests itself materially and affects the material world. Nothing is changed by the fact that it sometimes happens that one and the same thing can be incorporated into several structures, that the structures can interpenetrate, and so on. All of this is only a consequence of the fact that the structures which concern the social sciences are immaterial and are charged with energy.

7

Art as a Semiotic Fact

It has become increasingly clear that the framework of individual consciousness is constituted, even in its innermost layers, of contents belonging to the social consciousness. As a result, the problems of sign and meaning become more and more urgent, for all psychic content exceeding the limits of individual consciousness acquires the character of a sign by the very fact of its communicability. The study of the sign (semiology according to Saussure, sematology according to Bühler) must be elaborated in its entire scope. Just as contemporary linguistics (cf. the research of the Prague School, that is, the Prague Linguistic Circle) enlarges the field of semantics by treating all the elements of the linguistic system, even sounds, from a semantic point of view, the findings of linguistic semantics should be applied to all other series of signs and should be differentiated according to their special characters. There is even a whole group of disciplines particularly interested in the problems of the sign (as well as those of structure and value which, we would add, are closely connected to those of the sign; thus the work of art is at the same time a sign, a structure, and a value). These are the so-called humanities (*Geisteswissenschaften, sciences morales*), all working with materials which have, thanks to their dual existence in the sensory world and in the social consciousness, a more or less pronounced semiotic character.

The work of art cannot be identified, as psychological aesthetics has wished, with its author's state of mind or with any of the states of mind which it evokes in perceiving subjects. It is clear that each state of subjective consciousness has something individual and momentary that renders it ungraspable and incommunicable in its totality, whereas the work of art is designed to serve as an intermediary between its author and a collectivity. Still the "thing" representing the work of art in the sensory world remains and is

"L'Art comme fait sémiologique," *Actes du huitième Congrès international de philosophie à Prague 2–7 septembre 1934* (Prague, 1936); trans. Wendy Steiner.

unrestrictedly accessible to the perception of everyone. But the work of art cannot be reduced to this "work-thing" (*oeuvre-chose*) either, since the work-thing happens to change completely in appearance and internal structure through temporal or spatial shifts. Such changes become palpable, for example, if we compare several consecutive translations of a single literary work. The work-thing functions, then, only as an external symbol (the *signifiant* according to Saussure's terminology) to which corresponds in the social consciousness a meaning (sometimes called the "aesthetic object") consisting of what the subjective states of consciousness evoked in the members of a certain collectivity have in common.

In addition to this central nucleus belonging to the social consciousness, there are, of course, in every act of perception of a work subjective, psychic elements which closely resemble what Fechner meant by the term *the associative factor* of aesthetic perception. These subjective elements themselves can also be objectified but only as their general quality or quantity is determined by the central nucleus situated in the social consciousness. For example, the subjective state of mind which accompanies any individual's perception of an Impressionist painting is of a completely different nature from that which a Cubist painting evokes. As for the quantitative differences, it is evident that the quantity of subjective images and emotions is greater for a Surrealist literary work than for a Classicist work. The former leaves to the reader the task of imagining almost the whole contexture of the theme; the latter almost completely suppresses his liberty of subjective associations by means of concise expression. It is in this fashion that the subjective components of the perceiving subject's psychic state acquire, at least indirectly through the mediation of the nucleus belonging to the social consciousness, an objectively semiotic character, similar to the one that the "accessory" meanings of a word have.

To conclude these few general remarks we must add that in refusing to identify the work of art with a subjective psychic state, we are at the same time rejecting hedonistic aesthetic theories. For the pleasure evoked by a work of art can, at most, attain an indirect objectification as potential "accessory meaning." We would be wrong to affirm that pleasure is necessarily part of the perception of every work of art. There are periods in art which tend to arouse it; there are others which are indifferent to it or even seek its opposite.

According to the usual definition, the sign is a sensory reality relating to another reality that it is supposed to evoke. We are thus obliged to ask ourselves what this other reality replaced by the work of art is. It is true that we could simply state that the work of art is an *autonomous* sign characterized only by its serving as an intermediary among the members of the same collectivity. But if we were to do so, we would simply be dismissing the question of the contact of the work-thing with the intended reality without resolving it. Although there are signs not relating to any distinct reality, something is always referred to by the sign, and this follows quite naturally from the fact that the sign must be understood in the same way by the one who expresses it and by the one who perceives it. But since this "something" is not distinctly delimited for autonomous signs, what is this indistinct reality referred to by the work of art? It is the total context of so-called social phenomena—for example, philosophy, politics, religion, and economics. For this reason art is more capable of characterizing and representing the given "epoch" than any other social phenomenon. For a long time, therefore, the history of art has been confused with the history of culture in the broad sense of the term, and conversely general history tends to borrow its periodization from the history of art. Admittedly, the connection between certain works of art and the total context of social phenomena appears loose. The works of the so-called *poètes maudits,* for example, are alien to the standards of contemporary values. But it is just for this reason that they remain excluded from literature and are only accepted by the collectivity at a moment when, as a consequence of the evolution of the social context, they become capable of expressing it.

We must add one more explanatory remark to prevent any possible misunderstanding. If we say that the work of art refers to the context of social phenomena, we are by no means affirming thereby that it necessarily coincides with this context in such a way that, without qualification, we could take it for a direct testimony or a passive reflection. Like every *sign,* the work of art can have an indirect relation, for example, metaphoric or otherwise oblique, to the thing signified without thereby ceasing to refer to it. From the semiotic nature of art it follows that a work of art should never be

exploited as a historical or sociological document without a preliminary interpretation of its documentary value, that is, the quality
of its relation to the given context of social phenomena.

To summarize the essential features of what we have set forth so
far, we may say that the objective study of the phenomenon of art
must regard the work of art as a sign composed of a sensory symbol created by the artist, a "meaning" (= aesthetic object) lodged
in the social consciousness, and a relation to the thing signified—
a relation that refers to the entire context of social phenomena.
The second of these constituents contains the structure proper of
the work.

We have not yet, however, exhausted the problems of the
semiotics of art. Besides its function as autonomous sign the work
of art has yet another function, that of *communicative* sign. Thus
a literary work functions not only as a work of art but also and
simultaneously as *parole* expressing a state of mind, a thought, an
emotion, and so forth. There are arts in which this communicative
function is very apparent (literature, painting, sculpture), and
there are others in which it is veiled (dance) or even invisible
(music, architecture). We leave aside the difficult problem of the
latent presence or the total absence of the communicative element
in music and architecture, although even here we are inclined to
recognize a diffuse communicative element (the relation of musical
melody to linguistic intonation, the communicative power of
which is evident); we shall address ourselves only to those arts in
which the functioning of the work as a communicative sign is beyond doubt. These are arts with a "subject" (= theme, content) in
which the subject seems at first glance to function as the *communicative* meaning of the work. In reality, each of the components of
a work of art, even the most "formal," has its own communicative
value independent of the subject. Thus the colors and lines of a
painting signify "something," even in the absence of any subject
(cf. Kandinsky's "absolute" painting or the works of certain
Surrealist painters). It is in this virtual semiotic character of the
"formal" components that the "diffuse" communicative power of
arts without a subject lies. To be precise, then, we must say that it
is the entire structure which functions as the meaning, even the
communicative meaning, of the work of art. The subject of the
work simply plays the role of an axis of crystallization in relation

to this meaning which, without it, would remain vague. The work of art therefore has two semiotic functions, autonomous and communicative, the second of which is reserved especially for arts with a subject. In the evolution of these arts we can thus see a dialectic antimony, more or less pronounced in appearance, between the functions of the autonomous sign and communicative sign. The history of prose (the novel, the short story) offers especially typical examples of this.

But the subtlest complications arise as soon as we question from a communicative standpoint the relation of art to the thing signified. It is a different relation from that which links all of art in its capacity as autonomous sign to the entire context of social phenomena, for as a communicative sign, art is oriented toward a distinct reality, for example, a definite event or a certain personage. In this respect art resembles purely communicative signs except for the essential difference that the communicative relation between the work of art and the thing signified does not have an existential value, even if the work asserts something. We cannot postulate the documentary authenticity of the subject of a work of art as long as we evaluate the work as a product of art. This is not to say that the *modifications* of the relation to the thing signified lack importance for the work: they function as factors of its structure. It is very important for the structure of a given work that we know whether it treats its subject as "real" (sometimes even as documentary) or "fictive," or whether it oscillates between these two poles. We might even find some works based on a parallelism and counterbalancing of the dual relation to a distinct reality, the one without existential value and the other purely communicative. Such is the case of the painted or sculpted portrait, which is at the same time a communication about the person represented and a work of art devoid of existential value. In literature, the historical novel and the biographical novel are characterized by the same duality. Modifications of the relation to reality thus play an important role in the structure of every art working with a subject; but the theoretical study of these arts must never lose sight of the true essence of the subject, which is to be a unity of meaning and not a passive copy of reality, even if the work is "realistic" or "naturalistic."

To conclude, we would like to point out that as long as the semiotic character of art is insufficiently illuminated, the study of the structure of the work of art will necessarily remain incomplete. Without a semiotic orientation the theoretician of art will always be inclined to regard the work either as a purely formal construction or as a direct reflection of its author's psychic or even physiological dispositions, of the distinct reality expressed by it, or of the ideological, economic, social, or cultural situation of the given milieu. Hence he will treat the development of art as a series of formal transformations, or deny it completely (which is the case of certain currents in psychological aesthetics), or finally conceive it as a passive commentary on a development external to art. Only the semiotic point of view will permit theoreticians to recognize the autonomous existence and essential dynamism of artistic structure and to understand its development as a movement which is immanent but in constant dialectic relation to the development of the other spheres of culture.

The purpose of this brief outline of the semiotic study of art is first to provide a partial illustration of a certain aspect of the dichotomy, natural sciences/humanities (*sciences morales*), which occupies an entire section of this Congress and second to stress the importance of semiotic questions for aesthetics and the history of the arts. Perhaps we shall be permitted, at the end of our paper, to sum up its principal ideas in the form of theses:

A. In addition to the problems of structure and value, the problem of the sign is one of the essential problems of the humanities which all work with materials having a more or less pronounced semiotic character. This is why the results obtained by the research of linguistic semantics should be applied to the materials of these disciplines—especially to those whose semiotic character is most clear-cut—so as to differentiate them according to the specific characteristics of these materials.

B. The work of art has the character of a sign. It cannot be identified with the individual state of consciousness of its author, with any state of consciousness of the perceiving subjects, or with the work-thing. It exists as an "aesthetic object" lodged in the consciousness of a whole collectivity. In relation to this immaterial object, the sensory work-thing is only its external symbol; the individual states of consciousness evoked by the work-thing represent the aesthetic object only through what is common to all of them.

C. Every work of art is an *autonomous* sign composed of: (1) a "work-thing" functioning as a sensory symbol; (2) an "aesthetic object" lodged in the social consciousness and functioning as "meaning"; (3) a relation to the thing signified, a relation which does not refer to a distinct existence—it is an autonomous sign— but the total context of social phenomena of the given milieu (science, philosophy, religion, politics, economics, etc.).

D. The arts with a "subject" (= theme, content) have yet a second semiotic function which is *communicative*. In this case the sensory symbol naturally remains the same as in the preceding case; here also, meaning is furnished by the entire aesthetic object, but among the components of this object there is a privileged vehicle which functions as an axis of crystallization of the diffuse communicative power of the other components. This is the subject of the work. The relation to the thing signified, as in every communicative sign, is oriented toward a distinct existence (event, person, thing, etc.). In this respect the work of art resembles purely communicative signs. However, and this is an essential difference, the relation between the work of art and the thing signified does not have existential value. It is impossible to postulate the documentary authenticity of the subject of a work of art as long as we evaluate the work as a product of art. This does not mean that the modifications of the relation to the thing signified (that is, the different degrees of the scale "reality–fiction") lack importance for a work of art. They function as factors of its structure.

E. The two semiotic functions, communicative and autonomous, which coexist in arts with a subject, together constitute one of the essential dialectic antinomies in the development of these arts; their duality manifests itself in the course of development by constant oscillations in their relation to reality.

8

Intentionality and Unintentionality in Art

The work of art stands out among human products as the prime example of intentional creation. Practical creation is also intentional, of course; however, man takes into account only those properties of the object being produced which are supposed to serve a planned aim. He does not consider all its other properties which are indifferent with respect to this aim. This fact has been manifest particularly since the time when a distinct differentiation of functions came into being. We still find a consideration for "useless" properties (ornamental decoration with a symbolic and aesthetic function, etc.), for example, in folk implements that originated in a milieu where functions were undifferentiated, but a modern machine or even a tool implements a perfect selection of properties relevant to a purpose. Consequently the difference between practical and artistic creation—at one time (and in folk creation, insofar as it exists, even up to the present) not evident enough—is more marked today. In the work of art neither a single property of the object nor a single detail of its organization is beyond the range of our attention. Only as an integral whole does the work of art fulfill its function as an aesthetic sign. Evidently the impression of absolute intentionality by means of which the work of art affects us has its source and its justification here.

But in spite of this, perhaps even precisely because of this, it is—and has been from ancient times—strikingly apparent to the more careful observer that there is much in the work of art as a whole and in art in general which defies intentionality and which in particular cases exceeds the given intention. The explanation for these unintentional moments has been sought in the artist—in the psychic processes accompanying creation, in the participation of the subconscious during the origin of the work. Plato's famous statement made through Socrates in *Phaedrus* explicitly attests to this: "A third kind of possession or madness comes from the

"Záměrnost a nezáměrnost v umění," a lecture at the Prague Linguistic Circle on May 26, 1943; published in *Studie z estetiky* (Prague, 1966).

Muses. It takes hold upon a gentle virginal soul, awakens and inspires it to song and poetry and so, glorifying the innumerable
deeds of our forefathers, educates posterity. He who without the
Muses' madness in his soul comes knocking at the door of poetry,
thinking that art alone will make him fit to be called a poet, will
find that he is found wanting and that the verse he writes in his
sober senses is beaten hollow by the poetry of madmen."[1] "Art
alone," hence conscious intentionality, does not suffice; "madness," the participation of the subconscious, is necessary; moreover, only this gives the work perfection.

The problem of the conscious and the subconscious in artistic
creation was not a concern of the Middle Ages, which regarded the
artist only as an imitator of the beauty of divine creation[2] and as a
producer similar to artisans.[3] But we find mention of this problem
again during the Renaissance; for example, we read in Leonardo da
Vinci's *Art of Painting*: "When the work is equal to the knowledge
and judgment of the painter, it is a bad sign; and when it surpasses
the judgment, it is still worse, as is the case with those who
wonder at having succeeded so well."[4] Here the participation of
the subconscious, hence unintentionality, in artistic creation is
naturally condemned, for Renaissance art and its theory tend to
rationalize the creative process so that art competes with scientific
knowledge.[5] Precisely for this reason, however, it is important that

1. *Phaedrus,* trans. W. C. Helmbold and W. G. Rabinowitz (New York, 1956), p. 26.
2. H. H. Glunz, *Die Literarästhetik des europäischen Mittelalters* (n.p., 1937): "God
alone is the true Creator who creates so that something arises from nothing. Nature does
not create in this sense but only reveals and develops what has already been created in
embryo; it provides what has been created with its various discernible forms. Man cannot even do this. He unites or separates only what is already at hand, he only reshuffles
parts and believes that in creating new combinations, he creates at least as nature [does].
But his art is only a forgery of nature, it is an untrue, falsified and falsifying, forging and
aping art, an *ars adulterina*. It is indicative that a medieval etymology links the names of
craft art, the only art of which men were capable, '*ars mechanica*,' to '*moechus*'
[adulterer]. *Ars moecha* falsifies and stains what has been created by God and nature, the
true work of art, by dragging it down to earth" (p. 216).
3. J. Maritain, *Art and Scholasticism with Other Essays,* trans. J. F. Scanlan (New
York, 1930): "In the powerfully social structure of mediaeval civilisation the artist
ranked simply as an artisan, and every kind of anarchical development was prohibited
to his individualism, because a natural social discipline imposed upon him from without
certain limiting conditions" (p. 17).
4. *The Art of Painting* (New York, 1957), p. 214.
5. Cf. H. Nohl, *Die ästhetische Wirklichkeit* (Frankfurt am Main, 1935): "Thus the
aesthetics of the Renaissance, in fact, takes into account only the beauty of nature,
whose secret it seeks to reveal, and art is only an instrument for conceiving it and for

an allusion to the subconscious in the process of artistic creation occurs even during the reign of such a tendency.

Subconsciousness as a factor of the process of artistic creation becomes especially valued in the theory of art at the beginning of the nineteenth century. The whole theory of the genius is based upon it: "No work of genius can be improved, or be freed from its faults by reflection and its immediate results, . . ." says Goethe in a letter to Schiller.[6] Similarly, Schiller writes: "Unconsciousness combined with reflection constitutes the poet-artist."[7] Interest in the subconscious in the process of artistic creation has not waned since that time. As scientific psychology has developed, it has seen more clearly the participation of the subconscious in mental life in general—its activity.[8] The participation of the subconscious in the process of scientific and technical creation, as well as other kinds of creation, is also being studied according to the model of the process of artistic creation (Ribot, Paulhan). Moreover, special studies devoted to the participation of the subconscious in the process of artistic creation itself have been appearing,[9] just as the participation of the subconscious in mental life in general, especially its role in the structure of personality, is being investigated (Janet and others). Depth psychology has been studying the course of subconscious processes in detail, with a strong inclination toward art; the initiating activity of the subconscious is a fundamental premise for depth psychology.

The problem of the conscious–subconscious in art has therefore not only a long tradition but also a still unexhausted vitality. The

---

the perfect further elaboration of patterns available in nature. Only if one views the art of the Renaissance in this context, will one understand its most intrinsic meaning: It seeks to comprehend the world and to shape it further according to its own law" (p. 26). "One can comprehend the entire meaning of the work of these artists only if one conceives it in connection with the great work of contemporary natural science; only then does one perceive its most profound intention: It is a forerunner of the new science" (p. 30). "The art of the Renaissance is accompanied by a great many treatises which seek to rationalize this artistic work. Whoever approaches these treatises with the expectation of finding beautiful feelings and experiences will be astonished by their dry earnestness and mathematical matter-of-factness" (p. 29).

6. *Correspondence Between Schiller and Goethe, from 1794 to 1805,* trans. L. D. Schmitz (London, 1879), 2, 374–75.

7. *Ibid.,* p. 372.

8. "*The subconscious is an accumulator of energy*: it saves so that consciousness can spend"–T. Ribot, cited according to G. Dwelshauvers, *L'Inconscient* (Paris, 1916), p. 5.

9. O. Behaghel, *Bewusstes und Unbewusstes im dichterischen Schaffen* (Leipzig, 1907).

fact that the question of the subconscious has an immediate importance for artistic practice itself contributes to this vitality.
Again and again artists are compelled to ask themsevles to what
extent they can rely on their subconscious during the creative
process. That the answer sounds different according to trends and
circumstances—now in favor of the conscious creative process
(Edgar Allan Poe, "The Philosophy of Poetic Composition"), now
in favor of the subconscious (Goethe's and Schiller's statements
above)—changes nothing.

All those who have raised the question of the subconscious in
artistic creation since antiquity have apparently often had in mind
not only the psychological process of creation but also to a considerable extent the unintentionality obvious in the product itself
(cf. Plato's aforementioned statement). However, the subconscious
in creation and the unintentionality in the product have seemed
identical to them.

Only modern psychology has perceived that even the subconscious has its own intentionality, and it has thus established the
premise for separating the problem of the intentional–unintentional from the problem of the conscious–subconscious. In showing that even a subconscious *norm,* hence intentionality concentrated into a rule, can exist, contemporary theory of art has
attained similar conclusions independently of psychology. We have
in mind some studies in modern metrics such as Josef Rypka's "La
Métrique du mutaqárib épique persan."[10] By means of a statistical
analysis of Old Persian verse the author has demonstrated in an
absolutely objective manner that parallel to the quantitative
metrical scheme there is a tendency toward a regular distribution
of stresses and word boundaries about which the poets themselves
had no knowledge and which had also remained completely hidden from modern European scholars until his discovery. Nevertheless, as Rytka states, this tendency is an active aesthetic factor.
The variances between a very regular quantitative scheme and a
latent tendency toward a regular distribution of stresses and word
boundaries ensured, as it were, the rhythmic differentiation of the
line, which, had it been based on quantity alone, would have been
rhythmically monotonous.

The fact that unintentionality can participate in the creation of
a work of art, even without any conscious or subconscious inter-

10. *Travaux du Cercle linguistique de Prague* 6 (Prague, 1936), 192 ff.

vention on the part of the artist, testifies further to the need for separating the question of intentionality–unintentionality from the psychological question of the conscious–unconscious in artistic creation. Today, for example, when artificial torsos occur so frequently in sculpture, it can hardly be disputed that in perceiving the sculptural torsos of antiquity, we spontaneously comprehend the truncation as a component of their aesthetic effect. If we stand before the Aphrodite of Melos, we do not complete the contour of this statue with a helmet and a hand holding a pomegranate, as one reconstruction wishes, or with a shield resting on a thigh, as another reconstruction imagines;[11] and we may even say in general that the idea of any completion of the present state of a statue would have a disturbing effect on our perception. Yet, the perfect three-dimensionally enclosed contour of a statue, as we see it and as it has been emphasized in recent years by a revolving pedestal, is largely the result of the intervention of external accident which the artist could not have controlled in any way whatsoever.

Although psychology has already accomplished a great deal toward solving the problem of the conscious and the subconscious elements of the creative process, we must still pose the question of intentionality and unintentionality in artistic creation again—and independently of psychology. This is what we want to attempt in the present study. If we wish to free ourselves radically from the psychological consideration, however, we must proceed not from the originator of the activity but from the activity itself, or, better, from the product that has originated by means of it.

We shall begin with intentionality, leaving aside for the time being its opposite, unintentionality, and we shall ask: In what way does intentionality make itself felt in the activity or the product? In practical activities, which are the most normal cases of behavior, intentionality expresses itself primarily as a tendency toward a specific aim that is to be attained by a given activity. The activity originates from a specific subject. If it concerns a product that has originated by means of the activity, this tendency toward a goal manifests itself as a certain mode of its organization. From this organization we also deduce the subject's participation during the origin of the object. Only if we know both of these boundary points, is the activity (or its product) satisfactorily characterized for us; our evaluation of the activity (or its product) also occurs

11. With respect to both reconstructions, see A. H. Springer, *Handbuch der Kunstgeschichte* (Stuttgart, 1923), 1, 413.

with respect to these two points. Naturally, during the evaluation, we shall sometimes be interested in the goal (Was the activity adequate enough with respect to the given goal?), and sometimes, conversely, in the subject (Was the goal chosen by the individual actually desirable, and how was the goal related to the individual's ability?). This fact does not, however, alter the fundamental knowledge that the center of attention is not the activity itself (or its product) but the starting point and the point of issue, hence two instances which are *outside* the activity itself (or outside its product).

A different situation exists in artistic creation. Its products are not oriented toward any specific external goal but are themselves the goal. This is valid even when we realize that a work of art can acquire *secondarily*—on account of its extra-aesthetic functions which are, however, subordinate to the aesthetic function—a relation to the most varied external aims. None of these secondary goals suffices to characterize fully and unequivocally the intent of the work insofar as we regard it as an artistic product. The relation to the subject is also different and less specific in art than in practical activities. Whereas in the latter the originator of the activity or product is unequivocally the only subject who matters, in art the fundamental subject is not the originator but the individual to whom the artistic product is addressed, hence the perceiver. Insofar as the artist assumes a relation to his product as an artistic product (not as an object of production), even he himself sees and judges it as the perceiver. The perceiver is not, however, a specific person, not a particular individual, but anyone. All of this follows from the fact that a work of art is not a "thing" but a sign designated to mediate among individuals. In fact, it is an autonomous sign lacking an unequivocal relation to reality so that its mediating task is all the more striking.[12] Hence not even the intent of an artistic work can be unequivocally characterized by its relation to the subject.[13]

12. Cf. our theses "Art as a Semiotic Fact" (above) and "Poetic Designation and the Aesthetic Function of Language," *The Word and Verbal Art: Selected Essays by Jan Mukařovský*, trans. and ed. John Burbank and Peter Steiner (New Haven, 1977), pp. 65–73.

13. The statement that a work of art cannot be unequivocally characterized by its relation to its originator may at first glance seem paradoxical, if we recall that there are entire aesthetic movements—Croce and his adherents—which consider a work of art to be an unequivocal expression of the originator's personality. A feeling characteristic only for a certain period and a certain attitude toward art must not, however, be generalized.

The two boundary points that suffice in practical activities for a characterization of the intention from which the activity or its product originated move into the background in art. Intentionality

---

As is well known, the originator of a work of art was of no concern to the Middle Ages; we have conclusive evidence, preserved in Vasari's biography of Michelangelo, about how a sense of authorship developed only during the Renaissance. Vasari relates the origin of Michelangelo's Pietà and adds to his narration: "Michelagnolo devoted so much love and pains [to] his work that he put his name on the girdle crossing the Virgin's breast, a thing he never did again. One morning he had gone to the place where it stands and observed a number of Lombards who were praising it loudly. One of them asked another the name of the sculptor, and he replied, 'Our Gobbo of Milan.' Michelagnolo said nothing, but he resented the injustice of having his work attributed to another, and that night he shut himself in the chapel with a light and his chisels and carved his name on it" [G. Vasari, *The Lives of the Painters, Sculptors and Architects,* trans. A. B. Hinds (London, 1927), 4, 115]. The anecdote indicates that even for a Renaissance artist, proud of his craft, a feeling of a fatal bond with his work was not the intrinsic motive for an explicit claim to it; rather it was jealousy, for only when the work was attributed to another did the author resolve to sign it. We find the same attitude toward the author, the same indifference to him as in the Middle Ages, though much later, in folkloric art: "If a simple rustic sees a cathedral which impresses him, then inside the cathedral a painting which he admires, and if he hears played and sung a mass, the sounds of which delight him, he will hardly ask the name of the architect, painter, or composer but will praise what seems to him praiseworthy and at most will want to know at whose expense the cathedral was built, who donated the painting for the altar, who plays and sings in the choir. And he behaves in the same way vis-à-vis his songs. Let us say, he himself has heard an improvisation and knows the improvisator; he has also memorized the words and melody of the song, and perhaps he helps to spread it by singing it himself; however, both he and the audience are more interested in the song itself than in the songster. Therefore the song has for a signature the place and the region from which it has come, or any other accidental external indicator, rather than some personal name" [O. Hostinský, *Česká světská píseň lidová* (The Czech secular folk song) (Prague, 1906), p. 23]. This quotation shows very clearly that it is not the originator's personality but the work that interests the rustic. If he turns his attention to some individual, it is much more likely to be someone among the perceivers—the one who had the cathedral built, who donated the picture, who plays and sings—than the originator. František Bartoš characterizes this interest directed at a perceiver—or better at a reproducing perceiver—even more distinctly: "The folk knew only good singers and esteemed them; they did not ask about the poets. The more new songs the singer knew, the more esteemed he was, but no one inquired about where he got these new songs, thinking that the singer had heard them from someone just as he himself was now hearing them from the singer for the first time" [cited according to N. Melniková-Papoušková, *Putování za lidovým uměním* (A quest for folk art) (Prague, 1941), p. 169]. The agreement of the medieval attitude toward the originator of a work with the folk attitude thus clearly testifies that a close connection between a work and its originator is a concern only of a certain period, not a phenomenon generally and essentially valid. Besides, and this is even more important, the "meaning" of a work, as we shall see, does not depend only on the originator but to a considerable extent on the way in which the perceiver apprehends it. Those who want to draw unequivocal conclusions from the work about the artist, his psychic organization, experiences, and so forth, are always in danger of imposing their own perceiving interpretation of the work upon the artist.

itself then comes to the fore. But what is intentionality "in itself" if it is not defined with respect to the goal and the originator? We have already mentioned that a work of art is an autonomous sign lacking an unequivocal reference. As an autonomous sign a work of art does not enter into a binding relation to reality, which it represents (communicates) by means of its theme, through its separate parts, but only *as a whole* can it establish a relation to any one of the perceiver's experiences or to a set of his experiences in his subconscious. (A work of art "means," then, the perceiver's existential experience, his mental world.) This must be emphasized especially in contrast to communicative signs (e.g., a communicative verbal utterance) in which each part, each partial semantic unit, can be verified in the reality to which it refers (cf. a scientific proof).

Thus semantic unity is a very relevant condition in a work of art, and intentionality is the force which binds together the individual parts and components of a work into the unity that gives the work its meaning. As soon as the perceiver adopts an attitude toward a certain object, which is usual during the perception of a work of art, he immediately makes an effort to find in the organization of the work traces of an arrangement that will permit the work to be conceived as a semantic whole. The unity of a work of art—for which theoreticians have so often looked outside the work, sometimes in the artist's personality, sometimes in experience as a unique encounter of the originator's personality with reality—which formalist movements unsuccessfully explained as an absolute harmony of all the parts and components of a work (a harmony which never exists in reality), can rightly be found only in intentionality, the force operating within the work which strives toward the resolution of the contradictions and tensions among its individual parts and components, thereby giving each of them a specific relation to the others and all of them together a unified meaning. Hence intentionality in art is *semantic* energy.

We must, nevertheless, remark that the character of a semantically unifying force also pertains to intentionality in practical activities where, however, this character is obscured by consideration for the goal and, in some cases, for the originator. As soon as we start to view any practical activity or object produced by it as an artistic fact, the need for semantic unification becomes startlingly clear (for example, if work movements become the object of self-oriented perception by analogy with the arts of dancing and mime, or if we view a machine—as has happened more often—as a work of visual art according to the model of sculpture).

Here again we encounter the importance of the perceiving subject in art. Intentionality as a semantic fact is accessible only to the view of the person who adopts toward the work an attitude unclouded by any practical consideration. The originator, being the producer of the work, must also have a purely practical attitude toward it. His aim is the completion of the work, and on the way toward this goal he encounters technical difficulties, sometimes pertaining to craftsmanship in the very literal sense of the word, which have nothing in common with intrinsic artistic intentionality. It is well enough known that artists themselves in judging others' works sometimes attribute considerable importance to the dexterity with which technical difficulties have been overcome in these works—a standpoint that is generally quite alien to the mere aesthetically oriented perceiver. Furthermore, the artist can be guided in his work (at least partially) by personal motives of a practical nature (a material consideration which is strikingly apparent, for example, among Renaissance artists—viz. the numerous testimonies in Vasari). These considerations also obscure self-oriented, "pure" intentionality. The artist, it is true, must constantly consider the work as an autonomous sign even while he is working, and a practical consideration always blends completely with pure intentionality in his attitude toward the work in progress. This does not matter, however. What is important is that at moments when he regards his product from the standpoint of pure intentionality in an effort (conscious or subconscious) to introduce traces of this intentionality into its organization, he behaves as the perceiver, and only from the perceiver's viewpoint does the entire scope of the tendency toward semantic unity become clearly and distinctly evident.

It is not the originator's attitude toward the work but the perceiver's which is fundamental, or "unmarked," for understanding its intrinsic artistic intent. However paradoxical this statement might seem, the artist's attitude appears secondary, or "marked," from the standpoint of intentionality, of course. Such a notion of the relationship between the artist and the perceiver with respect to the work does not after all lack evidence in real life. Again, we must only overcome in ourselves (as we have already emphasized above in a footnote) a current, purely contemporary view that we unjustly consider generally valid. When, for example, Vasari (in the biography of Pietro Perugino) searches for the reasons why Florence (of all the cities) raised the most perfect masters in all the arts, especially in painting, he does not place the greatest emphasis on the artists themselves, as we might perhaps today, but on "the spirit of criticism, the air making minds naturally free and not content with mediocrity, but leading them to value works for their beauty and other good qualities rather than for their authors."[14]

Nor is the relationship between the perceiver's and the originator's attitudes such that only the latter is active, while the former is passive. The perceiver, too, is active vis-à-vis the work. The semantic unification that he reaches during perception is, of course, evoked to a greater or lesser degree by the organization of the work. It is not, however, limited to pure perception, but rather it has the nature of an effort by means of which the interrelations among the individual components of the perceived work are bound together. This effort is even creative in the sense that the incorporation of the components and parts of the work into complex and unified relations gives rise to a meaning not contained in any of them taken by itself or even resulting from their mere sum. The inevitable result of the unifying effort is predetermined to a certain, sometimes considerable, extent by the organization of the work, but it always depends in part on the perceiver who decides (it does not matter whether consciously or subconsciously) which component of the work he will take as the basis of semantic unification and how he will regulate the interrelations of all the components. The perceiver's initiative—which is as a rule individual only to a small degree, being determined for the most part by general factors such as time, generation, and social milieu—provides the possibility that different perceivers (or rather different groups of perceivers) will invest the same work with a different intentionality, sometimes considerably divergent from that which its originator gave it and to which he also adapted it. Not only can a shift in the dominant component and a regrouping of the components that were the original vehicles of intentionality take place in the perceiver's conception, but those components which were

14. *The Lives*, p. 125.

originally outside the intention can even become vehicles of intentionality. This will happen, for example, when obsolete but once simply necessary modes of linguistic expression strike the reader of an old literary work as poetically effective archaisms.

The perceiver's active participation in the formation of intentionality gives this intentionality a dynamic nature. As a resultant of the encounter between the viewer's attitude and the organization of the work, intentionality is labile and oscillates during the perception of the same work, or at least—with the same perceiver—from perception to perception. It is a common experience that the more vividly a work affects a perceiver, the more possibilities of perception it offers him.

The perceiver's active participation in intentionality in art, however, can also become explicit. This happens when the perceiver intervenes directly in the organization of the work. Cases of this kind are quite frequent. The very fact that the artist takes the public into account while he is creating is evidence of this phenomenon. Sometimes the public's influence is limited to a negative inhibition;[15] at other times it is positive. When the artist fights against the prevailing taste by means of his work, however, we have, in fact, a case of an indirect expression of the viewer's activity during the formation of intentionality. The critic is also a perceiver, and his participation in artistic creation is the more evident.[16] We even know of cases in which an artist, before making his work public, presents it tentatively to persons whom he considers representatives of his audience (the anecdote about Molière's maid). The artist need not, of course, have in mind the audience which will perceive his work upon publication. He is sometimes at variance with this audience and appeals to a future one (in some cases, totally nonexistent); compare the case of Stendhal (I will be read around 1880). Even this notion, however, affects the

15. "The sagacious artist, while respecting himself, will respect the idiosyncrasies of his public" (Arnold Bennett about himself, cited according to L. L. Schücking, *The Sociology of Literary Taste*, trans. E. W. Dickes [London, 1944], p. 37).

16. "In the conclusion of the article 'Herec a kritik' [The actor and the critic], Hilar himself confesses to an almost physiological need for agreement: 'Such are all of us theater people. We must be believed, and something must be desired of us. We accomplish the superhuman. A word of distrust and doubt will upset and crush us. A word of trust elates and inspires us. The critic's word has such great power and responsibility'" [cited according to M. Rutte's study *K. H. Hilar: Člověk a dílo* (K. H. Hilar: The man and his works) (Prague, 1936), p. 94].

artist's intentionality. But the perceiver is not the only public: the buyer is another public, and it is well known what a great influence Renaissance buyers had in all respects upon the creation originating from their initiative. Folk art, where the boundary between the perceiver and the author is often completely obliterated, is a case in itself. Let us mention, for instance, the folk song. As soon as the product has been accepted by collective agreement, it immediately undergoes an infinite series of changes; those who are the originators of these changes are no longer authors, in the sense in which we understand this word in high art, but are much more perceivers.

Intentionality in art can therefore be grasped fully only when we look at it from the perceiver's standpoint. Naturally, in making this statement, we do not want to create the impression that we consider the true perceiver's initiative as basically predominant over the originator's initiative, or even as equal to it. By using the term "perceiver," we are characterizing a certain point of view toward the work of art, a point of view which the author also takes insofar as he perceives his work as a sign, hence precisely as a work of art, not only as a product. It would be patently wrong if he wished to designate the originator's active relation to the work as basically secondary (even though such a case is, of course, possible in practice, as can be seen in the example of folk art). We would have to show distinctly the interval separating intentionality in art from the artist's psychology, from his private mental life. This is possible only when we clearly realize that the perceiver is the one who perceives the artist's work most purely as a sign.

Intentionality has been depsychologized by disengaging it from an absolute direct and strictly one-sided connection with the originator. Its proximity to the perceiver does not render it a psychological fact since the perceiver is not a specific individual but any person. What the perceiver introduces into the perceived work during perception, hence the perceiver's private "psychology," changes from perceiver to perceiver and thus remains outside the work considered as an object. With the depsychologization of intentionality, however, the form of the problem at which our study is primarily directed, namely the question of unintentionality in art, changes radically, and a new path to its solution opens up. All of this will be discussed in the following paragraphs.

First, however, we must come to terms with the question of

whether there is anything in a work that could be called unintentional from the perceiver's standpoint. If the perceiver necessarily
makes an effort to apprehend the entire work as a sign, hence as a
form that has originated from a unified intention and that acquires
a unified meaning from this intention, can there be anything
unintentional in the work as far as the perceiver is concerned? We
shall actually find views in the theory of art which attempt to
exclude unintentionality completely from art.

The conception of the work of art as purely intentional has
naturally been especially close to movements constructed upon
the perceiver's point of view, particularly formalist movements. In
the last half-century or so formalist movements in art have gradually arrived at two notions which reduce the work of art to pure
intentionality: the notions of stylization and deformation. According to the first of them, which originates in the visual arts, art is
merely the conquest and digestion of reality by the unity of form.
In programmatic theory of art this notion had currency especially
in the period when post-Impressionist movements in painting were
renewing a sense for the formal unification of represented objects
and the picture as a whole and when Symbolism in literature was
reacting similarly to Naturalism. The notion of stylization even
penetrated scholarly objectivist aesthetics which was then developing (our countryman Zich, for example, used this concept). Deformation, the second notion, came into vogue after the notion of
stylization—again in connection with the evolution of art itself—
when, for the purpose of emphasizing form, formal conventions
began to be forcibly violated and broken so that a feeling of formal dynamism arose from the tension between the methods of
organization which had been overcome and the new ones.

If we now look at the notions of stylization and deformation
retrospectively, we recognize that in both cases it was essentially
a matter of attempts to obscure the necessary presence of unintentionality as a factor of the impression which the work of art
makes. The notion of stylization tacitly but effectively pushes
unintentionality outside the work of art itself into its antecedent
state, into the reality of the represented object, or, better, into
the reality of the material that is used for the work. This "reality"
is overcome, or "digested," by the creative process. The notion of
deformation then attempts to reduce unintentionality to the disagreement between two intentionalities, the one being overcome

and the actual one. Today we can calmly say that these attempts have resulted in failure despite their usefulness for solving certain problems, for intentionality *necessarily* evokes in the perceiver the impression of an artefact, hence of a real opposition to the immediate, "natural" reality. But a living work which is not automatized for the perceiver necessarily evokes *besides* an impression of intentionality (or rather: integrally along with it) an immediate impression of reality, or rather: an impression *from* reality.

This intrinsic polarity of intentionality and unintentionality in artistic perception will be most apparent to us in cases where one or the other pole prevails (in perception). For this purpose we shall use the testimonies of two perceivers, one of whom apprehends the work of art predominantly as a sign, while the other reacts to it predominantly as if it were immediate reality. We borrow these testimonies from R. Müller-Freienfels' *Psychologie der Kunst.*[17]

Two theatergoers speak about their attitude toward the work of art. This case is especially advantageous for the documentation and comprehension of the unintentional elements in perception, for the theater is one of the arts which clearly addresses itself quite directly to the spectator's ability to experience an artistic creation as unmediated reality. The viewer who nevertheless understands the theater as predominantly intentional art says: "I sit in front of the stage as if it were a picture. Every moment I know that the events before me are not reality; at no time do I completely forget that I am sitting in the audience. Of course, once in a while I experience the feelings or passions of the depicted characters, but this is indeed only material for my own aesthetic feeling. And this feeling does not rest in the depicted passions but remains *above* the depicted events. Meanwhile my judgment stays

---

17. Vol. 1 (Leipzig-Berlin, 1912). These are the statements of two anonymous theater spectators. The author of the work uses them for a different purpose than we do. He is concerned with establishing three types of perceiver according to the manner in which the participation of the spectator's "I" asserts itself in perception. The types at which he arrives are: *Extatiker, Mitspieler,* and *Zuschauer.* The testimonies that we cite in the text are supporting material for the so-called *Zuschauer* and *Mitspieler* types. If we were to confront our conception of the polarity between intentionality and unintentionality with Müller-Freienfels' typology, we would say that the *Extatiker* type is only a variation of cases with a prevailing sense for the semioticity of the work of art and hence a close relative of the *Zuschauer* type. The *Extatiker,* as Müller-Freienfels renders him, is completely "inside" the perceived creation and sees reality, as far as possible, only through its medium; even when he stands before reality itself, he perceives it according to the model of a work of art (cf. the citation from George Sand in Müller-Freienfels).

alert and clear. My feeling always remains conscious and clear. I never get carried away, but if this does happen, it is unpleasant for me. Other people who let themselves be carried away by love or fear have completely unartistic feelings. Art begins only where the 'what' is forgotten and interest in the 'how' remains" (pp. 170–71). The other witness understands the theater in just the opposite way. This is a woman who expresses herself as follows: "I completely forget that I am in the theater. My own everyday existence totally escapes me. I experience within myself only the feelings of the characters on stage. Soon I am raging with Othello, soon I am shaking with Desdemona. Soon I feel like intervening on someone's behalf. In this I am drawn from one mood to another so quickly that I am incapable of rational judgment. In general this is strongest in modern plays, but I remember that at the end of an act in *King Lear* I noticed that out of fear I was holding quite fast to my girlfriend" (p. 169).

Müller-Freienfels considers such a mode of perception completely primitive. He is right to a certain extent, as long as he has in mind so clear-cut a case. It is certain, however, that there are elements of such an immediately experiencing attitude even in perception focused on artistic intentionality. The first of these two witnesses clearly attests to this fact himself when he admits that "of course, once in a while I experience the feelings or passions of the depicted characters" and that even sometimes, albeit against his conscious will, "I am carried away."

This *Mitreissung,* this immediate transport, which renders the work a direct part of the viewer's life (there are even well-known cases in which a spectator lets himself be stirred to a physical reaction—Don Quixote in the marionette theater), is outside of intentionality. For the viewer the work ceases to be an autonomous sign which is carried by a unifying intention. In fact, it ceases to be a sign at all and becomes an "unintentional" reality.

We shall now take a closer look at this unintentionality in art. In order not to leave anything unclear, we shall go back to the fundamentals and begin with at least a cursory glance at how unintentionality looks from the perspective of the creator of the work.

We have already demonstrated above that what is subconscious for an author in the process of creation and its results need not be unintentional in any way. This is valid for other kinds of "authorial" unintentionality as well.

In addition to subconscious unintentionality there is even unconscious unintentionality, which derives from an abnormal course of psychic events during creation. This involves an author's mental abnormality—temporary (intoxication of various kinds) or permanent—as a factor of the creative process. At first glance it might appear that such an unintentionality is completely unequivocal for the perceiver, but this would be a mistake. It is rather well known from the history of modern art that unusual artistic creations have sometimes been judged as manifestations of mental abnormality, whereby intentionality, often entirely conscious from the author's subjective standpoint, has been interpreted as unintentionality. Conversely, works that have originated from absolutely unconscious unintentionality can function as intentional works. With unconscious unintentionality it is appropriate to include artlessness, which manifests itself as ignorance of generally accepted technical principles or in an insufficient mastery of the material. Such artlessness is exemplified by the non-observance of the principles of perspective (the lack of a unified central point, etc.) in painting or by an imprecise observance of meter in poetry. The artlessness resulting from an insufficient mastery of the material is, for instance, a writer's imperfect knowledge of the language in which he writes. Of course, "artlessness" is a very relative notion. What seems artless from the standpoint of a later period might even appear as a technical advance to contemporaries. The unintentionality of artlessness is also very uncertain. It is extremely difficult to distinguish what of the "artlessness" in a work is genuine artlessness and what is intentional (the favorite polemics against new, unusual trends that intentionally violate accepted convention: according to the critics the violations arise from artlessness). Even genuine artlessness can appear as a component of intention (Henri Rousseau's primitivism, an insufficient knowledge of the language among writers of foreign origin or upbringing). Therefore unconscious unintentionality, just like subconscious unintentionality, does not permit generally valid and specific conclusions.

Another kind of unintentionality intervening in the process of creation is a coincidence of accidental, external circumstances. These can especially come into play wherever the work process takes place with the participation of material means, as in the theater, the visual arts, and so on. Yet, according to the circumstances, even unintentionality of this kind can function as a component of intention as well as its violation. (In such a case the perceiver learns of this unintentionality only from the artist's direct admission.)

Finally, we have the unintentionality which can be called impersonal, namely, accidental interventions that affect a work that is already finished. A striking example of this kind of unintentionality is the damage to a statue which renders it a torso. We have already shown above that this damage can become an integral component of the impression which the work makes thereafter and can thus change into intentionality. Hence not even here do we find a specific criterion for differentiating intentionality from unintentionality.

There are thus many ways in which elements independent of the artist's conscious intentions can penetrate the work. The variety could be enriched even more were we to introduce the category of the "semiconscious." There are frequent cases in the complexity of the mental processes wherein a poet consciously implements a certain general tendency, but the details of the execution originate subconsciously. In poetry, for example, we can hardly presuppose that a radical orientation toward euphony could have remained outside the poet's consciousness, but individual groupings of phonemes—and, of course, groupings of appropriate words and meanings—can nevertheless arise from subconscious associations.

Besides spontaneous unintentionality in the creator we must take into account intentional unintentionality—devices which are supposed to affect the viewer as a violation of semantic unity but which the originator has consciously introduced into the work for this purpose. Unintentionality thus becomes, in fact, a formal device. An example is the artificial torso in sculpture. All these kinds and nuances of authorial unintentionality that we have enumerated, and still others that could be revealed by a more detailed analysis, have great importance for the study of the genesis of a work as well as for the study of the relations between the work and its originator. They do not provide any firm support whatsoever for the relationship between intentionality and unintentionality in art itself. Everything that is really unintentional from the standpoint of the origin of a work can appear as intentional, and, conversely, what functions in a work as unintentional may have been introduced into it intentionally. Moreover, if we

lack direct testimonies, the estimation of what in a work is genetically intentional and what is unintentional is sometimes extremely
difficult, even impossible. Hence even here we have no other choice
but to take the perceiver's standpoint, or rather to look at the
work from the perceiver's perspective.

We have already demonstrated above that two moments are
necessarily present in every act of perception. One is determined
by an orientation toward what has semiotic validity in the work;
the other, on the contrary, tends toward an immediate experiencing of the work as reality. We have also said that intentionality,
viewed from the perceiver's standpoint, appears as an orientation
toward the semantic unification of the work because only a work
of unified meaning appears as a sign. Everything in the work that
resists this unification, that violates its semantic unity, is felt by
the perceiver to be unintentional. During the act of perception, as
we have already shown, the perceiver constantly fluctuates between a feeling of intentionality and one of unintentionality; in
other words, for him the work is simultaneously a sign (a self-
referential sign lacking an unequivocal relation to reality) and a
thing. By calling the work a *thing,* we wish to indicate that,
because of what is unintentional, semantically ununified in it, the
work appears to the viewer as similar to a *natural* fact, that is, a
fact which in its organization does not answer the question "For
what?" but leaves the decision about its functional use to man.
The immediacy and urgency of its effect upon man have their
origin precisely in this condition. As a rule, of course, man leaves
unnoticed natural facts unless their mysteriousness compels his
emotional involvement, or unless he intends to use them practically. The work of art, however, demands attention precisely
because of the fact that it is simultaneously a thing and a sign. The
internal unification provided by intentionality evokes a *particular*
relation to the object and creates a fixed axis around which
associated images and feelings can accumulate.

On the other hand, since a semantically unregulated thing (which
the work is because of its unintentionality) acquires the capacity
to attract to itself the most varied images and feelings, which need
not have anything in common with its own semantic charge, the
work thus becomes capable of being closely connected to the
entirely personal experiences, images, and feelings of any perceiver—capable of affecting not only his conscious mental life but

even of setting into motion forces which govern his subconscious. The perceiver's entire *personal* relation to reality, whether active or contemplative, will henceforth be changed to a greater or lesser degree by this influence. Hence the work of art has such a powerful effect upon man not because it gives him—as the common formula goes—an impression of the author's personality, his experiences, and so forth, but because it influences the *perceiver's personality, his experiences,* and so forth. Of course, all of this, as we have just ascertained, is due to the fact that an element of unintentionality is included and felt in the work. If and only if the work as a sign were intentional, would it necessarily be *res nullius,* common property, without the capacity to affect the perceiver in what is peculiar to himself alone.

Someone may quite rightly object that there are works of art, even entire periods, in which intentionality is exclusively emphasized and that works of these periods have nevertheless frequently outlived their authors by many years. Certainly art has rarely sought intentionality so strongly as during the period of French Classicism, the poetics of which actually demanded—in the person of Boileau—maximal intentionality:

> Il faut que chaque chose y soit mise en son lieu;
> Que le début, la fin, répondent au milieu;
> Que d'un art délicat les pièces assorties
> N'y forment qu'un seul tout de diverses parties;
> Que jamais du sujet le discours s'écartant,
> N'aille chercher trop loin quelque mot éclatant.[18]

And among the Classicist poets Racine is the one who maximally realized the canons of this movement for the semantic unification of creation. He perfectly observes the demands for unity of place, time, and action; he makes the climactic moment in the development of a passion the subject of his tragedies; he motivates peripeties precisely and fully. Yet, in the eyes of his contemporaries his tragedies contain elements that extend beyond and break through the circle of an intentionality carried to its conclusions; they cannot therefore be designated otherwise than as unintentional. Racine's contemporaries who experienced his works as perfectly

18. Boileau-Despréaux, *L'Art poétique: Poème en quatre chants* (Paris, 1882), 10, ll. 177–82.

alive were so strongly aware of this unintentionality that they even
condemned it as a defect: "Quinault satisfied them [his contempo-
raries], and Racine struck them as a brute. This Pyrrhus, whom we
find stylish and gallant, shocked them as a lout, and Racine was
obliged to write this explanation: 'Achilles's son had not read our
novels: these heroes are not, to be sure, Celadons.' Did they not
find Nero even too evil? He was not loving enough toward Junie.
Racine fought to obtain the right to do otherwise than Quinault
and to present pure passion in these crises in which natural
brutality reappears, shattering the thin varnish of our civilization.
His efforts seemed too crude and offended the gallant optimism of
the salons: Saint-Evremond, a spirited man, found *Britannicus* too
gloomy; indeed, the play is not 'consoling.'"[19]

Thus does a literary historian write about the effect of Racine's
plays on his contemporaries. Their criticisms which he quotes and
Racine's defense testify that there was something in Racine's plays
which for his contemporaries' sensibility went beyond the intention upon which the works were structured. That his contemporaries felt this unintentional element to be destructive is natural,
and as a rule, as we shall see in still other cases, it happens in new,
living art. What is important for us here is to establish that even
such an earnestly intentional artistic movement as French Classicism did not manage to stamp out unintentionality as a potent
component of artistic effect.

The painting of the Italian Renaissance provides another example. There are few cases in the history of art in which intentionality and even conscious intentionality so strongly governed every
effort of the artists. The painting of the *quattrocento* struggles
painstakingly for a faithful presentation of nature, especially for
the attainment of the illusion of space and volume; the battle for
perspective and the effort to comprehend the anatomical structure
of the human body make the art of that time a champion of
science.[20] And yet Squarcione reproaches his pupil, Andrea
Mantegna, one of the boldest proponents of these ideals and the
discoverer of perspective ceiling painting,[21] because "he had imitated marble antiques, from which it is impossible to learn painting
properly, since stones always possess a certain harshness and never

---

19. G. Lanson, *Histoire de la littérature française,* 7th ed. (Paris, 1902), pp. 537–38.
20. Nohl, *Die ästhetische Wirklichkeit,* p. 30.
21. Cf. R. Muther, *The History of Painting,* trans. G. Kriehn (New York, 1907), 1, 122.

have that softness peculiar to flesh and natural objects, which fall in folds and exhibit various movements."[22] Vasari, who gives us an account of this in the biography of Mantegna, adds that after these reprimands Mantegna "recognized that there was a great deal of truth in them, and so he set himself to drawing living persons"; but Vasari nevertheless remarks that Mantegna's paintings are "somewhat sharp, more closely resembling stone than living flesh."[23]

Even today, a historian of painting writes about Mantegna that "he disrobes nature, as it were, and lays bare her stony skeleton. He proceeds in the same manner with plants, being especially fond of grapes and leaves of vines. Just as wonderfully as they can be imitated to-day—the fruit in glass, and leaves in tin—so he painted them, equally true and equally hard. Greater changes were necessary in order to make trees harmonise with his style. They seemed to wear heavy iron armour, and their leaves, which no breeze could disturb, hang fast as steel from the branches. The branches stretch into the air, jagged and barbed as the points of javelins. Even the plants which grow in this stony soil have something metallic and crystalline about them. Some look like zinc sprinkled with white lead; others as if painted over with a coat of greenish bronze through which the white leaves of the steel still shimmer."[24] At one point a painting brings to mind a statue, at another materials which are neither present nor depicted in the picture: steel, bronze, and so on. It is quite evident that in this case the painting exceeds the limits of its semiotic range and becomes something other than a sign. Its individual parts suggest realities which do not belong to the semantic realm of the work, and they thus acquire the nature of a peculiar, illusory objectivity.

Hence intentionality is not prejudicial to the perceiver's sensing something in the work which goes beyond intention; he can perceive the sign simultaneously as a thing and experience immediate feelings deriving from the impact of a non-semiotic reality as well as "aesthetic" feelings (i.e., feelings linked to the sign).

Now that we have realized that unintentionality in art is not merely an occasional phenomenon, occurring perhaps just in some "decadent" artistic movements, but an intrinsic one, we must ask

22. Vasari, *The Lives*, 2, 104.
23. *Ibid.*
24. Muther, *The History of Painting*, pp. 119-20.

ourselves how unintentionality is expressed in the work of art if
we look at it from the perceiver's standpoint. We have already been
compelled to say something about this theme in the preceding
sections, but now we must attempt a more systematic analysis.

Let us return again for a moment to intentionality. We have said
that it involves a semantic unification. For greater clarity let us add
that this semantic unification is wholly dynamic. In discussing it,
we do not have in mind a static total meaning that has been called
in traditional aesthetics "the idea of the work." We do not deny,
of course, that some artistic movements or some periods can construct a work so that its semantic structure is experienced as the
exemplification of some general principle. Art last passed through
such a period in the immediate post-war years—Expressionism. The
theater in those days saw a series of plays in which according to
one critic the stage was no longer "the physical space of the action
but primarily the space of an idea. Staircases, platforms, steps . . .
did not have an intrinsic origin in spatial perception but rather
arose from a need for an ideal articulation, from a penchant for a
symbolic hierarchy of characters. . . . Movement and rhythm became not only the basic means of the ideational structure but also
the basis of a new form of stage direction and a new method of
acting." At that time novelistic visions were written which were,
in fact, thesis novels portraying characters of a strongly allegorical
nature. All of this, however, was just a trend of the time, and only
forcibly can we pose the question of "the idea" with respect to
forms of art other than that and ones similar to it.

But what does have supratemporal import as a principle of
semantic unification is the unifying semantic intention which is
essential for art and always operates in every work of art. We have
called it the semantic gesture.[25] This semantic intention is dynamic
for two reasons. On the one hand, it unifies the contradictions, or
"antinomies," on which the semantic structure of the work is
based; on the other, it takes place in time, for the perception of
every work, even a visual work, is an act whose temporal span has
even been sufficiently documented by experimental studies. An-

25. See my study "Genetika smyslu v Máchově poezii" [The genesis of meaning in
Mácha's poetry] in *Torso a tajemství Máchova díla* [The torso and the mystery of
Mácha's works], ed. J. Mukařovský (Prague, 1938) and the treatise "On Poetic Lan-
guage," *The Word and Verbal Art: Selected Essays by Jan Mukařovský*, trans. and ed.
John Burbank and Peter Steiner (New Haven, 1977), pp. 1–64.

other difference between "the idea of the work" and the semantic gesture is that the idea quite obviously pertains to content and has a definite semantic quality, whereas for the semantic gesture the difference between content and form is irrelevant. In the course of its duration the semantic gesture is gradually filled with a concrete content without our being able to say that this content enters from without. It simply originates in the range and the sphere of the semantic gesture which forms the content immediately upon its birth. The semantic gesture can therefore be designated as a concrete, though qualitatively not predetermined, semantic intention. If we examine the semantic gesture in a specific work, we cannot therefore simply express it, we cannot designate it by its semantic quality (as current criticism often does in speaking—with a slight trace of unwitting humor—of "the cry of birth and death," for example, as the real content of the work). We can only show how individual semantic elements of a work, from the most external "form" to whole thematic complexes (paragraphs, acts in a drama, etc.), group together under its influence. But not only the author and the structure that he has imposed upon the work are responsible for the semantic gesture which the perceiver experiences in the work. A considerable share falls to the perceiver, and it would not be difficult to demonstrate by a more detailed discussion of more recent analyses and critiques of older works that often the perceiver appreciably modifies the semantic gesture of a work contrary to the author's original intention. This accounts for the perceiver's activity as well as for the intentionality viewed from his standpoint.

The perceiver, then, introduces into the work of art a certain intentionality. This intentionality, to be sure, is evoked by the intentional structure of the work (otherwise there would not be an external impulse for the perceiver's assuming the same attitude toward the object that he is perceiving as toward an aesthetic sign); furthermore, the intentionality is considerably influenced by the quality of this structure, which, nevertheless, as we have just seen, has its own independence and intrinsic initiative. With the aid of this intentionality the perceiver binds the work into a semantic unity. All the components of the work invite his attention. The unifying semantic gesture with which he approaches the work strives to encompass them all in its unity. The fact that some components may stand outside of intention for the author is not relevant for the perceiver, as we have already shown. (In fact, the perceiver need not even be informed of how the author himself views the work.) Naturally, the unification does not occur smoothly. Contradictions can appear among individual components or, better, among the meanings of which they are the vehicles. Even these contradictions are resolved in intentionality precisely because—as we have remarked above—intentionality—the semantic gesture—is not a static, but a dynamic, unifying principle. Therefore we again confront the question: Does not perhaps everything in the work appear intentional to the perceiver?

If we are successful, the answer to this question will lead us to the very kernel of unintentionality in art. We have just said that intentionality is capable of overcoming the contradictions among individual components so that even semantic discord can appear intentional. Let us presume that a certain component of a poem, for example, the vocabulary, will strike the perceiver as "low" or even vulgar, whereas the theme will produce a different semantic impression, for example, a lyrically sentimental one. It is entirely possible that the reader will know how to discover the semantic resultant of these two contradictory components (an *intentionally* suppressed lyricism); but it is also possible that his concept of lyricism will be so rigorous that he will not come to this conclusion. What will happen in these two cases? In the first case, when the perceiver knows how to combine the contradictory components into a synthesis, their contradiction will appear as an *internal* contradiction (one of the internal contradictions) of the given poetic structure. In the second case, the contradiction will remain *outside* the structure; the vulgar vocabulary will appear to clash not only with the lyrically colored theme but with the entire structure of the poem: one component in opposition to all the others taken as a whole. The reader will then perceive this component which opposes all the others as an extra-aesthetic matter, and the feelings which will be evoked in him by its contradiction with the others will also be "extra-aesthetic," that is, connected with the work not as a sign but as a thing. It is possible, even probable, that these feelings will not be pleasing in any way; at the moment this is of no consequence to us. What is certain is that the component which *opposes* all the others will be experienced as an element of *unintentionality* in the given work.

The example that we have presented here is not fictional. We had in mind the case of Neruda's poetry, especially his youthful poetry, on which F. X. Šalda comments in his well-known study "An Avenue of Dream and Meditation to Jan Neruda's Grave": "In Neruda there are stanzas and lines which at the time of their origin stood on the very edge of daring and ridiculousness and at first tottered on paper weights in uncertainty between the two. Today the feeling and meaning of this escapes us; today we no longer easily perceive their boldness: they have triumphed, have been assimilated, have become common property, and thus we have lost their powerful immediacy, and we can only imagine it in reflection. . . . Well, at one time the following stanzas from two of Neruda's earlier poems were not far from ridiculousness. They embody the typical tragic nature of a young and proud soul imprisoned in an empty and lazy era and stifled by the fullness of its own unneeded and unused inner life, and many of us have scanned their bitter cadence in our time, if not with our lips, at least with our hearts:

Z uzlíčku boty čouhají	Shoes protrude from [my] little bundle
a mají podšvy silné,	and they have strong soles,
vždyť jsem si na ně kůži dal	for I had put on them the leather
z své pýchy neúchylné.	of my unbending pride.
. . . .	. . . .
V chladné trávě, v palných snech svých	In cool grass, in my scorching dreams
zas se povyválím,	I'll toss about again,
mysle, jak as rok zas žití	thinking how I might vainly idle away
marně prozahálím."[26]	another year of my life.

Šalda's words brilliantly grasp the oscillation between intentionality and unintentionality which appears in a work that is still fresh and unusual. Neruda's verse "at the time of [its] origin stood on the very edge of daring and ridiculousness and at first tottered on paper weights in uncertainty between the two." "Daring" is a feeling of the contradiction of the intentional that has been projected within the structure; "ridiculousness" has its source in unintentionality: the contradiction is felt outside the structure as involuntary. If the perceiver's overall attitude toward the work is governed by his effort to understand it as a perfect semantic unity

26. "Alej snu a meditace ku hrobu Jana Nerudy," *Boje o zítřek* (Prague, 1905), pp. 45–46.

resulting from a single intention, this still does not mean that the work will completely yield to this effort. It is always possible that some component of the work will develop such a radical resistance to the perceiver's effort that it will remain completely outside the semantic unity of the others.

As long as unintentionality is intensely felt by the perceiver, it always evokes an image of a deep rupture which splits the impression of the work into two. Tomíček's criticism of Mácha's *Máj* vividly attests to this: "Having adorned himself with colorful flowers, [the poet] threw himself into an extinct volcano, or perhaps better: his poem *is the slag which was ejected from an extinct volcano* and fell among flowers. We can and should have a liking for flowers but not for a cold, dead meteor which has been discharged from sundered entrails. *In this we find nothing beautiful, nothing vivifying, nothing poetic* in the strict sense of this word." A meteor ejected from a volcano, beautiful flowers, a poem, and the antithesis of the poetic, thus may a critic express his impression of what in Mácha's work has had a dangerously immediate effect upon him as a fact of life, as a question directly addressed to man, without the mediation of aesthetic semioticity.

Chmelenský comprehends this same contradiction somewhat differently in his criticism. If Tomíček projects unintentionality into the reflective aspect of Mácha's poem, Chmelenský sees it in the thematic aspect—the splitting of the impression made by the poem—, but its radical cleft remains the same: "*Máj*—at least to *me*—is too offensive, for I reluctantly turn away my eyes from a hanged man and an angel who has fallen so unpoetically. Even though Mr. Mácha has sown beautiful flowers here and there and has hung pretty pictures in gilded frames, the fragrance of his flowers and the splendor of his pictures do not hide the stench and haggardness of a hanging criminal and do not screen from our eyes an abominable wheel and a gallows, even if the poet himself has also appeared in the background."[27] Chmelenský, therefore, also senses in *Máj* a contradiction between artistically intentional elements and what functions extra-aesthetically, immediately. "The stench and haggardness of a hanging criminal," "an abominable wheel and a gallows" are not for him mere poetic requisites but a distinctly tormenting reality.

27. Both of these critiques are cited according to *Vybrané spisy K. Sabiny* [The selected writings of K. Sabina] (Prague, 1912), 2, 88 and 90-91.

It is, of course, the fate of every unintentionality that in time it will cross over into the artistic structure of the work, begin to be perceived as a component of it, and become intentionality. Neruda's case demonstrates this clearly enough, and Šalda explicitly shows that "today the feeling and sense of this escapes us . . . : [Neruda's stanzas and lines] have triumphed, have been assimilated, have become common property, and thus we have lost their powerful *immediacy,* and we can only imagine it in reflection." If however, a work of art outlives the time of its origin, if it again functions after some time as a living work, unintentionality will again revive in it, for it is precisely that which allows the work to be experienced as an immediately urgent fact. It is precisely Mácha's works that provide very telling evidence of this fact. Long after the time of its origin, almost a hundred years after its creator's birth, *Máj* once again excited such a polemical critique that one might have thought it was a new work. We have in mind Kamper's study "K. H. Mácha."

What excited Chmelenský in Mácha's *Máj*—the corpse, the scaffold, and so on—does not, of course, affect Kamper as unintentional, for the later, post-Máchovian era experienced all of this merely as Romantic requisites. Even the reflective aspect of the poem, its provocative metaphysical nihilism, is not unintentional for him, because eventually the refelction had passed into the poetic structure of *Máj,* and its antithesis to natural portrayal had already been experienced by the post-Máchovian generations merely as a poetically effective contrast. But a new unintentionality appeared: the incompleteness, the fragmentariness of the theme which contemporaries living in the actual atmosphere of Romanticism had not felt disturbing. Kamper is frankly shocked by this incompleteness: "Everything here [in *Máj*] is unclear, vague; everything hangs between heaven and earth. We do not know whether the girl sitting on the shore of the lake, to whom the friend of her lover Vilém brings the news that Vilém will be executed the next day because he has killed her seductor, his father, had been on intimate terms with Vilém's father or whether she had merely become the victim of a fateful mistake, chance, or guile. And it startles us that Jarmila does not seem to have any suspicion that her lover has killed her seductor, although 'today the twentieth day has passed' since she last met with him. She hears of the catastrophe only from the mouth of a stranger who, moreover, curses her. Vilém's character is equally enigmatic for us. . . ."[28]

The enumeration of the discrepancies violating the semantic unity of the theme in *Máj* continues even further in Kamper; for us, however, the passage cited suffices to make clear that the unintentionality in *Máj* was again perceived seventy years after its origin; but it was experienced differently and was different from the unintentionality Mácha's contemporaries felt. Once again it was perceived as a disturbing element; of course, this means only that it was felt intensely. This case is interesting because we can follow its further development, that is, how the unintentionality which Mácha's poetry newly acquires in this way begins again to turn into intentionality—still experienced, of course, as a potent element, but already as a component of the poetic structure itself.

About thirty years after Kamper we find in a contemporary poet the following understanding of thematic structure in Mácha (the sentences which we shall quote refer in this case to "Křivoklad"): "There is no doubt that this scene [from "Křivoklad"]— from the moment the king is awakened in the afternoon by hoof beats and discovers Milada's existence to the moment she utters the words: 'Good night—midnight!' and motions toward the prison tower—has a poetic effect. Likewise we know by what means this effect is achieved: by the lack of a causally justified connection between separate elements, by their acute concentration, by their surprising dramatization and replacement. . . . In truth, this entire scene produces a powerful dreamlike impression; it is characterized by dreamlike distortion. Only after reading the whole 'Křivoklad,' will we arrive involuntarily at an explanation of this scene. The executioner was the lover of the beautiful girl Milada, who appeared to us in the scene described as a phantom, and his father was the bastard son of the last Přemyslid so that the words 'O king! good night' belonged, as we surmise when we have finished reading 'Křivoklad,' to the Přemyslid executioner and not to King Václav. In no way does this explanation change the dreamlike appearance of the scene with which we have been concerned, just as nothing is changed in the structure of the dream when we have succeeded in additionally determining from what elements of reality it is constructed."[29] What interests us about this statement

28. J. Kamper, "K. H. Mácha" in J. Hanuš et al, *Literatura česká devatenáctého století* [Czech literature of the nineteenth century] (Prague, 1905), 3, pt. 1, 24 ff.

29. V. Nezval's contribution to "Básnický dnešek a K. H. Mácha" [Contemporary poetry and K. H. Mácha], *Slovo a slovesnost* 2 (1936): 75.

is that the same "lack of a causally justified connection between separate elements" which had exasperated Kamper is evaluated positively here; moreover, even the unintentionality of this procedure is emphasized, but this time interpreted as the result of the author's subconscious psychic processes.

The examples which we have cited instruct us that unintentionality, viewed from the perceiver's standpoint, appears as a feeling of disjunction in the impression which the work creates. The objective basis for this feeling lies in the impossibility of semantically unifying a certain component with the entire structure of the work. This was especially evident in the example from Neruda's poetry as Šalda interprets it (from a perceiver's standpoint). Even the interpretations of Mácha by his contemporary critics are essentially similar phenomena: certain thematic elements appeared to his contemporaries as incompatible with other thematic elements. In the case of the later understanding of Mácha's work (Kamper, etc.) there appears to be a semantic incompatibility between the expressed and unexpressed meaning.[30] Šalda's interpretation of Neruda demonstrated very clearly how unintentionality tends to turn into intentionality—how a component excluded from the structure tends to become part of it. It has been shown in the two successive conceptions of unintentionality in Mácha's work (in fact, in its revival in another form) that viewed from the perceiver's standpoint unintentionality is by no means rooted in the work unequivocally and invariably. Different components can appear as unintentional in the course of time. What we have al-

---

30. The duality of the expressed and unexpressed meaning is a general property of the semantic structure not only of a literary work but of every utterance. The share of unexpressed meaning in the semantic structure of an utterance can, of course, be different. A scientific statement, for example, generally avoids it as much as possible, whereas the share of unexpressed meaning in an everyday conversation is considerable. Sometimes unexpressed meaning is intentionally exploited even outside of literature, for example, in diplomatic agreements and the like.

Thus the relationship between unexpressed and expressed meaning is often very different. Sometimes the unexpressed meaning almost completely fits into the context of the expressed meaning; sometimes it is removed from this context, or better it creates its own special context, independently paralleling the context of expressed meaning and contiguous with it only at some points which may only alert the attentive listener to the presence of an unexpressed context without, however, informing him of its course. Literature can very profitably exploit the relation between the expressed and unexpressed meaning for the purpose of its intentionality (Symbolism did so very consistently), but the unexpressed meaning can also—as we have seen in the case of Mácha's work—affect the perceiver as unintentional in contrast to the intentional expressed meaning.

ready repeatedly emphasized follows from this. There is by no means a direct and constant relation between unintentionality viewed from the author's standpoint (whether it concerns a genuine unintentionality or an unintentionality deliberately inserted into the work by the author for the perceiver) [and unintentionality seen from the perceiver's standpoint].[31] Although the perceiver will always derive his feeling of intentionality and unintentionality *from the organization of the work,* this organization admits various interpretations in this respect.

The two unintentionalities which different generations successively perceived in Mácha's work have shown us that although the perceiver becomes aware of unintentionality in the work as something conditioned, or objectively provided in the structure of the work, unintentionality is not unequivocally predetermined by this structure. Consequently, by no means should we presuppose that what appears unintentional in the work was, in fact, unintentional for the author.

All the examples of unintentionality cited so far have concerned works which have outlived the time of their origin, hence permanent values. At the same time, however, we have seen that elements perceived in them as unintentional have often been evaluated negatively. Thus we must ask whether unintentionality is detrimental or beneficial to the effect of a work and what in general is its relation to artistic value. As long as we take the position that the intrinsic purpose of art is to arouse aesthetic pleasure, it is beyond dispute that unintentionality will appear to us as a negative factor impairing aesthetic pleasure, for pleasure derives from the impression of the overall unity of the work, a unity as little disturbed as possible. Contradictions contained in the very structure of the work necessarily introduce an element of displeasure into this structure—this will be more likely, of course, if the contradictions violate the very fundamental unity of the structure (and the semantic structure) by opposing one component to all the others. This fact also explains the protest of perceivers which accompanies instances of undisguised (and still fresh) unintentionality in art. It has already been frequently pointed out, however, that aesthetic displeasure is not an extra-aesthetic fact—only

31. *Editors' note.* We have deemed it necessary to complete what otherwise appears to be an incomplete statement by means of an interpolation (the words set in brackets).

aesthetic indifference is—and moreover that aesthetic displeasure is an important dialectic antithesis of aesthetic pleasure and in essence an omnipresent component of aesthetic effect. Let us add further that in the case of unintentionality displeasure is indeed only a concomitant phenomenon of the fact that in the impression made by the work "real" feelings contend with feelings associated with the work of art as a sign (so-called *aesthetic feelings*). "Real" feelings are those that enable man to affect only immediate reality, that is, the reality toward which man is accustomed to act directly and by which he is also directly influenced.

Hence we find ourselves at the very crux of the problem concerning the essence or rather the effectiveness of unintentionality as a factor in the perception of the work of art. The immediacy with which components outside the unity of the work affect the perceiver renders the work of art, which is an autonomous sign, an immediate reality, a thing, as well. As an autonomous sign the work transcends reality: the work relates to reality only figuratively, only as a whole. For the perceiver every work of art is a metaphoric representation of reality, both as a whole and as any of the realities experienced by him. As for the facts and incidents represented by the work of art, the perceiver is always aware that ". . . this is only a passing feeling, that the world is 'in fact' as he knows it independently of such an experience, that this [what he experiences in the work of art, J. M.], no matter how beautiful it may be, nevertheless is and remains only a 'beautiful dream.'"[32]

Aesthetic theories of art as an illusion (K. Lange) or as a lie (Paulhan) have their origin in this fundamental "unreality" of the work of art. It is not without significance that these theories emphasize precisely the semioticity and unity of the work of art. Paulhan, for example, says: "To adopt an artistic attitude toward anything at all . . . is to isolate it from the real world and make it part of a sort of imaginary and fictive world, tacitly or explicitly disregarding its real qualities and the ends for which it has been produced and is commonly used; this means to appreciate it for its beauty, not for its utility or its truth. . . . It is possible to adopt an artistic attitude toward a locomotive, for example. In this case, we do not use its speed and power to go on a business trip or to admire the countryside, but we account for the arrangement of its

32. F. Weinhandl, *Über das aufschliessende Symbol* (Berlin, 1929), p. 17.

mechanism, its boilers, its levers and its wheels, its fire-box and its coal; we notice the combination and the interdependence of its parts, we understand the special activity of each of them, and we grasp their convergence and system; we perceive the ultimate unity, the long and heavy row of cars which the locomotive is going to pull, and at the same time we comprehend its social function. . . . It symbolizes an entire human civilization. . . . If we consider this entire system organized in this way from its own standpoint, without thinking about how we could use it for our own needs or how we could learn some true information from it, if we simply admire its internal harmony and its special beauty, we think and feel as artists."[33]

In this connection we must also mention theories which have constructed their concepts of the aesthetic and art on feelings. Although feeling is a very evident aspect of the aesthetic attitude, especially of the perceiver's attitude, on the other hand, it is man's most direct and most immediate reaction to reality. Therefore, problems arose in constructing theories of the aesthetic on feelings; these problems were caused by the need to reconcile in some way aesthetic "disinterest" (deriving precisely from the semiotic nature of the work of art) with the *involvement* that is typical of feeling. Thus it turned out that "aesthetic" (in the proper sense of the word) feelings were declared as feelings associated with images, in contrast to "serious" feelings (*Ernstgefühle*) tied to reality: "The subject's aesthetic state of being is essentially a feeling (of pleasure or displeasure) combined with concrete representation [*anschauliches Vorstellen*] and, moreover, in such a manner that the representing [*Vorstellen*] constitutes the psychic precondition of the feeling. Aesthetic feelings are representational feelings [*Vorstellungsgefühle*]," states Witasek,[34] one of the leading representatives of a psychological aesthetics based on feelings. Other theoreticians even speak about "illusory feelings" or "illusions of feelings," that is, mere "images of feelings" or "notional" feelings (*Begriffsgefühle*).[35] Still others try to solve the difficulty with the notion of "technical" feelings (that is, those relating to the artistic structure of the work), which they declare to be the very essence of the aesthetic. For us it is interesting to see how even those

33. F. Paulhan, *Le Mensonge de l'art* (Paris, 1907), pp. 73–75.
34. S. Witasek, *Grundzüge der allgemeinen Ästhetik* (Leipzig, 1904), p. 181.
35. K. Lange, *Das Wesen der Kunst* (Berlin, 1901), 1, 97 and 103 f.

theories constructing a concept of the aesthetic on emotions emphasize the gulf between the work of art and reality.

We have not cited the views of aesthetic illusionism and emotionalism in order to accept them or to criticize their legitimacy. We have simply intended them to be evidence—considering all of their one-sidedness obvious today—of the fact that the work of art, to the extent that we perceive it as an autonomous aesthetic sign, appears severed from *direct* contact with reality, and not only with the external reality but also—and above all—with the reality of the perceiver's mental life. Hence the "imaginary and fictive world" in Paulhan and the *Scheingefühle* in Witasek.

This does not, however, exhaust the entire range of art—the entire capacity and urgency of its activity. The aestheticians of illusionism perceive this themselves: "Even the most idealistic and abstract art is often troubled by real and human elements. A symphony arouses feelings of sadness or mirth, love or despair. This is not its highest purpose, but our nature expresses itself in this way."[36] And the same author states elsewhere: "We must not expect art ever to give us an absolutely harmonious life, and sometimes even its life will be essentially less harmonious than real life; however, at certain moments it will correspond better to repressed needs which at the given moment are rather acute."[37] The oscillation of the work of art between semioticity and "reality," between its mediated and immediate effect, is very keenly grasped here. Nevertheless, we need a more detailed analysis of this "reality." Above all, it is clear that we are not dealing with a more precise or less precise, more concrete or less concrete, "ideal" or "realistic" *representation* of reality but, as we have already indicated, with the relation of the work to the perceiver's mental life. It is also now clear that the basis of the semiotic effect of the work of art is its semantic unification; the basis of its "reality," its immediacy, is what opposes unification in the work, in other words, what is perceived as unintentional. Only unintentionality is capable of making the work as mysterious for the perceiver as is a mysterious object, the purpose of which we do not know; only unintentionality is able to exasperate the perceiver's activity by its resistance to semantic unification; only unintentionality, which paves the way to the most varied associations in its unregulated

36. Paulhan, *Le Mensonge de l'art*, p. 99.
37. *Ibid.*, p. 110.

nature, can set into motion the perceiver's entire existential experience, all the conscious and subconscious tendencies of his personality, upon his contact with the work. Because of all of this, unintentionality incorporates the work of art into the sphere of the perceiver's existential interests and endows the work of art with an urgency unattainable by a pure sign, behind whose every feature the perceiver senses the intention of someone other than himself. If art again and again appears to man as new and unusual, the primary cause lies with the unintentionality perceived in the work. But intentionality is also renewed with every new artistic generation, with every artistic personality, and even, to a certain extent, with every new work.

From the studies of contemporary theory of art, however, we know with enough certainty that despite this continual renewal the regeneration of intentionality in art is never absolutely unexpected and unpredetermined. An artistic structure develops in a continuous series, and each of its new stages is only a reaction to a preceding state, its *partial* transformation. Unintentionality does not develop in a discernible succession: it *originates* again and again in the discord of a structure with the overall organization of the artefact which at a given moment is the vehicle of this structure. If new artistic trends of any kind—for example, extremely "non-realistic" ones—claim in their struggle against previous trends that they are renewing a sense of reality in art of which it has been deprived by earlier movements, they are, in fact, claiming that they are reviving an unintentionality which is necessary if the work of art is to be perceived as a matter of vital import.

It might, of course, seem odd that unintentionality—which, we claim, makes it possible for the work to establish contact with reality, to become, in fact, a part of reality—is often evaluated negatively, as is apparent from our examples. Whatever strikes the perceiver as violating the semantic unity of the work is usually condemned. How is it therefore possible to consider unintentionality as the essential component of the impression that a work of art makes upon the perceiver? Above all, we must not forget that unintentionality appears to be a disturbing factor only from the standpoint of a certain conception of art which evolved during the Renaissance and reached its peak in the nineteenth century, namely, a conception whereby semantic unification is the basic criterion for evaluating the work of art. Medieval art took a completely different view of this matter. To put it better, the perceiver's attitude toward the work of art was completely different. As evidence let us cite a brief but characteristic editorial note which accompanies "The Life of St. Simeon" (a story from *The Lives of the Holy Fathers*): "The more detailed portrayal of Simeon's stay at the monastery and the hardships that he had to suffer there, which in the Latin text motivate his flight from the monastery and the abbot's anxiety about him, is lacking in the Czech translation [of this story]; it is interesting that this lack of motivation did not matter to any of the copyists—nor apparently to any of the readers—of the five Old Czech manuscripts."[38] Here we have the most fundamental violation of semantic unity—the destruction of thematic unity. (Above we explained a violation of this kind as a disproportion in the relation between the expressed and unexpressed meanings.) Yet the successive copyists, and evidently the readers too, accepted this violation as a matter of course.

The violation of semantic unity is also a common phenomenon in folk poetry. In the folk song, for example, we often find side by side stanzas, one of which praises a thing or a person and the other of which derides the same thing or person. At times the comic and the serious come together so abruptly that the overall attitude of the song can actually remain unclear. Evidently these sudden semantic shifts do not bother the perceiver of the song. On the contrary, their unexpectedness (intensified by the possibility of continual improvisational variations of the song) ties the song to a real situation during its performance. If the singer addresses the song to a specific person who is present (e.g., solo songs at dances, songs as parts of ceremonies), the unexpected change in evaluation can strike this person very effectively—for good or bad. Finally, let us mention the colorful blends of incongruous stylistic elements in folk art, the disproportion of individual parts in folk representational painting and sculpture, and also the disproportionate size and accentuation of separate parts of the figure, and even the face, in folk pictures and sculptures.[39]

38. J. Vilikovský, "Svatý Simeon," *Život svatých otců* in *Próza z doby Karla IV* [Prose of Charles IV's era] (Prague, 1938), p. 256.

39. K. Šourek, *Lidové umění v Čechách a na Moravě* [Folk art in Bohemia and Moravia] (Prague, 1942), p. 118.

All of this strikes the perceiver as the semantic disunity of the work, as unintentionality, and it has been condemned as artlessness by those who have viewed folk art from the standpoint of high art. This unintentionality, however, constitutes an integral part of the impression for an adequate perception of folk art. Hence unintentionality is evidently a negative element only for that perception of art to which we are accustomed; even so, as we shall see immediately, it is only *seemingly* negative.

In the above examples, whether we were concerned with Racine or Mácha, we saw that what contemporaries criticized as a "mistake" later turned into an obvious component of the effect of the work (as soon as the component which had opposed the others and resisted unification got *into* the structure of the work for the perceiver). And it certainly is not too risky to claim that the very resistance that the intensely felt unintentionality has aroused in the perceiver can attest to the fact that the work has made a vivid impression upon him and has been experienced as something more immediate than just a mere sign. In order for us to admit this, we need only realize that aesthetic pleasure is by no means the unique and unconditional feature of the aesthetic and that only the dialectic union of pleasure and displeasure intensifies the fullness of the artistic experience.

After everything we have said about unintentionality one might presume that we consider it (viewed, of course, from the perceiver's, not the originator's, standpoint) as something more important and more essential for art than intentionality; that in regarding it as the reason why the work of art affects the perceiver with immediate urgency, we even wish to proclaim the unintentional element in the impression made by the work of art as something more desirable than the moment of semantic unification and hence intentionality. That would, of course, be a mistake which we may have occasioned quite involuntarily by placing too much emphasis on unintentionality in a polemic against the current conception. We must emphatically refer once more to the basic assertion from which we proceeded: the work of art in its very essence is a sign, an autonomous sign which directs attention to its internal organization. This organization is, of course, *intentional* both from the originator's and the perceiver's standpoint, and intentionality is therefore the fundamental—let us say, the unmarked—factor of the impression that a work of art makes.

Unintentionality is perceived only against its background; a feeling of unintentionality can arise in the perceiver only if obstacles stand in the way of his effort to unify the work semantically.

We have said that the work of art resembles a natural reality, untouched by man, on account of its unintentional aspect. We must, however, add that in a true natural reality—for example, a fragment of stone, a rock formation, the striking form of a branch or the root of a tree—we can perceive unintentionality as an active force affecting our feelings and image associations only if we approach such a reality with an effort to conceive it as a sign of unified meaning (that is, semantically unified). Excellent proof of this fact is provided by mandrake root formations which have been at least partially finished off by an artificial intervention. This has helped to realize the tendency toward semantic unification. Mandrakes are therefore special artefacts which, though retaining the accidental character of a natural reality and hence the predominant semantic disunity of their appearance, have nevertheless compelled perceivers to conceive them as representations of human figures, hence as signs.

Unintentionality is therefore a concomitant phenomenon of intentionality; we could even say that it is, in fact, a certain kind of intentionality. The perceiver's impression of unintentionality occurs wherever and whenever he fails in his striving for a semantically unified understanding of a work, for a summing up of the entire artistic artefact with a single uniform meaning. Although they are in constant dialectic tension, intentionality and unintentionality are essentially one. The mechanical—no longer dialectic—antithesis of these *two* is semantic indifference about which we may speak when a certain part or component of a work is indifferent for the perceiver, when it is outside his effort at a semantic unification.[40]

This more detailed elucidation of the close correlation between

40. For example, the frame of a picture, which separates a work from the surrounding surface of the wall, can be indifferent for the perceiver in this way. There are, of course, other cases where the frame belongs to the semantic structure of the work. Such a duality is very well illustrated by panel paintings (frequent in Dutch art) which have a double frame: one painted constituting a part of the picture, the other molded framing the pictorial panel. But even a "genuine" frame—as a rule indifferent with regard to the semantic structure of the picture—can become a part of it. Compare cases—not at all rare—in which Art Nouveau painting continues onto the frame in some manner (whether as a painting or as a woodcut), so that it exceeds the actual pictorial plane.

intentionality and unintentionality in art has perhaps removed a possible misunderstanding of the relative importance of these two factors in the impression made by a work of art. We must still, however, add that precisely because of its dialectic nature the relationship between the participation of intentionality and that of unintentionality in the impression made by the work of art is exceedingly variable during the concrete development of art and is subject to frequent oscillation. Sometimes greater emphasis is placed on intentionality; sometimes unintentionality is more strongly emphasized. But this statement is, of course, schematic. Their interrelations can be very diverse, for it is not the quantitative predominance of one or the other that matters but the qualitative nuances which intentionality and unintentionality acquire in this process. Of course, the wealth of these nuances is practically inexhaustible. In a more detailed study they could probably be grouped into more general types. For example, sometimes intentionality can stress a maximally smooth semantic unification which excludes or veils as many contradictions as possible (as in the period of Classicism); sometimes it can manifest itself as a force overcoming clear and pronounced contradictions (art after World War I). Unintentionality can be based sometimes on unexpected semantic associations, sometimes on abrupt reversals in evaluation, and so on. Naturally, the interrelation of intentionality and unintentionality changes whenever the appearance of one or both of them changes.

Finally, we must mention yet another possible misunderstanding, pertaining this time to the relationship between the problem of unintentionality in the work of art and the problem of the extra-aesthetic functions of art. Since in the course of our study we have frequently characterized intentionality as a phenomenon closely related to the aesthetic effect of a work and unintentionality as the connection of the work of art to reality, confusion of the problem of unintentionality with that of extra-aesthetic functions or the identification of these two problems may have resulted. This was certainly not our intention, however. The extra-aesthetic functions of art—especially the practical function in all its nuances—are, of course, directed at reality which is outside the work; they cause the work to affect reality; however, they still do not render the work itself an immediate reality but rather preserve its semiotic character. Extra-aesthetic functions are fulfilled by the work as a sign. Because of a pronounced and unambiguous extra-aesthetic function, the work of art becomes even more unequivocal than it is as a purely aesthetic sign. Extra-aesthetic functions, of course, oppose the aesthetic function but not the semantic unification of the work. Proof of this lies in the fact that an obvious adaptation of some extra-aesthetic function can become an integral component of both the aesthetic and the semantic structure of the work.

The opposition of intentionality and unintentionality is therefore something quite different from the opposition of the extra-aesthetic functions and the aesthetic function. An extra-aesthetic function can also, of course, become a component of the unintentionality perceived in the work of art, but only if it appears to the perceiver as something ununifiable with the remaining semantic structure of the work. In Czech literature, for example, František Pravda's stories incline toward such an unintentionality of an extra-aesthetic function (viewed from the perceiver's standpoint, of course). The reader feels their moralizing tendency as something alien in comparison to the objectifying nature of the narration and characterization: "Throughout his literary career František Pravda appears, on the one hand, as a Catholic author of calendar stories, an exhorter in the novel and a practical theologian in belles lettres, a forceful moralist, and a concerned educator of the folk; on the other hand, he is distinguished by a profound predilection for character portrayal of typical folk figures and a keen sense for the distinctive character of country folk whom he depicts with touching primitiveness and epic breadth."[41] Extra-aesthetic functions, then, become a component of unintentionality only sometimes, and there is no basic affinity between them and unintentionality in the work of art.

By elucidating the possible misunderstandings that might have been caused by some of our formulations, we have reached the end of our study which simplifies an extremely complex state of affairs in the interest of a lucid exposition. We do not intend, however, to conclude our study with the customary summary of the basic theses, for such a summary in its radical simplification would lead to further simplifications. We are, of course, aware that

---

41. A. Novák in J. Hanuš et al, *Literatura česká devatenáctého století* (Prague, 1907), 3, pt. 2, 124.

the basic assertions of this study lead to some conclusions which are rather different from generally accepted views; we would therefore like to formulate explicitly the major conclusions among these in place of a summary.

1. If the work of art is understood only as a sign, it is deprived of its direct incorporation into reality. It is not only a sign but also a thing immediately affecting man's mental life, causing direct and spontaneous involvement and penetrating through its action to the deepest levels of the perceiver's personality. It is precisely as a *thing* that the work is capable of affecting what is universally human in man, whereas in its semiotic aspect the work always appeals eventually to what is socially and temporally determined in him. Intentionality allows the work to be perceived as a sign, unintentionality as a thing; hence the opposition of intentionality and unintentionality is the basic antinomy of art. Mere intentionality does not suffice for an understanding of the work of art in its entirety, nor does it suffice for an understanding of development, for it is precisely in the process of development that the boundary between intentionality and unintentionality constantly shifts. Insofar as the notion of deformation reduces unintentionality to intentionality, it veils the true state of affairs.

2. Intentionality and unintentionality are semantic, not psychological, phenomena: the semantic unification of a work and the negation of this unification. A genuine structural analysis of a work of art is therefore semantic; a semantic analysis then pertains to all the components of a work, those pertaining both to its "content" and its "form." We must, however, take into account not only the force which unites the individual components of a work into an overall meaning but also the opposite force which tends to violate the unity of the overall meaning. A semantic analysis is not therefore synonymous with a formal analysis, even though it involves the internal structure of the work and not what is outside the work: the psychic preconditions from which the work arose (the author's disposition, the structure of his personality and his experience). However, in all of its objectivity—its non-psychologism—semantic analysis is capable of establishing a much more immediate connection with psychological study than an analysis of "content" or "form."

9

Dialectic Contradictions in Modern Art

If we wish to attempt an outline of the dialectics of modern art, we should first define what we consider modern art. The notion of "modernism" is very indefinite. Its instability results from its being conceived as a specific value on the one hand, and as a mere temporal definition on the other. In using the term, we are not at all concerned with an evaluation but simply with a temporal delimitation. Nevertheless, we must still decide this for ourselves, because even if we have definite reasons for our delimitation, someone else could make a different decision and have his own reasons for it.

For our purposes modern art begins with the boundary between the periods of Realism-Naturalism and Symbolism in literature and between Impressionism and post-Impressionism in painting.[1] The common denominator of this period beginning with a dual boundary is the suppression or—if we wish—the dissolution of the individual. In order to clarify what we mean, we shall go back further into the past, into the first half of the last century, to Romanticism. There is no doubt that Romanticism is closer, at least in its particular phenomena, to contemporary art than the period immediately following it, namely the period of Realism, Naturalism, and Impressionism. We could cite much evidence for this. Contemporary Czech poetry, for example, returns again and again to Mácha's poetry not out of platonic admiration but for help in solving the structural problems which confront it. The answer to the question of where the similarity between Romanticism and contemporary art lies is not difficult to find. In both periods the work is intensely experienced as a mere sign; and there is no absolute and necessary agreement between this sign and reality. In the intervening period, on the other hand, there were progressively increasing tendencies to minimize the factors stand-

"Dialektické rozpory v moderním umění," *Listy pro umění a kritiku* 3 (1935).

1. Impressionism is, of course, both an extreme case of the Realist-Naturalist tendency and the first stage in the abandonment of the imitation of nature.

ing between the work of art and reality—above all, subjective feeling and any evaluation, even an objectified one. The literary
Naturalist's aspiration is to present a scientific document; the
Impressionist's is to capture adequately bare sensory perceptions
prior to any interpretation as immediate equivalents of physiological reactions to an external impulse. We are speaking, of course,
only about a tendency, not about the possibilities and degrees of
its realization.

The common sign of Romantic and contemporary art is thus the
tendency to distance empirical reality from its reflection in art.
This distance is achieved by the deformation of empirical reality.
Nevertheless, there is a substantial *difference* between these
periods resulting from the individual's varying participation in this
deformation. In Romanticism the individual reshapes this reality
on his own responsibility. It is the revolt of an individual against
a reality already modified by social convention at the moment of
perception. It is not important whether the individual feels strong
enough to bear this responsibility (titanism) or yields to it (spleen,
Wertherism). The strong assertion of emotionality—for example,
the lyricization of epics in the so-called Byronic poetic tale—is connected with the individual's responsibility.

In the "modern" period the situation differs, as literature
demonstrates especially well. The individual in his function as the
sustaining point of epistemological certainty is suppressed. The
only role which Zola attributed to him in his famous statement
"La nature vue à travers un tempérament" was the function of the
rather secondary coloring of presented reality.

At the moment that the tendency toward deformation again
appears in a natural developmental opposition to this period of
documentary fidelity, there is no longer an individual who will
take upon himself responsibility for the violation of social convention with which empirical reality is permeated at the very
moment of sensory perception. Symbolism, the poetic movement
standing on the threshold of this period, proves this clearly in its
desire for an extreme objectification of artistic expression. It
yearns for an "absolute" work which is maximally separated from
empirical reality. Although this empirical reality would be the
most likely basis upon which people of the same period and social
sphere would agree, the work would nevertheless be accepted—in
fact, precisely because of this—as an unchangeable value regardless

of time, place, or social milieu. In striving for objectification, Symbolism goes so far that the sheer weight of this objectification smothers the poet's creative potential. The Symbolist experiment resulting in Mallarmé's desperate slogan "Never does a single throw of the dice destroy chance" (in other words, it will never be possible to create an absolute work independent of man) graphically demonstrates the *horror individui* to which this movement succumbed as well as the impasse it leads to.

Never again did modern art reach a formulation so heavily weighted against the individual; however, the suppression of the individual as the bearer of responsibility for the deformation is common to all phases of artistic development up to the present. For example, Futurism proclaims expressly in the words of its initiator, Marinetti, that "in literature I must be abolished." Though Dadaism asks for the ultimate destruction of empirical reality, at the same time it annihilates any personal responsibility on the part of the individual so completely that it leaves decision-making to absolute chance.[2] Someone could object by pointing to Expressionism, art based on feeling, indeed on gradations of feeling. We would answer, however, that Expressionism provides quite contrary evidence in its nature as well as in its collapse. "Boundless feeling" (*das masslose Gefühl*[3]), from which angle this artistic movement views reality, aims at an almost ontological objectification; the ambition of Expressionism is to construct art as metaphysics. And precisely the impossibility of such an objectification is the cause of its collapse. Thus Hausenstein could write in his polemic against Expressionism: "We find ourselves tempted to assume that Expressionism is not only far from providing an objectification of the world, but it is also the most extreme excess of subjectivity which has ever existed."[4] Hence even Expressionism tends toward objectification and collapses at the impossibility of it.

Given this state of affairs, we cannot, of course, speak about the individual's epistemological responsibility, which is totally

---

2. Dadaist depersonalization is, however, different from that of the Symbolists. The Symbolists exclude chance in the name of order, whereas the Dadaists exclude order in the name of chance.

3. K. Edschmid's term; cf. "Über den dichterischen Expressionismus," *Über den Expressionismus in die Literatur und die neue Dichtung* (Berlin, 1921), pp. 39–78.

4. W. Hausenstein, *Über Expressionismus in der Malerei* (Berlin, 1919).

destroyed: "The old conception of personality is threatened. What kind of personality can there be, after all, when everything is in flow, in flux, when discontinuity and disaggregation rule so that man loses himself, dissolves himself into a series of discrete reactions and explosions which are not connected by any thread of reasonable purpose."[5] Contemporary art is tossed about by two antipodal tendencies. One leads to the deformation of empirical reality, to its corrosion; the other makes it impossible to base this deformation on the epistemological responsibility of the individual as a measure of all things. However, this also closes the path to material reality—the realm where all the impulses activating man's senses originate and which thus exists independently of man, even though man is a part of it. Although Romanticism, like modern art, revolted against empirical reality, unlike modern art, it had an access to reality independent of man and his relation to the world. This was created by the individual whose free will, unbounded by social convention, appeared as a direct testimony of the existence of the reality of which man is a part. Realism, on the other hand, gave up the individual as a guarantee of the existence of this reality and found a new guarantee in its belief in the precise parallelism between empirical and material reality. As a result of the Realist period modern art has no doubt remained distrustful of the first, Romantic, guarantee; in developmental antithesis it has also rejected the second guarantee accepted by Realism.

We must not, of course, interchange or identify different things. If in modern art the individual is relieved of epistemological responsibility, the artist's individuality is in no way removed as a factor in the structure of the work. In this respect, his individuality is completely liberated and strengthened by this divestment of epistemological responsibility so that it asserts itself today more than ever before and is at the same time demanded by critics and the public as a particular shading or nuance of a work. Even single works by the same author or particular periods of his creation become individualized in relation to one another. Structural individuality—uniqueness—even becomes one of the significant criteria of the value of the work.[6]

5. F. X. Šalda, "O dnešním položení tvorby básnické" [On the current state of poetic creation], *Šaldův zápisník* (Prague, 1933), 5, 331.

6. Cf. F. X. Šalda, "Introduction" to *Duše a dílo* (Prague, 1913): "Real evaluation consists in nothing but proving the uniqueness of a studied phenomenon, its tragic creative drama, which never repeats itself again" (p. 6).

We must add that in recent years the artistic movement appears more and more programmatic, setting as its goal the reinstatement of the individual in his function of fulcrum in the contact of art with material reality. This is Surrealism. Its deformative relation to empirical reality incorporates it into the evolutionary cycle of modern art; traces of Dadaism are especially discernible in it. From an epistemological viewpoint, however, it is guided by the effort to establish contact with material reality through the mediation of personality. Surrealism does not, however, attempt the reconstruction of the Romantic psychological individual who supported his epistemological validity by means of conscious will; instead it turns to a biological personality. Personality is a natural phenomenon for the Surrealists, which explains their effort during artistic creation to penetrate as deeply as possible to those levels of spiritual life which seem to be closest to the biological base, that is, to various types of psychic automatism, dreams, and so on. Through the help of the biological individual free of social relations, the Surrealists intend to gain immediate contact with material reality which should be newly revealed to man.

Furthermore, if the Romantic individual separated his bearer from other people as much as possible, Surrealism presupposes that the biological individual, though typologically differentiated by his dispositions, nevertheless contains enough features accessible to universal supra-individual understanding. These differences between Romanticism and Surrealism cannot, however, prevent us from ascertaining analogies. The interest of Surrealism in dreams, for example, coincides closely with the similar interest of Romantic art: of the Czech Romantics not only Mácha recorded and poetically exploited his dreams, but so did Erben, as the materials recently published by Grund show.[7]

Finally, we must remark that the picture which we have tried to draw in these paragraphs is inevitably schematic. Terms such as Romanticism, Realism, and so forth, cannot be considered a true picture of the total heterogeneity of the actual state of affairs. Therefore, the boundaries which we have marked and everything that we have constructed upon this delimitation are valid only in the roughest contours. We must not forget that as early as the period of Realism-Naturalism, during the eighteen seventies, a pleiad of poets directly aligned with modern art (Rimbaud, Lautréamont) arose.

7. A. Grund, *Karel Jaromír Erben* (Prague, 1935).

As we have shown, the common denominator of modern art is the suppression of personality, especially the complex and hence strikingly unique psychological personality which stresses the unity of the work by its very presence. Under these conditions the perceiver confronts an objective artistic structure along with the numerous dialectic contradictions which permeate it. It is no accident that in conjunction with modern art the theory of art arrives in its own ways at the notion of artistic structure as a continuous developmental series existing in the social consciousness and developing under the influence of the contradictions which it contains. Structure appears free from dependence upon the individual and material reality, but its equilibrium is disturbed because of this; antinomies which always function latently in art come right to the surface. The work of art appears as a set of contradictions. Each of its components is simultaneously itself and its contrary; similarly the whole work is the antithesis of what is outside it.

Heightened dialectic tension in modern art often manifests itself in the one-sided emphasis of a single member of a given antinomy. For example, if it concerns the contradiction between the aesthetic function and other subordinated functions of art, the aesthetic function is sometimes stressed to an extreme (cf. "art for art's sake" which has programmatically appeared in modern art several times) and is sometimes completely rejected (cf. modern architecture). The tendency to go to extremes (cf. the predilection for experiment) is connected with this conspicuous dialectic quality. For example, if painting is to be purged of non-painterly means, what results is Suprematism and Neoplasticism which remove from the picture not only the representation of objects but also plasticity, contours, and, finally, even the frame so that color remains the only element on which the painting is based. The ultimate consequences of a similar effort at "pure" poetry were the rejection of all poetic elements except for speech sound elements and their arrangements (poems in "artificial language").

We must, however, remark that in modern art there are sometimes cases in which a heightened dialectic quality is achieved through an intensive oscillation between the two members of the antinomy rather than through the emphasis of a single member. We shall cite examples of this when we deal with the pairs truthfulness/fictiousness of the theme and subjective expressiveness/semiotic objectivity of the work of art.

We shall start with the dialectic contradiction between art and society. In no period and in no art is the relationship between these two spheres so direct and harmonious that art fully expresses some kind of *Zeitgeist*. To begin with, this is because society itself is always stratified and never escapes either the tension among its individual parts or their interchanges. Art which is as a rule bound to a certain stratum, its bearer, becomes part of this tension and movement. Likewise it can happen that bearers of different arts and even different genres of the same art are different strata in a given period and society.

Today, however, affairs have reached the culminating point of a movement which gained momentum throughout the nineteenth century, namely, art deprived of a solid social basis provided by its association with a specific stratum. There is no longer an unequivocal relation between the artist and the buyer; the artist frequently creates his works for an unknown and socially indeterminate buyer. Painters and sculptors, for example, create mostly for exhibitions where the work is the object of a free market, or they entrust their work to dealers who often not only direct their purchases according to contemporary taste but also speculate on probable future taste. The audience, a group of socially indeterminate and heterogeneous individuals, intervenes between art and society in the place of the buyer who represents a precisely defined social milieu for the artist. The development of art criticism, especially journals and newspapers beginning in the last century, is a symptom and a yardstick of the alienation between art and society. The critic stands between the audience and art as a mediator; his influence reaches both sides, but his basic attitude is polemic both toward the artist and toward the audience. He pushes through his demands against the will of both and prefers to be on his own, unbound by any obligations.[8] In this respect, it is also characteristic that the more heterogeneous and accidental the group of individuals representing the audience, the stronger the critic's influence. Theatrical criticism is, as we know, always more immediately influential and feared than literary criticism because the theatrical audience, frequently varying from one performance to another, is much less homogeneous and continuous in its

---

8. Cf. F. X. Šalda, "Kritika patosem a inspirací" [Criticism through pathos and inspiration], in *Boje o zítřek*, 3rd ed. (Prague, 1918), pp. 257–77.

composition than the reading public which is relatively stabilized and hence faithful to the authors whom it once favors.

We can therefore observe a considerable separation between art and the social organization in the entire realm of modern art. The audience stands between art and society, and criticism stands between the audience and art, but neither criticism nor the audience undertakes the task of passively uniting the two; on the contrary, they are restless elements—the audience because of its social heterogeneity and changeability, and criticism for its double-edged polemical focus. It is not, therefore, an exaggeration to claim that art is socially uprooted in the contemporary world. One of the conspicuous consequences of this abnormal state is the accelerated tempo of the development of art. Schools and movements follow one another quickly, and there are considerable contradictions among them; this is due to the slackening of the retarding influence of the social milieu which in the past bound art by its demands. This loosening results in the emphasized autonomy of art which under the weakened pressure of society is left to its own evolutionary dynamics, unretarded by anything. Moreover, the weakened ties with society influence the external organization of certain arts. The theater, for example, tends more and more to create small avant-garde theaters which, by addressing themselves to a narrow segment of the theatrical public, limit its social indeterminacy.

Naturally, artists suffer from the divorce between society and their works. Hatred of the public, the changeable element, arises. In the beginnings of modern art there were efforts to push the public out of the artist's view. The Symbolists who, as we have already mentioned, longed for the absolute work proclaimed that, if need be, they could do without a single reader (Mallarmé). Similarly, Futurism declares in Marinetti's words: "I do not care for the comprehension of the multitude. . . ."[9] Even if the artist does not deny the audience but, on the contrary, desires it, the path toward mutual understanding remains blocked. André Breton says: "One audience for which we speak and from which we should learn everything, if we are to continue to speak, does not listen; another audience, indifferent or hostile, listens."[10] Denial of the

9. "Destruction of Syntax—Imagination Without Strings—Words-in-Freedom," in *Futurist Manifestos,* ed. U. Apollonio (London, 1973), p. 106.
10. *Les Vases communicants,* 8th ed. (Paris, 1932), p. 101.

audience does not necessarily entail a denial of the relation between art and society. Although we may suppose that Symbolism —at least in its most extreme forms—tended not only to desocialize but also to dehumanize art in the sense of an absolute value independent of the perceiver, we may not claim this about later phases of modern art. There it is simply a matter of polemics against the art public, a socially diverse crowd unable to provide art with certainty through the stability and unidirectionality of its demands. The aim of this polemic is, however, to renew a direct relationship between art and society itself, no longer only with one of its strata—the complete return to a past stage is impossible here as elsewhere—but with the entire range of its homogeneous social organization. Proof of this aim may be found in the constantly repeated statements of contemporary artists that art will be redundant in future society because all people will be artists. Disregarding what is unrealizable in this idea, on account of the different degrees and kinds of aesthetic propensity among individuals, at the outset nothing prevents us from interpreting such statements as an expression of longing for a genuine incorporation of artistic creation into the life of society as a whole.[11]

The dialectic contradiction between art and society is always one of the most powerful factors in the history of art as well as an important force in the development of society. This contradiction is obviously heightened in modern art because of the alienation of these two spheres, but at the same time it is emphasized by the bilateral need for a new reconciliation. Yet we must remark that the effectiveness of this new, unprecedented relationship between these two spheres is also reflected in the structure of artistic works. As evidence let us cite the strong tendency toward exclusiveness which is frequently a structural component in modern art; compare the different ways of concealing part of a theme or obfuscating verbal expression in poetry, the complication and hindrance of the total perception of the image in painting, and so forth. All these different devices parallel the effort to limit the audience about which we spoke above.

11. The special position of film among the other modern arts is symptomatic of this tendency. Film is the youngest art and therefore corresponds most to the demands of its time. Whereas other arts, especially theater, the closest to film, tend to limit the heterogeneity of their audience, film tends to occupy the broadest social spectrum. Figures such as Chaplin, who appeal equally to all standards of taste, are more frequent in film than in any other art.

A further contradiction in modern art is the antinomy between art and the individual's psychic life which can be expressed by the formula: the work of art as an immediate expression of a subjective mental state and as an objective sign mediating among the members of the same collectivity. Pure subjective expression is, for example, a spontaneous cry of pain or joy. We cannot deny that there is something of this cry in the work of art. The work can appear as an equivalent of the mental state of either its creator or its perceiver. Aside from this, however, the work of art is also a supra-individual sign detached from any psychological subject and emphasizing only what is accessible to general understanding. The work of art can tend toward either one of these extremes. The contradiction between Romanticism and Realism corresponds to this polarity in certain respects. Modern art, especially in some of its phenomena, prefers, however, to oscillate between the two extremes, evoking what appears to be a highly subjective excitement while at the same time making clear that the quality of this excitement is irrelevant with respect to the real individual and functions merely as an element of the structure of the work.

This game is naturally most pronounced in lyric poetry. Nezval incorporated it into his poetics and expressed it directly in several of his poems. Let us take, for example, the lines:

> Dnes skočil básník z kazatelny
> Má měkký klobouk místo helmy
> Nepíše dávno při luně
> Dal sbohem už i tribuně
> Má fantazii místo citu

> Today the poet has jumped down from the pulpit
> He wears a soft hat instead of a helmet
> For a long time he has not written in the moonlight
> He has even said farewell to the dais
> He has imagination instead of emotion
> ["Dopis Mukařovskému," *Zpáteční lístek*]

For Nezval emotion as a component of a poem is "the cranberry in the crêpe." Somewhere else he says:

> Nesmírná blaženost vytváří ve mně osu
> na níž se otáčím jak hvězdná tělesa
> Houpám se na tišinách houpám se na patosu
> dobývám na vlně sváteční nebesa

> Boundless bliss creates an axis in me
> around which I revolve like sidereal bodies
> I swing on the lulls I swing on pathos
> On the wave I conquer the holiday skies
> ["Jízda na mořské vlně," *Sbohem a šáteček*]

This antinomy cannot be poetically expressed more clearly: pathos as an expression of an immediate excitement, and pathos as a game fully incorporated into the structure of an objectified sign outside of which it loses its validity. Of course, insofar as criticism is oriented toward unequivocally expressive lyrics, such "trifling with the emotions" usually appears to be a poet's cynicism.

Another antinomy based on the semiotic character of art is the antithesis between the work of art as an autonomous sign and as a communicative sign. It mainly occurs in those arts which work with a distinct theme (content), such as painting (of course, not ornamental) and literature. The theme is always to a certain extent a communication about reality. If we nevertheless call a thematic work of art an autonomous sign, we have in mind the fact that its content is not bound to a specific concrete reality so that we could pose the essential question of its truthfulness/untruthfulness. If we perceive and evaluate a novel, for example, as a work of art, we do not require that the events which it narrates correspond to some real facts localized in a certain point of real time and space, though such a requirement would be quite natural and proper with respect to any other—communicative—utterance. But even in this connection we must understand art dialectically, because a message is always potentially included in a literary or painted work regardless of its autonomy. From the viewpoint of art itself, however, the message operates only as a component of artistic structure. For example, the characteristic feature of Realist novels and paintings is the effort to evoke an *impression* of truthfulness in what is narrated, portrayed, or depicted. It is, of course, only a matter of the impression or, as the case may be, the illusion, evoked by the formal devices of the work, not its obligatory documentary nature.[12]

Thematic art thus constantly oscillates between the poles fictitiousness/truthfulness; sometimes one member of the antinomy

---

12. Cf. R. Jakobson's article "O realismu v umění," *Červen* 4 (1921): 300–04. *Editors' note.* English translation: "On Realism in Modern Art" by K. Magassy, *Readings in Russian Poetics*, ed. L. Matějka and K. Pomorska (Cambridge, Mass., 1971), pp. 38–46.

is emphasized, sometimes the other. In addition, modern art frequently emphasizes the antinomy between fictitiousness and truthfulness through an intensification of this oscillation. It does so
through a complex accretion of transitional shades between these
two poles. In Vančura's *Konec starých časů,* for example, the play
on the border between truthfulness and fictitiousness is achieved,
as Jakobson has recently shown,[13] through the juxtaposition of
two systems of fictitious values, the feudal world and the post-war
nouveau riche world, both of which pretend to be real. At other
times, the real and the fictitious are juxtaposed so that there will
be no certainty about which of the two planes the individual details of the theme belong to (as in Nezval's *Jak vejce vejci* or
Monaco). After all, the Symbolists had already used transitions
from the plane of fiction to the plane of reality. The Symbolist
poets handled meaning in such a way that the developed poetic
image changed instantly into direct designation and vice versa.

In painting, shifts from objectivity to non-objectivity and back,
as well as the divestment of objectivity from objects depicted
realistically, are related though not identical with the above situation in poetry. Thus even here objectivity and non-objectivity
constitute a dialectic antinomy, the tension of which is heightened
in contemporary painting. For example, Cubist painting on the
one hand breaks up the object by destroying its actual outline but,
on the other hand, emphasizes its objectivity by allowing it to be
viewed (of course, synecdochically) simultaneously from many
perspectival points in order to make its unity felt as a crystalizing
point in space, independent of changes in the viewer's perspective.
Futurist painting frequently makes metonymies for immaterial
events out of things characterized as material objects by depicting,
for example, a bundle of seemingly disparate things which in fact
represent the noise of the street whereby single sounds are expressed through the persons and objects that produce them. Even
more intensive is the transition from extreme objectivity to extreme non-objectivity in Surrealist painting where the objectivity
of every single depicted thing is emphasized, but where it is
simultaneously suggested that these objects are merely metaphors
for the totally non-objective, hidden meaning of the whole through

13. "Rub literární vědy" [The other side of literary studies], *Slovo a slovesnost* 1
(1935): 131–32.

the unmotivated assembling of mysteriously disparate objects within the frame of the same picture.

Nor do movements which seem totally to exclude objectivity from the picture lose their relation to objectivity. We can even find cases in which the dialectic shift from an absolute non-objectivity to a new, complete objectivity becomes patent. We have in mind Suprematism which in its polemics against objectivity has gone so far as to exclude draftsmanship and plasticity. The painting, which is composed of colored rectangles functioning as mere color-quanta, not as contours, and hence totally non-objective from the painterly viewpoint, becomes a thing in itself. The theoretician of Suprematism (Behne) claims that "the new painting is not governed by the object, which is created by color only secondarily through symbolism, fiction, representation, suggestion; rather it is governed directly by colors which are used here not as allusions to some object but as what they really are and what they mean in themselves, such as red, light blue, dark green, and so on."[14] A Suprematist painting tends to become an object among other objects to such a degree that the idea of the machine production of paintings ceases to be absurd for the Suprematists.

This brings us to the antinomy between material and its application in the work of art. There is a contradiction here between the work of art as an aesthetic structure and the same work as an object. Let us proceed from a simple example. A semiprecious stone such as a piece of jasper is an object of specific, material (physical, chemical, etc.) characteristics about which our senses inform us. As soon as we adopt an aesthetic attitude toward it, a change occurs. Each of its characteristics, while retaining its material value, at the same time becomes—in its relation to the others as a component of their total set—a factor of an aesthetic attitude (*Verhalten*) which this set evokes in the observer. Similarly, the work of art is both an object and an aesthetic structure. The vehicle of its material characteristics is also a material; these characteristics then become components of artistic structure with respect to its aesthetic effect.[15] Material therefore has a consid-

14. A. Behne, *Von Kunst zur Gestaltung* (Berlin, 1925), p. 75.
15. Here we have in mind primarily the material of the visual arts, because the material of literature, language, is a much more complicated case. Even before its

erable significance for the structure of an artistic creation. A marble statue is not only materially, but also artistically, different from the same statue cast in metal.

The specific properties of every material can be exploited in a work of art either positively, that is, when the material is taken into account in the creative process, or negatively, that is, when it is violated. In both cases the material functions as a component of the structure of the work. Here as well as in other respects modern art is dialectic to a high degree. It draws attention primarily to the raw physicality of material by leaving to it enough of its own nature to let it stand in opposition to the artistic structure, though it is incorporated into this structure. Typical of all contemporary art is its predilection for unusual materials, in some cases brand new ones which for this very reason draw attention to their specific characteristics and their physicality. If we leave aside architecture, where new materials can be at least partially explained by the upsurge of industrial production and commerce, which provides an unusually rich selection, we can cite as an example from painting the pictures of Moholy-Nagy who uses glass mirrors or metallic sheets not fully covered by paint as a base. Instead of oil paints he frequently uses lacquers and even brand new materials such as celluloid, galalith, and so on. Frequently, in order to emphasize its material as an object, painting calls attention to the rawness and crudeness of this material; compare the pieces of paper, in some cases printed newspaper, playing cards, and so forth, glued into the painted space of Cubist paintings. A similar example from the same school of painting is the realistic depiction of the structure of materials, for instance, the growth rings in wood in the middle of a picture which breaks up the outlines of the depicted object and typifies details into stereometric forms, hence an unrealistic picture. Finally, let us mention the relief modeling of some depicted objects from a colored paste which is spread equally on the remaining surface of the painting. Both the multiplication of the stock of materials and the conspicuous exploitation of their characteristics are especially prominent against the background of nineteenth-century painting

---

entrance into the work it is not only an object (perceptible through hearing) but also —and especially—a sign.

which worked mainly with a very limited repertoire of materials and left others to lower forms of art.

The dialectic contradiction between material and the aesthetic function which it acquires in the work points to the antinomy between art and non-art, that is, between products with a dominant aesthetic function and those in which the aesthetic function is either subordinated to another dominant function or is altogether absent. This antinomy is not limited only to modern art either. The aesthetic function is always at variance with the others. Even in art itself it is sometimes displaced by another function; on the other hand, even outside of art it often exhibits a tendency to become the dominant function.[16] In modern art, however, oscillations are more pronounced. Sometimes the absolute supremacy of the aesthetic function is programmatically declared and artistically realized (as in the art for the sake of art of Symbolist and Dadaist poetry); sometimes its exclusion is proclaimed (as in the theory of functional architecture). Both the extreme emphasis and the denial of the aesthetic function are, of course, transformed into their direct opposites. The maximal exclusion of all functions other than the aesthetic causes the aesthetic function to change into other functions such as the moral ("What offends a man of taste when he looks at vice is its deformity and lack of proportion"—Baudelaire[17]) or the intellectual ("The cognition of the beauty of the world is the goal of our effort"—Březina[18]). On the other hand, the maximal denial of the aesthetic function in functional architecture becomes a means of aesthetic effect (maximal functionality equals maximum aesthetic value).

There is yet another tendency in modern art; it emphasizes, we believe, the antithesis between art and other products of human activity. It exploits products which no doubt at some time or in some place functioned or are functioning as art but which do not fit the aesthetic canon of art in the milieu for which the artist creates; instead they directly contradict it. In this respect, compare the relation between African plastic art and modern sculpture

16. For more detail about this antinomy see my study *Estetická funkce, norma a hodnota jako sociální fakty* (Prague, 1936). *Editors' note.* English translation: *Aesthetic Function, Norm and Value as Social Facts,* by M. E. Suino (Ann Arbor, 1970).

17. "Théophile Gautier," *L'Art romantique* (Paris, 1889), p. 152.

18. "Krása světa" [The beauty of the world], *Hudba pramenů* in *Spisy Otakara Březiny* (Prague, 1933), 2, 30.

or the tendency toward "peripheral" art in poetry[19] and painting.[20]
Since, however, such contacts between "high" art and "primitive"
or "low" art result at the same time in the introduction of an
alien aesthetic canon into the artistic structure of the work, we
shall mention them in more detail when we speak about the
antinomy of "beauty" and its negation.

Furthermore, the intense relationship between modern art and
machine technology (civilizationism in poetry, the close relation
between machine production and the plastic arts, the emphasis on
the involvement of the machine as an aesthetic factor in film and
photography) is also characteristic of the relation between art and
non-art. Somewhat similar to the contradiction between art and
non-art are the contradictions among the individual arts. However,
since these contradictions do not belong to the relationship between art and the extra-aesthetic, we shall return to them later.

The antinomy between art and non-art drew our attention to
the aesthetic function which is the basis of art. Let us therefore
turn to the internal antinomies of the aesthetic function itself,
that is, the discrepancies which arise in the work among components functioning as aesthetic factors. The first of these is the
antinomy called (not very precisely) the contradiction between
content and form. The relationship between these two bundles of
components into which the work of art divides (as far as thematic
art is concerned) can be defined in various ways. We shall use a
definition that, we admit, is not totally comprehensive, but for
our purpose it grasps the essence of the matter. The components
of content in the work of art are those which appear as a rule to be
the determining ones; the formal components are those which
appear to be determined. In reality, of course, the content is always simultaneously determining and determined, likewise the
form, because the dialectic contradiction between content and
form is based precisely on the tension between determining and
being determined. Modern art heightens this tension and allows
the content/form antinomy to obtrude by shifting the weight to
its negation, emphasizing the determining role of form. For ex-

19. See the articles in Karel Čapek's *Marsyas* (Prague, 1931) or Nezval's introduction
to *Pět prstů* (Prague, 1932) and some symptomatic phenomena in the poetry of both
writers.
20. Cf. Josef Čapek's book *Nejskromnější umění* [The humblest art] (Prague, 1920)
and Henri Rousseau's paintings.

ample, modern poetry frequently allows content to grow directly
from form in deriving its theme from linguistic elements; compare
some of Nezval's lyric poems in which the only continuous (though
variable) thematic thread is provided by a semantic chain of
rhymes or poems from Biebl's collection *Zlatými řetězy* (1926) in
which the thematic contexture is explicitly carried by euphonic
figures. The peak of this tendency in painting is a certain kind of
expressionism, the so-called absolute painting of Kandinsky,
Kupka's Orphism, some of Josef Šíma's pictures, and the Artifi-
cialism of Štýrský and Toyen, where the rudimentary thematiza-
tion (e.g., space, outline) is vaguely suggested by the distribution
of colors (e.g., warm colors come to the fore, and cold colors sink
into the background) and by the way the line is handled (cf. the
vague suggestions of objectivity furnished by closed and unclosed
contours).

It is also possible for the pronounced antinomy of content and
form to manifest itself in such a way that form becomes content
without losing its formal character. The poetic images of Symbolism provide a good example. The poetic image is a matter of
form in its very relation to the object which it suggests only indirectly. Nevertheless, the Symbolists often exploited the image in
such a way that the developed image became a minute thematic
whole in itself. Frequently the narration of the whole episode was
presented only through an image and only as an image. Let us
look, for example, at Březina's lines:

> Sem nikdo z živých nezbloudí. Jen vzkříšen zraky mými
> vstal smutek těchto míst a kroky bázní ztlumenými,
> by bratří neviditelných ze spánku nevyrušil,
> mi vyšel naproti.

> None of the living sets foot here. Just resurrected by my gaze
> the sadness of these places has risen and in steps muffled
>   by fear,
> lest it awake the invisible brethren from their sleep,
> it has come to meet me.
>
> ["Smutek hmoty," *Stavitelé chrámu*]

The image of sadness approaching with muffled steps is more than
mere form; it is form dialectically changing into content.

The poetic images which Breton calls "doubles" in *Les Vases communicants* provide another example. These doubles are poetic images in which one and the same word in the text functions simultaneously as an image, hence a matter of form, and as a designation proper referring directly to the theme. Nezval presented the poetics of this kind of image in his book *Chtěla okrást lorda Blamingtona*. Let us quote one example: "The novel. The setting of the sun in a room. There are writers who wish to paint this sunset in words. They study the furniture piece by piece; they search for reflections. The older literary schools used mythological apparatus. This mystery can be evoked by a single sentence: The sun has set. And the memory of it remains in the room. A rose in a glass behind the window."[21] Here a rose is simultaneously the image of the sun, thus form, and a real rose with all of its properties, thus content. We can also cite an example of the opposite type, one in which content becomes form without losing its nature. We have in mind the works of Cubist painting, the content of which is unequivocally indicated only by the title. The title— for example, "Man with a Pipe"—determines the formal interpretation to a certain extent. If the picture lacked a title, the interpretation of its form would often be uncertain; if it had a different title, the interpretation would change. Here the theme functions explicitly as a formative factor.

The contradiction between content and form becomes acute in modern art as a result of these processes—the determination of content by form and the dialectic transformation of form into content and vice versa. But each of these groups of elements also has an internal antinomy which is likewise utilized with great effectiveness in works of contemporary art. The internal antinomy of form consists in the fact that form is at the same time an organizing and a disorganizing factor in the work. The unmarked member of the antinomy is, of course, the organizing power of form; as a rule form is understood and defined in this way. Modern art, however, emphasizes negation, specifically the disorganizational potential of form which, in reaching its culmination, changes through a dialectic reversal into a new affirmation: a reorganization by means of form. Cubist painting furnishes one of the most illuminating proofs. Here form disorganizes the object by depriving it of the unity of perspective and reduces the parts into which the

21. V. Nezval, *Chtěla okrást lorda Blamingtona* (Prague, 1930), p. 77.

object is dissolved to the regularity of stereometric forms. At the same time, however, it organizes the object into a new unity of plane and contour. Similarly, the poetry of Poetism breaks down the causal continuity of events carried over from external reality by the theme and substitutes for it a new formal continuity (compositional, purely semantic, rhythmic, etc.).

Content (theme) parallels the internal contradiction within form with its own internal antimony which lies in the contradiction between unity and multiplicity. The content of a work of art is *ex definitione* a semantic whole; at the same time, however, it is also a multiplicity because of its articulation into subordinate units whose semantic relations violate and emphasize the total unity. In the normal structure of the narrative plot, for example, tension originates from an unexpected sequence of events which are impossible to connect into a semantic unity at the beginning. Only the resolution consolidates the theme by tying together all its parts *post factum* into a unified meaning. Modern art frequently heightens the dialectic antinomy between the continuity and discontinuity of the theme by presenting the theme so discontinuously that each of its parts retains an independent reference (i.e., a presupposed relation to reality beyond the work—in fact, beyond its theme). Surrealism proceeds furthest along this path by composing the theme out of completely heterogeneous facts in literature, out of objects unconnected by anything except the common frame in painting. Here even a unification made possible by form (e.g., by means of composition or rhythm) is rejected; instead the documentary nature of each fact mentioned in a literary work or the objectivity of each thing portrayed in a pictorial work is emphasized in order for them to affect the perceiver more strongly as discrete forces. The connection of discrete facts into a semantic unity is left to the viewer or reader. This underlines the internal antinomy within the theme.

We could examine an entire structure in descending order down to individual components and discover the antinomies with which the structure is permeated down to its foundations, but this would require a detailed and specific analysis with respect to particular arts which we cannot carry out here. Nevertheless, we cannot ignore one of the most important antinomies, the contradiction between beauty and its negation. We do not have in mind the conventional problem of the aesthetics of "ugliness" but the fact that the work of art, especially in its initial freshness, evokes not only aesthetic pleasure but also strong elements of displeasure by violating traditional aesthetic norms. Modern art likes to intensify this sense of violation, which does not, however, entail the suppression of normativism, but rather its exposure and emphasis. The stronger the violation of regularity is to be emphasized, the stronger the regularity must be felt. Contemporary art therefore delights in crossing one norm with another. A canon existing as a system and achieving its own unequivocal ideal of beauty, while valid somewhere outside of contemporary "official" art, is juxtaposed to the reigning canon of norms (i.e., taste). We mentioned a few examples above when we discussed the contradiction between art and non-art. Instead of the rejection of only one set of norms (the canon) there is an oscillation between two sets. As a rule this occurs within the structure in such a way that some groups of elements are subject to one canon and some to another (e.g., in literature, the sentence structure versus the word selection). The clash can, of course, originate outside the structure if a work created on the basis of an alien canon is incorporated into the context of official art whose canon then serves as the background for the perception of the work.

The last antinomy we must briefly discuss is the opposition among the individual arts, in other words, the opposition between an art oriented toward another art and a so-called *pure* art (i.e., "pure" poetry, painting, etc.). Every art can seek a path toward other arts in such a way that it stresses components which it has in common with them (e.g., theme connects literature, drama, painting, and film; rhythm and sound values link literature and music; the distribution of light and shadow, proportion, and outline are common to painting, sculpture, and film); on the other hand, every art strives by its own specific means to compete with the specific means of another art (e.g., literature trying to compete with the visual possibilities of painting, film competing with drama, and drama with film). Even the usual metaphoric clichés used by criticism, such as the "musicality" of a poem or even a painting, the "poeticness" of music or painting, and the "plasticity" of a poem or a painting, attest to the interrelation of the individual arts. Interrelations among the arts can be very complex. For example, the composition of Richard Wagner's musical works (the characteristic motif, musical quotations) is directly influenced by literature. The novelist Thomas Mann, on the other hand, consciously adopts the Wagnerian principle of composition as a model for the structure of his own literary works.[22]

Of course, it is also possible for a particular art to attempt to be itself in such a way that it emphasizes only the specific characteristics which differentiate it from other arts: for example, literature stressing purely linguistic elements, painting color, and so forth. These tendencies toward "pure" art and toward a merging with another art are usually heightened to an extreme (e.g., poetry in an "artificial" language and Suprematism in painting; at the opposite pole, Symbolist poetry merging with music and Surrealist painting identifying itself with literature). At the same time it is interesting to note that this dialectic pair frequently crosses with the pair subordination/domination of the aesthetic function. Compare Symbolist poetry connecting the tendency toward another art (music) with the pronounced domination of the aesthetic function; or Constructivism in architecture stressing the specific nature of architecture and simultaneously striving for the subordination of the aesthetic function.

We have attempted to demonstrate that modern art is based on dialectic contradictions. We do not, of course, mean that these contradictions do not exist in other phases of art—indeed, they are the constant moving force of development—but rather that contradictions which generally make themselves felt gradually stand out forcibly in modern art and function openly by mingling with one another. At the beginning of this study we pointed out the reasons for this particular state. We have been concerned neither with a criticism of nor with an apology for modern art but rather with an experimental epistemological characterization. Modern art is too often characterized as a manifestation of the crisis of contemporary culture and society. Such a characterization is justified only insofar as it is not a manifestation of hatred for any living art, and only if it is accompanied by an awareness of how much effort at an axiological reconstruction there is in modern art and how strongly it strives for order—a dynamic order, naturally—in its seeming chaos.

---

22. Cf. W. Schaber, "Klang und Wort im Kontrapunkt," *Thomas Mann zu seinem sechzigsten Geburtstag* (Zurich, 1935), pp. 21-48.

10

Personality in Art

Today we are indeed in a somewhat paradoxical situation. As soon as the critic begins to think about a work seriously, he will strive to ascertain to what extent the artist has implemented his experiences, expressed his personality, or exposed his psychic *privatissimum* in it. If the artist is asked a question about his work, he feels obliged to speak about the subconscious elements of his creation, his emotional life, and so on, with the utmost confidence in the value of personality and in the universal relevance of each of its slightest vibrations. But in so doing, all of us distinctly feel that we have gone beyond the time of our fathers when subjectivity predominated over objectivity, when in literature and in life people could afford the luxury of speaking about the purely inner, externally undetermined suffering which in their view comprised the only dignified spiritual atmosphere for a cultivated man living, as they liked to say, "an intense inner life." Development itself and time have taught us well enough that we cannot live with our eyes closed to objective, external reality, that every individual's own psychic *privatissimum* is incommunicable in its entire uniqueness— we no longer believe in the mysterious power of "suggestion," as the generation of the Symbolists did—and that this *privatissimum* is also altogether indifferent for other individuals, for what really matters is only what can be communicated.

Thus arises the contradiction between this conception of the artistic personality and artistic creation itself which has been based for a long time upon other than subjectively psychological foundations. I do not want to analyze in detail here what the consequences of this paradoxical indefiniteness in the conception of the artist's personality are for his feelings about life, his frame of mind, and his attitude toward his audience and society in general. Certainly it is not comfortable to bear in one's consciousness the contradiction between one's, let us say, "civic" view of personality

"Osobnost v umění," a lecture at Mánes on February 3, 1944; published in *Studie z estetiky* (Prague, 1966).

and one's professionally artistic view of it. It is also certain that the artist, conscious of his obligations to his audience and society and, on the other hand, of the justification of his demand to be independent in his creation, has to have a clear idea of the artistic personality. It is not, however, my ambition to attempt to answer this question and say what the artist's attitude toward his own creation and society *should* be henceforth or how the artist *should* reconcile his personal feelings about life with his artistic ones. Given such a critical state of affairs, the task of a scholarly study can only be to indicate the problem and to formulate it.

In order to grasp the scope of our problem, let us glance at the past, at least for a moment. It is generally known that the Middle Ages were not even aware of the very notion of the artistic personality or, of course, the related notion of individuality—the individuality of the artistic creation. Let us take the poet. From the viewpoint of the Middle Ages his task is by no means undignified. The poet knows, and others know, that he presents divine beauty in a form which is accessible to human senses and is generally perceptible. But a mere imitation, indeed a supremely imperfect imitation of this divine beauty, remains the highest that he can achieve. He is absolutely bound by the Bible or by moral and metaphysical truths. Nowhere is there room for free choice and creativity on his part; hence there is not even room for his personality. We know that medieval works were frequently anonymous. It sounds almost inconceivable to us that some medieval poet was bitterly reproached for attempting to go his own way in his writing. Even during the Renaissance we find evidence (in Vasari) that imitation, hence the denial of one's own personality, was considered not a detriment but a virtue. In Titian's biography we read: "When he [Titian] first adopted Giorgione's style, at the age of eighteen, he made the portrait of a noble of ca Barbarigo, his friend . . . . It was so excellent that, if Titian had not written his name on the dark background, it would have been attributed to Giorgione."[1]

As concerns the visual arts, it is commonly known that they were classified among the *artes serviles,* the crafts. This fact, of course, clearly indicates a view of the artistic personality. Only at

1. G. Vasari, "The Works of Titian of Cadore, Painter," in *The Lives of Painters, Sculptors and Architects,* trans. A. B. Hinds (London, 1927), 4, 199–200.

the end of the Middle Ages does artistic creation begin to be sub-
jectivized: "And thus since the time of Charles [IV] the source of
artistic form has no longer been the thing itself and its organization, comprehensible only through a concept and an abstraction,
but the optical and aural experience which it evokes in the creating
subject. The source, the primary cause, and the origin of artistic
form have been transferred from the created thing, an object, to
the creating subject."[2] We must not, of course, imagine the
subjectivity mentioned here by the art historian to be modern
subjectivity. It consists only in the fact that the artist ceases to be
an imitator of immaterial divine beauty, its translator into an imperfect human language. But a new limitation immediately arises
for him: the organization of the reality which he depicts. This
organization becomes "beauty" for the artist, hence an obligatory
norm.

This is also valid, of course, for the Renaissance. We know what
efforts the Renaissance artists made to master perspective, an objective perspective, not a subjective optical one (the origin of
descriptive geometry from these efforts); and furthermore what
efforts they made in the study of anatomy; and so on. Therefore
subjectivism, starting with the Middle Ages and culminating in the
Renaissance, could in fact be called objectivism from our standpoint. Similarly we must not identify the Renaissance conception
of the artistic personality with the modern one. We see how the
artist's self-confidence grows; we see, for example, Michelangelo—
at the very peak of the Renaissance—defending his superiority and
independence as an artist against his entire surroundings and even
against the Pope (his famous statement to the painter and goldsmith Francia: "I am under the same obligation to Pope Julius,
who gave it to me [the bronze for the Pope's statue], as you are to
those who provide your paints."[3])

In all of this, however, the conception of personality is unlike
the modern conception, we could say more a quantitative than a
qualitative one. Of course, the artist esteems his own work; he is
aware that someone else could not do it better or even in the same
way as he has done it: he is jealous of his rivals, and so on. In

2. V. Mencl, "O dvojí povaze a funkci středověkého umění" [On the dual nature and
function of medieval art], Život 19 (1944): No. 2, 45.

3. Vasari, "Michelagnolo Buonarotti of Florence, Painter, Sculptor and Architect," in
The Lives of Painters, Sculptors and Architects, 4, 123.

brief, he is aware of his personality as a force. But he does not even dream of considering his work as a product of his personality—its traits, its dispositions. He does not think about this; he does not even know the psychological concepts appropriate for it. For him the work is a product of conscious will, of skill. We know, for example, what weight Leonardo da Vinci places—in *The Art of Painting*—on the practical and theoretical training which should be the painter's preparation. We do not find a single word about the painter's personality as the inspirer of the work of art; instead we find repeated contemptuous remarks about those who think that they can attain a goal by relying upon themselves alone, their fantasy, and so forth. He does not seek the value of the work of art in the fact that it may be an expression of its author but in the fact that it grasps the order and composition of nature. For this reason not even a judgment about a work of art is a matter of individual taste for him but a question of a quite objectively justifiable appreciation. A painter should not reject anyone's judgment in his work: "A painter ought not certainly to refuse listening to the opinion of anyone; for we know that, although a man be not a painter, he may have just notions of the forms of men; whether a man has a hump or a large hand; whether he be lame, or has any other defect."[4]

Since the conception of personality in the Renaissance viewed from the modern standpoint is, in fact, so "impersonal," that is, devoid of consideration for the individual's uniqueness, a close symbiosis of the artist and the scholar—even the specialist in the exact sciences of mathematics and physics—frequently occurs in the Renaissance man. Moreover, it is a symbiosis which in no way splits the personality into two alien aspects. For Leonardo there is no difference between painting and inventing instruments and machines. For him both of these activities are the same kind of work; both demand ingenuity and skill. This conception of personality advanced by the Renaissance is not, therefore, one which is a burden to man in any way, one which ties his hands or impedes his mental life. Rather it supports his triumphant self-confidence. This conception survived for a long time if we disregard various fluctuations, isolated cases, and foreshadowings of a further developmental stage.

4. Leonardo da Vinci, *The Art of Painting* (New York, 1957), p. 28.

Only the beginning of the nineteenth century brings a radical turn: its name is Romanticism. The Romantic conception of personality culminates in the notion of genius. Genius is no longer personality creating through a conscious will, attentive to the external reality which it cognizes or reshapes. Genius is creative involuntariness—spontaneity. It is just as spontaneous as the natural forces to which it is related. A genius does not create because he wants to but because he must. In fact, a genius does not even create, for something within him creates ("Es dichtet in mir" is the slogan of the Romantic artist). Spontaneity, of course, immediately changes the relationship between the artist and his work, between the artist and reality, and between the artist and other people, as well as the artist's attitude toward himself. A work suddenly appears as a genuine expression of the artist's personality, as a "material" replica of his mental organization. It is as involuntary a product as a pearl in an oyster's shell.

The artist no longer seeks the organization in sensorily perceptible nature but in himself. He himself is a natural force, and therefore the image of nature as he experiences it in his inner self and as he implements it in his work is more authentic than a mechanically reproducing testimony of the senses. Man, and especially man-the-artist, begins to experience the tension and contradiction between reality and himself. "The human spirit and nature, which were one, have fallen apart in time. Nature goes its eternal, peaceful, regular way, but man has obliterated all traces which lead to it, having thereby lost his original harmony and essence," says Mácha.[5] What a difference in comparison to the standpoint of Renaissance man for whom precisely the natural order was the basis of all creation! During Romanticism the relationship between the artist and other people changes in the sense that the artist feels himself to be unique, therefore different from other people, separated from them, whether he feels this separation to be a privilege or a curse. A Romantic artist would no longer repeat Leonardo's statement that in his work he must heed everyone's judgment because every man, even the non-artist, knows nature. For the Romantic, an artist is an artist precisely because he sees reality differently than others in his own unique way.

5. Cited according to K. Sabina, "Upomínka na K. H. Máchu" [A memoir of K. H. Mácha], in *Vybrané spisy K. Sabiny* (Prague, 1912), 2, 121.

Finally, the attitude toward one's self changes so that the Romantic artist, having discovered himself—his individuality, concentrates primarily on his own inner self, not on what is happening around him. Perhaps Mácha could have understood Leonardo's advice: "Whoever flatters himself that he can retain in his memory all the effects of Nature, is deceived, for our memory is not so capacious; therefore consult Nature for every thing."[6] But certainly Leonardo would not have understood Mácha's statement: "It often seems to me that I am looking into myself and that I see a vast wilderness in myself; a veritable chaos swarms before my eyes until eventually it merges into a dark cloud. This cloud weighs upon me like lead. I often feel that something lies beyond it but I don't know what."[7] This direction of looking, inward, simply did not exist in Leonardo's time; it had not yet been discovered.

In light of this brief description of Romanticism, we must not, of course, suppose that Romanticism, in comparison with Renaissance self-confidence, meant some kind of degeneration, a loss of powers. The conviction about the force of personality—what we have called the quantitative aspect of personality in the Renaissance—remained unshattered in the Romantic man and artist. Only in the Romantic sphere of thought could the notion of artistic *creation* in the proper, literal sense of the word have originated. Only when the artist felt himself to be independent of the order of external reality, and perceived himself to be the originator of the order which appears in his work, could he feel himself to be the creator, the maker of a certain universe, the code of which is the work. The divide between the Renaissance and Romantic conceptions of the artistic personality is deep, but it is not a severance of continuity. After all, the way in which Romanticism conceived personality has sufficed without any essential change up to the present as a firm foundation of the artist's situation vis-à-vis his work and the world that surrounds him. There have been developmental changes, but the basic feature of the Romantic conception—the relation of spontaneity, which links the work and personality—has remained untouched by these changes.

Even when psychological aesthetics replaced the previous

6. *The Art of Painting,* p. 214.
7. Cited according to K. Sabina, "Upomínka na K. H. Máchu," p. 116.

speculative aesthetics in the second half of the nineteenth century, it was constructed on the premise of creative spontaneity. Only because psychological aestheticians, in proceeding from the premise of spontaneity, equated the work with a personality, could they have postulated that they were studying art itself by studying the psychic activity from which the work arose (or which it evokes in the perceiver). The sociological aestheticians of Taine's persuasion also, after all, proceeded on the basis of the premise of the spontaneous relationship between the artistic personality and the work. Taine's theory, of course, appears to be absolutely anti-Romantic in its strict determinism which explains the artist's personality completely by means of the causal effect of external influences; but since it conceives not only the artist's personality but also his work as a "copy of the surrounding mores and an indication of a certain mental state," it betrays that it too is firmly rooted in the conquests of Romanticism and that along with Romanticism it overlooks everything which in reality separates— as we shall see—the artistic personality and the work from one another. Thus in the pair personality/the work personality asserts itself more and more to the detriment of the work, the more it prevails over the work.

The situation at the end of the century is already such that the work appears to be a mere accidentality with respect to personality, whereas personality itself seems to be the main goal of artistic creation. We do not have to go far afield for an illustration. Let us quote several sentences from Šalda's essay "Personality and the Work": "Least of all does the rabble understand the mystery of transcendentality—the personality transcending its work. But indeed a work is a real artistic feat only when the creator's personality stands and breathes behind it like immense and inscrutable eternity and darkness behind a moment. The work is great only when it has been created from innermost necessity, under pressure which could not be resisted, for the author's need and only for it, for his growth and inner history—and not in order for him to present a passable sample of his dexterity and swiftness at fingering . . . . A great work of art, even the greatest, is merely a chip which has flown off a genius' chisel, from that beautiful inner statue which a great spirit is carving in darkness from himself and for himself."[8]

8. "Osobnost a dílo," in *Boje o zítřek* (Prague, 1905), p. 29.

We have now reached the peak of the evolution of that conception of personality in art which had its origin in the Renaissance. This conception culminates here in a paradox of crystal clarity and distinctness, but precisely for this reason a paradox from which it is impossible to proceed further. I do not make any claim that such a conception is incapable of life in itself. If I were to attempt to do so, that literary movement of which Šalda was a contemporary and, in fact, a lifelong member, namely Symbolism, would prove me wrong. Because Symbolism, which indeed attained more than respectable results, built its entire theory of the exclusiveness of art—its aristocratic nature, and so forth—precisely upon this paradox.

As I have said, however, it was impossible to proceed further. The Romantic conception of the relationship between the artist and the work was theoretically still alive, but *de facto* it had already degenerated. The requirement for uniqueness was more and more emphasized. Since the work is supposed to be an incontestable equivalent of its creator's psychic personality but at the same time one and the same creator can produce a whole series of dissimilar works, there arises the concomitant notion of the *experience,* which is nothing but the artist's personality limited to a specific moment of its existence. Experiences can, of course, change, and thus works also change (even though the premise of the work's identity with a psychic activity continues to be maintained). This is, of course, an atomization of personality. The requirement that every work of art be new and different arises concurrently with the theory of experience in criticism and in general evaluation. Individuality is now imposed not only upon the author but also upon the work. The result of this is a peculiar conceptual labyrinth in which it is difficult to orient oneself. Only one thing is certain: "Individuality" conceived in this atomistic way becomes by a peculiar reversal an argument for eclectics and imitators, for who else but an imitator can renew and change his individuality from work to work more often?

It is natural that such confusion gives rise to fatigue from an excessively hypertrophied personality. The symptoms are different, indeed extremely varied, precisely because it is more a matter of a feeling of negative resistance than of a conscious tendency toward another conception. Let us mention some of these symptoms. There is a predilection for the "humblest art," semi-folk and anonymous, where there is no emphasis at all on personality. Another such symptom is an effort—at least theoretical and programmatic—on the part of the artist to disappear in a crowd of other people, to make all people artists. Another includes attempts to place artistic activity among other human pursuits liberated from the burden of individuality. The artist is compared to a craftsman or a worker; in fact, he occasionally makes an effort to be considered among craftsmen or workers. There is still another symptom: In recent years we have experienced an artistic movement which clung very tenaciously to the automatic correspondence of the work to a psychic state while emphatically claiming that it did not seek those psychic states which are individual and unrepeatable but rather those which are generally human and which are therefore not necessarily bound to any personality. Finally, besides all of these symptoms which have occurred in artistic life, we should perhaps cite a parallel phenomenon in the development of scholarship. Psychological aesthetics has given way to objectivist aesthetics which is more and more inclined to view the connection between the artist's personality and the work as polysemic and indirect, hence not simply spontaneous.

This is how matters stand today, and so we conclude our historical survey of the question of personality in art. We have learned that the awareness of the artistic personality, which originated at the boundary between the Middle Ages and modern times, gradually underwent various modifications, none of which meant a return to the previous state when personality in art was simply not considered (though it necessarily existed and functioned). Moreover, it would be inappropriate today to believe that as a consequence of the crisis which we just mentioned the artistic personality could withdraw completely into the background and there could be a return to the idyllic past of the cathedral builders when the author simply did not matter or did not matter more than the craftsman following his orders. I am pointing this out explicitly so that there will be no doubt that I do not subscribe to such an antiquarian view, which still has its adherents. I am convinced that when society and art themselves create a new conception of personality in art, the need for which, though evident, has not yet been satisfied, it will be, as it always is in development, a conception constructed on the premises provided by the immediately preceding stage but imbuing these premises with a new meaning. It is possible to prepare for its arrival in many ways, and perhaps much of what is happening in art and in other cultural spheres is already tending toward this new conception of the artistic personality without its being apparent to us at the present moment. As we have said above, scholarship can perform no other task in this process than to indicate the existence of the problem and to attempt its formulation.

We shall try to do so now. At the beginning of our deliberations, however, we must disregard everything transitory, or historically determined, and attempt to reveal the unchanging essence of the matter. We undertook in advance a historical survey of the conception of personality in art precisely in order to expose what is historically determined as purely transitory. If we now say "personality in art," we are not thinking of either the way in which the Renaissance understood it or the Romantic or Symbolist conceptions. All of these are mere conceptions; we are now concerned with the *reality* of personality in art, independent of any conception—a reality that necessarily existed even in medieval art which was not aware of the artistic personality and that still exists in folk art and the art of primitive peoples who likewise are not aware of it. We have in mind nothing but the work of art and the fact that this work has an originator, for this is the only thing that distinguishes it from a natural object. The originator is necessary to the extent that we would automatically perceive him to be behind a natural object if it had affected us as a work of art through its accidental organization. But why did the originator create a work of art? There can, of course, be many different answers to this question, but they will all have one thing in common: While creating his work, the artist had in mind other people for whom he created it. Otherwise, what he was creating would not have been for him what we call a work of art but something else. For example, an actor does not and cannot play for himself.[9] There is, of course, someone who indeed "plays" only for himself and who

---

9. To play really "for himself" would be either completely impossible for him or at least difficult and nerve-wracking. It is said that while the actors of the mad Bavarian king Ludwig, who only had to play for the king himself, were on stage, they waited impatiently for the curtain in the royal box to sway in order to know that the king was in the theater. As long as they were not sure of this, they played in an unbearable mental state.

not only does not need spectators but rejects them. This is a child, but a child's activity is precisely something other than art; it is *play*.

Using the example of the theater, we have tried to illustrate something which is valid for art in general: Art is made for others—for listeners and spectators, in brief, for perceivers. If certain periods—I have in mind specifically the period of Symbolism—have denied the necessity of a listener or a spectator, it was only a programmatic requirement on their part. If we looked at the real situation, we would see that the necessity of a perceiver sounds as an undertone there. Sometimes they reject a large audience and address themselves to a narrow circle of "chosen spirits"; at other times they demand a future or ideal audience, not existing in reality but affecting the course of their creation in their imagination. There are therefore always two necessary parties in the work of art: the one who presents it and the one who receives it. We say "the artist and the spectator" or "the listener, the reader," and we are accustomed to seeing these two parties as sharply separated. The artist is active and has the initiative, whereas the spectator is passive. The artist is trained for his task; today he is generally a professional. The spectator, however, is not bound to art in this existential manner. We know, of course, that there are some transitional types, that there are in particular dilettantes who are also trained, but they essentially maintain the spectator's passivity in their creation (by imitating), and we are accustomed to overlooking such figures as secondary and unessential.

However, this is a historical situation which did not always exist. If we take only a few steps across the boundary of the art which we call *high* and turn our attention to folk art, the matter already looks completely different. Even in folk art, of course, cases in which the author is known are not rare. For instance, specialists in folk art have frequently discerned among the people an individual who is more gifted than the others. But the difference between the author and the perceiver has not been felt; it has not been emphasized at all. He who is known in his region as a songster by no means has to be a composer of songs but simply a preserver of them (on account of his memory, singing ability, etc.). We have an example in Eva Studeničová about whom Plicka has written a monograph and who is mentioned in Papoušková's book.[10] Even

10. N. Melniková–Papoušková, *Putování za lidovým uměním* [A quest for folk art] (Prague, 1941).

more telling evidence is mentioned by the German ethnographer Jungbauer from Šumava.[11] By chance he had an opportunity to write down a song about a village tragedy (a boy killed at night under his beloved's window) as it was sung by the author herself, an already elderly woman, sixty years after she had composed it. Thanks to her good memory the old woman reproduced her creation faithfully; it had twenty-one quatrains. At the same time the ethnographer succeeded in recording this same song as it existed among the people sixty years after its origin. It had only seven stanzas, but its entire nature had also changed. From the original broadside song extensively depicting the actual event with an emphasis on individual details, it had become in sixty years a very economical and really firmly constructed ballad. The stanzas which vanished along the way had vanished, of course, because they were forgotten. Apparently this forgetfulness was not simply mechanical but also artistically intentional. Who, in fact, is the author here? Obviously the authorship passes from hand to hand. The perceiver can be the author after a while and vice versa.

A similar thing happens in some forms of folk visual art: for example, the painting of Easter eggs or the painting of a cottage and its rooms in Moravian Slovakia. Although every such work has its author, and although some authors are obviously more talented than others, they are not authors in our sense of the word. Here, too, the boundary between the author and a mere spectator has been completely obliterated.

Finally, there is the folk theater. Ethnographers have on more than one occasion ascertained that there is almost no dividing line between the actor and the spectator. When the actor has concluded his role, or at a moment when he is not occupied with it, he mingles with the audience; and anyone from the audience can participate in the play when he has the urge to do so. We can conclude only that although there are always two parties, the artist and the perceiver, these two parties are not separated by any precise boundary. Just as in a conversation the speaker of one moment can become the listener of the next moment, so it is in art. And if we wanted to examine the histories of various arts in more detail, we would encounter frequent cases in which the author's and the perceiver's roles have interpenetrated in many respects even during periods when they had already been

11. "Zur Volksliedfrage," *Germanisch-romanische Monatsschrift* 5 (1913): 68 f.

differentiated. Such an interpenetration was, for example, the case with Chaucer who asked his aristocratic patron to correct his poem as he saw fit (for it was supposed to reflect the views of the aristocratic milieu to which the poet himself did not belong). In the visual arts such an interpenetration is, for example, the participation of enlightened Renaissance clients who provided the artist with themes.

We have basically equated the relationship between the artist and the perceiver to the relation between the addresser and the addressee. This equation is appropriate not only for them but also for the work of art itself. An utterance can pass between a speaker and a listener because it is a *sign* which both parties understand. In making his utterance, the speaker takes into account in advance how the listener will understand him; he formulates it with regard for the listener. It is exactly the same with the work of art. Its task is likewise that the perceiver will understand it in the same way as the author. In his creation the author heeds the perceiver, takes him into account; the perceiver, on the other hand, understands the work as the author's utterance and perceives the author behind it. Therefore theories which seek to reduce the work of art to a mere expression of the author's feelings and emotions are fallacious. Suddenly our view of artistic personality is completely different from the conventional view. We no longer see before us the author bound inseparably to a work and the spectator as a mere accidentality without any essential relation to the work. Instead we recognize that the author's attitude toward the work is not fundamentally different from the spectator's. They are simply two parties between whom the work mediates; and on account of this ability to mediate, the work is a *sign,* not an expression.

From this knowledge we should draw further conclusions. Before dealing with them, however, let us turn our attention for a moment to a possible objection. It might be said that there is nevertheless a fundamental difference between the word and the work of art. A word is current coin, common property; we do not recognize any traces of a specific personality in a word taken by itself, as we find it in the dictionary, whereas we do in a work of art. Here we must agree. It goes without saying that we perceive a personality behind a work of art in contrast to a word. We have already stated that this distinguishes it from a natural object. We perceive the work of art as "made," as intentional. And intentionality requires a *subject* from whom it proceeds, who is its source; hence it presupposes a man. A subject is therefore given not only outside of the work of art but within it. The subject is a component of the work of art and not only when it claims to be directly and explicitly subjective. The presence, indeed the omnipresence, of the subject in a work of visual art is obvious: the choice of theme, its conception, the selection and distribution of colors, the brush strokes (the painter's handwriting) and even the perspective seen from a specific point at which the position of the subject is abstractly presupposed—everything in a painting points to a subject.

It is the same in the other arts. The subject is an intrinsic principle of the artistic unity of a work. He is even present where he seems to be completely invisible, for example, in a dramatic dialogue. We see characters on the stage conversing with one another, one seemingly speaking only for another's sake without any witnesses; in reality, nevertheless, every one of their sentences is addressed not to their partner but to a third person not present on stage. Only for him do the words mean what they were intended to mean. The one who has calculated the words and their effect in this way is the subject; the one to whom they are addressed is also the subject. In essence, there are not two subjects but just one. Only, the subject's carrier the first time is the one whom we call the author and the second time the one whom we call the perceiver. This assertion sounds somewhat paradoxical at first. Let us realize, however, that the author and the perceiver are often combined in one person, and it is the artist himself in whose person they are combined most often, indeed as a rule. At the moment when in the creation of his work the artist evaluates it with respect to how it will affect the perceiver, when he actually perceives the work as an artistic sign and not as a mere product for the completion of which such and such technical knowledge and means are necessary—at these moments he assumes precisely the attitude of a perceiver with respect to it. And just as it is impossible to distinguish the author from the perceiver at such moments, it is equally impossible to differentiate the former from the latter in a work of art. There is only one subject contained in the work, and this subject is provided by its intentionality. If at a given moment the one who projects intentionality into the work, or the one who perceives this intentionality from an already completed work, is in contact with the work, it is a different matter which lies outside of the work itself.

By discussing the subject of the work of art, we have prepared the way for another question which we pondered just a little while ago. If there is no essential difference in the author's and the perceiver's attitudes toward the work, and if the work of art is not an expression of its creator's personality or mental states but a sign mediating between two parties, what, then, is the status of theories which interpret the work of art from the artist's mental states, dispositions, and so forth?

Let us begin with an anecdote. Once there lived among us an actress, a great actress who took the slogan "Art equals the expression of the artist's personality" literally. She wrote to a young novice in the art of acting: "Play naturally, without affectation; see to it that you experience everything first and only then play it—not really wanting to *play* but to *live*." This actress was Hana Kvapilová. On one occasion a leading critic, Jindřich Vodák, sharply condemned Kvapilová's performance in Ibsen's *Rosmersholm*. He wrote: "After the declaration in the fourth act we imagine Rebecca to be tired by the great disappointment of her life, dejected, eagerly awaiting the liberating password of death— Mrs. Kvapilová seemingly could have undergone those entire four acts again with an even worse Rosmer." Kvapilová answered this criticism with an entire article which, however, she never published. Jaroslav Kvapil included it in *The Literary Remains of Hana Kvapilová*. In this article we find the characteristic words: "I confess that in the first two performances I wanted to attempt an absolutely *non-histrionic* presentation, to suggest *in a lifelike manner* the consequence of the fatal blow, and I see that this attempt failed completely. Who else could have perceived and appreciated my work if not the reviewer who has thought everything through so well? But the reviewer did not see this . . . . The genuine, non-histrionic excitement of the moment was engulfed by the vast dimensions of the National Theater and its stage. The spectator's perception of the scene was also engulfed for the same reason; my Rebecca's contact with the audience was completely cut off; the entire subtle plan of my work in the last act was utterly lost."[12]

12. "Rebekka Westová," in *Literární pozůstalost Hany Kvapilové,* ed. J. Kvapil (Prague, 1907), p. 217.

Here we have a very good illustration of the abyss between expression and the artistic sign. The actress, oriented toward expression, a direct and immediate expression of a mental state, forgot that the work of art is a sign designated for a spectator, mediating between an artist and a spectator. She remained a prisoner of that view of spontaneity and immediacy by which the work of art (in the given case, the character which she was creating) is connected to the author. This negligence cost her dearly. The critic, a perceptive critic moreover, did not notice that immediacy of experience with which the actress wanted to imbue her performance. On the contrary, he condemned this performance for not being based on experience. The contradiction between immediate expression and the sign was, after all, the basic tragic contradiction of Kvapilová's entire artistic creation. We find a characteristic remark about this in another place in the *Literary Remains*: "I see that my Tanya was too intimate. The last act will destroy me physically and mentally for good. Would you believe that my fevers date from that moment? And I didn't even bring her closer to the audience! I'd like to know in what I was mistaken; would you tell me?"–she asks a critic in a letter.[13]

I hope that these quotations have made completely clear the important, indeed the most important, thing for us. There is no direct connection between an artist and a work; the Romantic thesis about the spontaneity and immediacy with which an artist creates has been overcome in practice and in theory (although it was artistically fruitful at the time of its full validity), and it is more than doomed to its downfall. There are many things between the artist and his work. The time has come to devote our attention once again to the *activity*, whether conscious or subconscious, which brought about the work, the activity which, as we have seen, was absolutely clear to the Renaissance artist and the Renaissance theory of art (e.g., Leonardo) as well. It is, of course, evident that this activity on the artist's part, which makes it impossible to conceive the relationship between the work and himself as involuntary, will appear to us now as much more complex than it did to the men of the Renaissance. In particular, we shall see the multitude of factors which the artist encounters, with which he collides and with which he struggles on the way to his work.

13. "Z dvou listů divadelnímu kritikovi," *ibid.*, p. 348.

First, closest to the work, we shall see what is called the *living artistic tradition*. The creation of a work is impossible without preconditions. By the very fact that the author intends to create a work of art he enters into contact with the previous conception of the work of art and art in general and the previous artistic devices, that is, the ways in which the individual components of the work of art were and are handled. Even if he is an artist-revolutionary who has the resolve and the power to change radically the state of art which he encounters upon his arrival, he cannot do more than change it and make the perceiver feel that he has changed it; but in doing so, he introduces the previous state of art into his work and makes it a background against which the work will be perceived as new and unusual. These traditional artistic devices make it impossible in advance for the work to become an immediate expression. Insofar as the artist's mental state enters the work at all, it has already been objectified by the previous situation in art, been severed from its source and been transformed into a sign.

In order to clarify what we mean, let us once again turn to Hana Kvapilová's case. We have seen that she was striving to present to the spectator—as a work of art—as exact an expression of her mental state as possible. We have seen that she sometimes foundered in this attempt, but there is no doubt that she actually succeeded many more times. According to the actress' subjective feeling, she was actually living on the stage at such moments. But did the audience perceive her performance in this way? We must realize what the state of the art of acting was before the advent of the generation of dramatic Realism to which Kvapilová belonged. Acting had been based upon conventions of facial expressions and declamation. "I love you" was always spoken with a particular customary gesture and "I hate you" with a different, but equally customary, gesture, and so forth. This gesture was at the disposal of every actor and every character without exception at the proper moment. As a result, one could not, of course, speak about the unity of character; this character had nothing which could individualize it or distinguish it from others. Then the young Realist actors, among them Kvapilová, reversed the situation. They emphasized the unity of the character, neglected up to then, and subordinated the gesture to this unity. They deprived the gesture of its independence and thereby of its conventionality. The actor's facial expressions and gestures could no longer spasmodically express in distinct contours at one time "I love you" and at another time "I hate you"; instead they merged into a continuous series resembling the "natural," non-artificial and non-artistic gesture and facial expression of everyday life. The audience immediately sensed this contrast between the old and new styles of acting. In this confrontation the new acting was also experienced as a sign, as a result of artistic intention, not as a spontaneous expression. At the moment when the confrontation of histrionic Realism with the older style of acting vanished from the audience's consciousness, the situation became even more conclusive for us; Realist acting, which had once been felt to be the opposite of conventionality, became a convention itself—in the hands of epigones— and thus revealed its semioticity quite distinctly. There is therefore no real immediate expression in art, for artistic intention (often even conscious artistic will) always stands between the artist and the work of art.

But there are yet other factors which stand between the artist and the work of art. First, on the part of the artist himself there are various extra-artistic motives for his creation, whether or not he is aware of them. There are, for example, economic motives which it has usually been deemed appropriate to overlook; but the Renaissance artist, for instance, very calmly acknowledged them; and they willy-nilly influence creation even in its highest forms. Furthermore, there are motives stemming from ambition, social considerations, and so forth. These too make it impossible for the artist's work to be related directly to his personality. What if, for example, one of these considerations causes the artist to conceal his actual mental state or to feign another? All of this deserves consideration.

Finally, there are all the external influences, the point of intersection of which is the artist's personality, whether they come from society or other spheres of culture. If we analyzed them in detail, the illusion to which Taine and his followers succumbed could easily come about. There is nothing but these influences; the artist's personality does not exist at all. But we would not want to go so far. On the contrary, if we assert that the path from the artist's personality to the work is not direct and immediate, especially not spontaneous, we are far from denying the artist's personality; rather we would prefer to emphasize it. Social, general

cultural, and artistic influences affect the personality only inso-
much and in such a manner as the personality itself (whether
consciously or subconsciously) allows. Personality is not a sum of
influences but their equilibrium—their subordination and superordination to one another, and it is for this reason that the artist's
personality proves to be an initiative force just as any other
personality.

In brief, we think that personality is by no means to be dissolved
into external influences like salt in water. And this also applies to
personality in art. If there is something which has been overcome
and something which requires correction, it is simply the view that
the glory and significance of the artistic personality consists in the
fact that it expresses itself through the work fully and, in fact,
passively. If, as we hope, the future development of art and the
artist's situation liberates the artist from something, what will disappear may be only the chore of looking after his individuality
and individualness in the same way as a gardener looks after a
hothouse flower or as a tenor takes care of his voice.

Film, Theater, and Visual Arts

11

An Attempt at a Structural Analysis
of a Dramatic Figure

Today the conception of a work of art as a structure, that is, a system of components aesthetically deautomatized and organized into a complex hierarchy, which is unified by the prevalence of one component over the others, is accepted in the theory of several arts. It is clear to theoreticians and historians of music and the visual arts that in the analysis of a certain work, or even in the history of a given art, we cannot either substitute the psychology of the artist's personality for a structural analysis or confuse the development of a given art with the history of culture or with that of ideology alone. Much of this is clear in the theory of literature as well, though certainly not everywhere nor for everyone. Nevertheless, it is quite risky to use the method of structural analysis for the art of acting, especially if it concerns a film actor who uses his real name for his performances and, moreover, even looks the same in all of his roles. The theoretician who tries to separate the appearance from the man and to study the structural organization of the dramatic figure, regardless of the actor's psyche and ethos, is in danger of being considered a scandalous cynic who denies the artist his human value. Permit him, therefore, for the sake of his defense and a lucid explanation to appeal to the recent photo-montage in the *Prager Presse* which juxtaposed a grey-haired man with an intelligent physiognomy and the simple-minded face of a black-haired man in a derby hat. . . . Despite its disadvantages a structural analysis of the dramatic figure has a certain small advantage: the equality of even quite different aesthetic canons is generally admitted in the dramatic arts more than in the other arts. The Hamlets of Kvapil and Hilar, Vojan and Kohout, are evaluated in a historical perspective without depreciating one another. Perhaps even this study, therefore, will not be criticized for lacking an evaluative orientation.

"Pokus o strukturní rozbor hereckého zjevu: Chaplin ve Světlech velkoměsta," *Literární noviny* 5, no. 10 (1931).

We must first draw attention to the fact that the structure of the dramatic figure is merely a partial structure which acquires unambiguity only in the total structure of the dramatic work. Here it appears in multiple relations, for example, the actor and the stage space, the actor and the dramatic text, the actor and the other actors. We shall consider only one of these relations: the hierarchy of characters in the dramatic work. This hierarchy differs according to period and milieu and, in part, in relation to the dramatic text. Sometimes actors create a structurally bound whole in which no one has a dominant position and no one is the focal point of all the relations among the characters of the work. Sometimes one character (or several) becomes a focal point, dominating the others who seem to be there only to provide a background or retinue for the dominant figure (or figures). Sometimes all the characters appear to be equal and to lack structural relations. Their relationship is merely ornamentally compositional. In other words, the tasks and rights of theatrical directing are evaluated differently in different periods and different milieux. Chaplin's case obviously belongs in the second category. Chaplin is an axis around which the other characters gather, for which they are there. They emerge from the shadows only insofar as they are necessary for the dominant character. This assertion will be developed and proven only later.

Let us now turn our attention to the internal structure of the dramatic figure itself. The components of this structure are many and varied; nevertheless, we can arrange them in three distinct groups. First, there is the set of vocal components. It is quite complex (the pitch of the voice and its melodic undulation, the intensity and tone of the voice, tempo, etc.), but in the given case this group has no importance for us. Chaplin's films are "pantomimes" (Chaplin uses this term himself to distinguish his latest movie from the sound-track film). Later we shall explain why his movies have to be silent. The second group cannot be identified otherwise than by the triple designation: facial expressions, gestures, poses. These are three different components both from an objective and a structural standpoint. They can parallel one another, but they can also diverge so that their interrelation is felt to be an interference (an effective comic means). Moreover, one of them can subordinate the others to itself or, conversely, all of them can be in equilibrium. What is common to all three of these components, however, is the fact that they are felt to be expressive, to be an expression of the character's mental state, especially his emotions. This property binds them into a unified group. The third group is composed of those movements of the body by which the actor's relation to the stage space is expressed and carried.[1] Frequently the components of this group cannot be objectively distinguished from those of the preceding group (e.g., the actor's walk can simultaneously be a gesture, an expression of a mental state, and can cause a change in his relation to the stage space); but functionally, as we have suggested, they are quite clearly distinct from the previous group and conjoin into an independent category.

We certainly do not have to provide extensive proof to propound the thesis that the dominant position in Chaplin belongs to the components of the second group. For the sake of expediency we shall simply call them gestures and thus extend this term to facial expressions and poses without undue distortion. As we have already said, the first group (vocal components) is completely suppressed in Chaplin, while the third group (movements) occupies a distinctly subordinate position. Even though movements which change the actor's relation to space occur, they are charged to the utmost with the function of gestures (Chaplin's walk sensitively reflects every change in his mental state). Hence the dominant position falls to gestures (expressive elements), constituting an uninterrupted series full of interferences and unexpected *pointes* which carries the entire dynamics not only of Chaplin's performance but also of the whole film. Chaplin's gestures are not subordinated to any other component; on the contrary, they subordinate all the other components. In this way Chaplin's acting distinctly differs from the usual cases. Even if an actor differentiates and emphasizes gestures, they usually serve a word, a movement, or the plot. They are a passive series whose peripety is motivated by other series.

But for Chaplin, the word which is most capable of influencing

---

1. Even in Chaplin, though he is a typical film actor, we can speak about the stage in the theatrical sense, that is, a static stage, because here the camera is almost passive. Even if it moves, it has only an auxiliary role—for the purpose of close-ups. To prove and elucidate this assertion let us recall the active role of the camera in Russian films where the changeability of standpoints and perspectives plays the dominant role in the structure of the work, whereas the dramatic figure is structurally subordinated.

gestures must be completely suppressed if the gestures are to be the dominant component. In a Chaplin film every distinct word would be a blotch: it would turn the hierarchy of components upside down. For this reason neither Chaplin himself nor the other characters speak. Typical in this respect is the introductory scene of *City Lights*, the unveiling of a monument, in which distinct words are replaced by sounds having only intonation and tone in common with words. As far as movements in the stage space are concerned, we have said that they are charged with the function of gestures; as a matter of fact, they are gestures. Moreover, Chaplin is a dramatic figure who does not move too much (his immobility is even stressed by an organic defect in his feet).

And now for the plot. The plot lacks any dynamism of its own: it is merely a series of events linked by a weak thread. Its function is to be the substratum of the dynamic sequence of gestures. The divisions between individual events serve only to provide pauses in the sequence of gestures and to render it coherent through this articulation. Even the incompleteness of the plot is an expression of its atomization. Chaplin's film does not end in a plot conclusion but in a gesture-*pointe,* indeed one of Chaplin's gestures (a look and a smile). This holds only for the European version of the film, but it is characteristic that such a way of concluding the movie is possible.

If we posit the sequence of gestures as the dominant component of Chaplin's dramatic figure, we must now define the character of this line. In a negative sense we can say that none of the three elements (facial expressions, gestures, poses) prevails over the others but that they assert themselves equally. A positive definition of the very essence of this sequence is: Its dynamics is carried by the interference (whether simultaneous or successive) of two types of gestures: gesture-signs and gesture-expressions. Here we must engage in a brief discussion of the function of gestures in general. We have already said that this function is essentially expressive in *all* gestures. But this expressiveness has its nuances. It can be immediate and individual; yet it can also acquire supra-individual validity. In such a case the gesture becomes a conventional sign, universally comprehensible (either in general or in a certain milieu). This is true, for example, of ritual gestures (a typical case: the gestures of a religious cult) or especially social gestures. Social gestures are signs which conventionally—like words—signal certain

emotions or mental states, for instance, sincere emotional participation, willingness, or respect. But there is no guarantee that the
mental state of the person who uses the gesture corresponds to the
mood of which the gesture is a sign. That is why all the Alcestes of
the world are so angry at the insincerity of social conventions. The
individual expressiveness ("sincerity") of a social gesture can be
reliably recognized only if it is involuntarily accompanied by some
nuance which alters its conventional course. It can happen that the
particular emotion coincides with the mental state of which the
gesture is the sign. In such a case the gesture-sign will be exag-
gerated beyond the conventional degree of its intensity (too deep
a bow or too broad a smile). But even the opposite can occur: The
particular mental state is different from the mood which is supposed to be feigned by the gesture-sign. In that case there will
occur an interference, either *successive,* that is, such that the
coordination of the series of gestures developing in time will be
disturbed (the sudden invasion of an individually expressive, involuntary gesture into the series of gesture-signs), or *simultaneous,*
that is, such that the gesture-sign provided, for example, by a
facial expression will at the same time be negated by a contradictory gesticulation of the hand based on individual expression or
vice versa.

Chaplin's case is typical of the interference of social gesture-
signs with individually expressive gestures. Everything in Chaplin's
acting is aimed at heightening and sharpening this interference,
even his special appearance: formal attire which is ragged, gloves
without fingers but a cane and a black derby. In particular, however, the social paradox of Chaplin contained in the very theme of
the beggar with social aspirations serves to sharpen the interference
of gestures. This provides the basis of the interference. The integrating emotional feature of the social gestures is the feeling of
self-assurance and superiority, whereas the expressive gestures of
Chaplin-the-beggar revolve around the emotional complex of
inferiority. These two planes of gestures interweave through the
entire performance in constant catachreses. To characterize this
interweaving in detail would mean providing an endless enumeration of the verbal paraphrases of the individual moments of the
performance. This would be monotonous and useless. Much more
interesting is the fact that the duality of the plane of gestures is
also reflected in the distribution of the supporting characters in

Chaplin's performance. There are two supporting characters: the blind flower girl and the drunk millionaire. All the others are demoted to the level of extras, either partially (the old woman) or completely (all the others). Each of the two supporting characters is modified so that he can perceive only one plane, one of the interfering series of Chaplin's gestures. Such a one-sided perception is motivated by blindness in the girl, by intoxication in the millionaire.

The girl perceives only the social gesture-signs. The deformed image which she gets of Chaplin is furnished toward the end of the film—through a remarkable process of realization. A man, a nondescript social type, comes to the now-seeing girl's shop to buy some flowers. His departure is accompanied by the caption: "I thought that it was *him*." All the scenes in which Chaplin meets the girl—they are always alone so that the presence of a third, seeing person will not shatter the girl's illusion—are founded upon the polar oscillation between the two planes of Chaplin's gestures: social and individually expressive gestures. Whenever Chaplin draws close to the girl in these scenes, the social gestures gain the upper hand, but as soon as he takes a few steps away from her, the expressive gestures suddenly prevail in each instance. This is especially evident in the scene in which Chaplin brings gifts to the girl and moves back and forth from the table where the bag of presents is lying to the chair on which the girl is sitting. Here the sudden changes in gestures, the transition from plane to plane, function almost like the *pointes* of epigrams. In this connection we shall also understand why Chaplin's film cannot have the usual "happy ending." A happy ending would entail the complete negation of the dramatic contradiction between the two levels of gestures upon which the film is based rather than upon its resolution. If concluded by the beggar's marrying the girl, the film would appear negligible in retrospect, because its dramatic contradiction would be impaired.

Now to the relationship between the beggar and the millionaire. The millionaire, as we have said, also has access to only one of the two interfering series of gestures, the individually expressive ones. He must, of course, be drunk for this deformation of vision to be operative. As soon as he becomes sober, he sees, as all the other people do, the comical interference of the two series, and he behaves toward Chaplin with the same disdain as all the others. But whereas the girl's deformation of perception (the ability to see only one series of gestures) is permanent, and the solution occurs only at the very end of the film, the millionaire's state of deformed vision alternates with states of normal vision. This, of course, provides the hierarchy of the two supporting characters. The girl comes more to the fore, because the permanent deformation of perception provides a broader and stronger basis for the interference of the two planes of gestures than does the millionaire's intermittent intoxication. The millionaire is, however, necessary as the girl's opposite. From the first meeting with Chaplin when by means of his expressive gestures the beggar sings a pathetic hymn to the beauty of life ("And tomorrow the sun will rise again") in front of the millionaire, their relationship is full of outpourings of friendship, from one embrace to another. And thus we have quite imperceptibly proceeded from the structural analysis of a dramatic figure to the structure of the entire film. This is another proof of the extent to which the interference of the two levels of gestures is the axis of Chaplin's film.

Let us stop here, for we have probably said everything of substance. In conclusion, though, permit us to make a few evaluative comments. What causes the spectator's awe of Chaplin's figure is the immense span between the intensity of the effect which he achieves and the simplicity of his devices. He takes as the dominant of his structure a component that usually (in film) occupies a secondary position: gestures in the broad sense of the term (facial expressions, gestures proper, poses). And to this fragile dominant of limited capacity he manages to subordinate not only the structure of his own dramatic figure but even that of the entire film. This presupposes an almost unbelievable economy in all the other components. If any of them became only a little more emphatic, called only a little more attention to itself, the entire structure would collapse. The structure of Chaplin's acting resembles a three-dimensional figure which rests on the sharpest of its edges but nevertheless is in perfect equilibrium. Hence the illusion of immateriality: the pure lyrics of gestures freed from dependence upon a corporal substratum.

12

A Note on the Aesthetics of Film

I

It is no longer necessary, as it was only a few years ago, to begin a study of the aesthetics of film with the argument that film is an art. Nevertheless, the question of the relation between aesthetics and film has not yet lost its immediacy, for the development of this young art is still disturbed by changes in its technical ("mechanical") basis. Therefore, more than traditional arts, film needs a norm both in a positive sense (something to observe) and in a negative sense (something to violate). Film artists are at a disadvantage because they face possibilities in their work which are too broad and undiversified. Arts with a long tradition always have at hand a whole series of devices which have gained a definite, stabilized form and conventional meanings through a lengthy development. For example, comparative studies of *plots* show that there are in fact no new themes in literature: the development of almost any theme can be traced back thousands of years. In *The Theory of Prose* Šklovskij cites the example of Maupassant's story "Le Retour" which is based on an adaptation of the very old theme of "a man at the wedding of his own wife" and counts on the reader knowing this theme from elsewhere. The same holds true for poetry, for example with metrical schemes. Every poetry has a certain repertoire of traditional verse schemes which through long years of use have acquired a fixed rhythmical (not only metrical) organization and semantic coloration under the influence of the genres in which they have been used. We can also characterize the poetic genres themselves as mere canonized sets of particular devices. This does not, however, mean that the artist cannot alter traditional norms and conventions; on the contrary, they are frequently violated (the contemporary theory of genres is based on the knowledge that the development of genres results from the constant violation of generic norms), and this violation is experienced as an intentional artistic device.

"K estetice filmu," *Listy pro umění a kritiku* 1 (1933).

What seems to be a limitation is thus, in essence, an enrichment of artistic possibilities, and until recently film had almost no really distinct norms and conventions; even now there are only a few. Film artists are therefore seeking norms. The word "norm," however, brings to mind aesthetics, which used to be, and sometimes even now is, considered a normative discipline. But modern aesthetics, which has given up the metaphysical notion of beauty in any form and which views artistic structure as a developmental fact, should not be expected to prescribe what should be. A norm can only be the product of the development of art itself, a petrified impression of developmental activity. If aesthetics cannot be the logic of art, judging its correctness and incorrectness, it can nevertheless be something else: the epistemology of art. That is to say, every art has certain basic possibilities provided by the character of its material and the way in which the given art masters it. These possibilities imply at the same time a limitation, not a normative one in the sense, for example, of Lessing and Semper who presumed that art does not have the right to overstep its boundaries, but a factual limitation, in that a particular art does not cease to be itself even if it trespasses upon the territory of another art. *Si duo faciunt idem, non est idem;* we therefore understand speeded-up motion in film as a deformation of temporal duration, whereas in theater we would experience the acceleration of the actor's gestures as a deformation of his personality, for dramatic time and film time are epistemologically different.

The transgression of boundaries is a very frequent phenomenon in the history of art. For example, literary Symbolism has often characterized itself as the *music* of the word; Surrealist painting working with poetic tropes (with "transfer" of meaning) claims for itself the name of *poetry*. After all, this is just a return visit of the kind poetry made to painting in the period of so-called *descriptive* poetry (eighteenth century) and during the period of Parnassianism (nineteenth century). The developmental significance of such transgressions of boundaries lies in the fact that art learns to experience its devices in a new way and see its material from an unusual perspective. At the same time, however, the given art remains itself, does not merge with the contiguous art, but attains different effects through the same device or attains the same effect through different devices. If, however, the approximation of another art is to be incorporated into the developmental order of the art which is striving for this approximation, one condition must be fulfilled: the developmental order and tradition must already exist. The basic precondition for this is certainty in handling the material (which does not mean a blind subordination to the material).

Film has already been in close contact with several arts: drama, narrative literature, painting, and music. However, this was in the days when film had not yet mastered its material, and therefore contact was more a matter of seeking support than a matter of regular development. The effort to master the material is connected with the tendency toward the purely filmic. This is the beginning of regular development. New approximations to other arts will surely come with time, but only as developmental stages. The epistemological inquiry into the conditions provided by the material of film parallels the effort at pure film. This is the task of the aesthetics of film. It should not determine the norm but should reinforce the intentionality of this development by exposing its latent preconditions. Our study is an outline of a particular chapter in the epistemology of film; we shall be concerned with the epistemology of film space.

II

Film space used to be, especially in the beginning, confused with theatrical space. This confusion does not, however, correspond to reality, even if the camera simply photographs the events on a theatrical stage without changing its position as the nature of theatrical space requires.[1] That is to say, theatrical space is three-dimensional, and three-dimensional people move within it. This does not obtain in film, which has the possibility of movement, but movement projected onto a two-dimensional plane and into illusory space. Also, as has already been stated many times, the actor's attitude toward space is quite different in film than in theater. The theatrical actor is a living and integral personality clearly distinguished from the inanimate surroundings (the stage and its contents), whereas the consecutive images of the actor (in some cases only partial ones) on the screen are mere components of the total projected picture, just as in painting, for example.

---

1. O. Zich, *Estetika dramatického umění* [The aesthetics of dramatic art] (Prague, 1931).

Russian theoreticians of film have therefore coined for the film actor the term "naturščik," that is, model, which does justice to his similarity with the model in painting.[2]

Now what about the relationship between film space and illusory space? It is clear that pictorial space really does exist in film, and with all the means of painterly illusoriness (if we disregard the more profound basic differences between perspective as a device in painting and perspective in photography). This illusoriness can be intensified greatly by certain means, but these means are also available to painting. One of them is that the usual conception of depth in illusory pictorial space is reversed: the viewer's attention which is usually directed toward the background is instead drawn outward from the picture. This device was often used in Baroque painting. The direction of a gesture (the person standing in the foreground of the picture aims a revolver at the audience) or the direction of movement (a train goes off as if at right angles to the pictorial plane) accomplishes this in film. Another way of intensifying spatial illusion is to look from underneath or above, for example to look from a high story into a deep courtyard. In such cases the illusion is strengthened by the change in the position of the axis of the eye. In reality the position is horizontal (for the perceiver viewing the picture); however, the position presupposed by the picture is almost vertical. Film has both of these means in common with painting.

Another possibility is the following. During filming the camera is mounted on a moving vehicle, and the objective is aimed forward. The movement then takes place in a street or an alley, in other words along a path that is surrounded on both sides by a continuous series of objects. We do not see the vehicle in the picture; we see only the street (the path) leading into the background of the picture but quickly running in the opposite direction, outward from the picture. Because of the motion it might seem that this is a matter of a specifically filmic device, but in fact it is only a modification of the aforementioned case (the reversal of the conception of spatial depth) which in some of its variants is totally accessible to painting.

The basis for film space is thus illusory pictorial space. But, in

2. There are, however, nuances in filmic practice; the actor's individuality can be emphasized in film, or, on the other hand, it can be suppressed. Compare the differences between Chaplin's film and Russian films.

addition, the art of film has at its disposal another form of space unavailable to other arts. This is the space provided by the technique of the shot. When there is a change from one shot to another, whether it occurs smoothly or abruptly, the focusing of the objective or the placement of the entire camera in space is, obviously, always changed. And this spatial shift is reflected in the viewer's consciousness through a peculiar feeling which has already been described many times as the illusory displacement of the viewer himself. René Clair explains: "The viewer who looks at a remote automobile race is suddenly thrown under the huge wheels of one of the cars; he observes the speedometer; he takes the steering wheel into his hands. He becomes the actor and sees how the trees falling down around the curves are swallowed up by his vision."[3] This presentation of space from "inside" is a specifically filmic device; only the discovery of the shot permitted film to cease being an animated picture.

The technique of the shot, moreover, has had a reverse influence upon the technique of photography itself. On the one hand, it has called attention to the interesting possibilities of the view from underneath and above obtained by circling the object from all sides; on the other hand, and this is more important, the shot has created the technique of the close-up. The pictorial effectiveness of the close-up consists in the unusual bringing close of an object (Epstein says about this: "I was turning my head, and I saw on the right side a gesture reduced to its mere square root, but on the left side this gesture had already been magnified to the eighth power."); the spatial effectiveness of the close-up is achieved by the impression of the incompleteness of the picture which appears to us as a slice of three-dimensional space felt to exist in front of the picture and around its sides. Let us imagine, for example, a hand in a close-up. Where is the person to whom this hand belongs? In the space outside the picture. Or let us assume a picture of a revolver lying on a table. It arouses the expectation that at any time a hand will appear and pick up the revolver, and this hand will emerge from the space lying outside the picture where we place its anticipated existence. Here is yet another example. Two people are fighting and rolling on the floor; a knife is lying near them. The scene is presented in such a way that we alternately see

3. "Le Rythme," *Les Cahiers du mois* (1925).

the fighting pair and the knife in close-ups. Every time that the
knife appears, there is suspense. When will the hand that will grab
it finally appear? When the hand finally appears in a close-up, there
is new suspense. Which one of the pair has taken hold of the knife?
Only where we have an intense awareness of the space outside the
picture may we speak about a dynamic close-up. Otherwise it
would be a matter of a static slice of a normal visual field. We
must, of course, remind ourselves that the awareness of its "pic-
torialness" does not disappear during the close-up; we do not therefore transfer the size of the close-up into extrapictorial space, and
the magnified hand is not the hand of a giant for us.

In shots, film space is presented successively through a series of
pictures; we feel it in passing from one picture to another. Sound-
track film has, however, introduced the additional possibility of
the simultaneous presence of film space. Let us imagine a situation
quite common in film. We see a picture, and at the same time we
hear a sound whose source we must place somewhere outside the
picture rather than inside it. For example, we see a person's face
and hear speech which is not uttered by the person in the picture;
or we see the legs of dancing people and simultaneously hear their
words; or we see a street from a moving vehicle which itself
remains hidden, and at the same time we hear the hoofbeats of
horses drawing a carriage; and so on. Through this arises an awareness of the space "between" the picture and the sound.

Now let us pose the question of the essence of this specifically
filmic space and its relation to pictorial space. We have named
three means through which filmic space can be achieved: a change
in shot, the close-up, and the extrapictorial localization of sound.
We shall proceed from the one which is fundamental among them,
the one without which film space would not exist at all, the shot.
Let us imagine any scene taking place in a particular space (like a
room). By no means does this space have to be presented to us in
a full shot; it can be presented by means of hints alone, by means
of a sequence of partial shots. Even then we shall experience its
unity; in other words, we shall perceive the individual pictorial
(illusory) spaces shown consecutively on the plane of the screen
as pictures of the separate sections of a unified three-dimensional
space. How will this total unity of space be presented to us? In
order to answer this question we must remind ourselves of the
sentence as a semantic whole in language. The sentence is com-

posed of words, none of which contains its total meaning. That
meaning is fully known to us only when we listen to the entire
sentence. Nevertheless, at the very moment that we hear the first
word we evaluate it in accordance with the potential meaning of
the sentence, a component of which it will be. The sense or meaning of the whole sentence is not therefore contained in any of its
words but exists potentially in the speaker's and the listener's consciousness in every word from first to last. At the same time we
can observe the successive unfolding of the meaning from the beginning of the sentence to its end. All of this can also be said about
film space. It is not fully provided by any of the pictures, but each
of the pictures is accompanied by an awareness of the unity of the
total space, and the image of this space gains definition with the
progression of the sequence of pictures. Thus we may presuppose
that specifically filmic space, which is neither a real nor an illusory
one, is space-meaning. Illusory spatial segments presented in consecutive pictures are partial signs of this space-meaning, the entirety
of which "signifies" the total space.

We can, after all, deduce the semantic nature of film space from
a concrete example. In a study on the poetics of film[4] Tynjanov
cites this pair of shots: (1) a meadow where a pig is running
around; (2) the same meadow, trampled down, but now without
the pig, where a man is walking. Here Tynjanov sees an example
of filmic simile: man–pig. But if we imagine these two scenes in
one shot (by means of which the interference of specifically filmic
space would be eliminated), we discover that the awareness of the
semantic link between the two phenomena yields to an awareness
of the mere temporal successiveness of the two scenes. Film space
thus operates as a semantic factor only through a change in shot.
Furthermore, the semantic energy of the close-up, one of the
means of creating filmic space, is well known. Epstein says:
"Another power of cinematography is its animism. An unanimated
object, for example, a revolver, is merely a prop in the theater. In
film, however, it has the possibility of being magnified. That
Browning which a hand slowly pulls from a half-open drawer . . .
suddenly becomes alive. It becomes a symbol of a thousand
possibilities." This polysemic quality of the close-up is facilitated

4. "Ob osnovax kino" [On the principles of film], in *Poètika kino* [The poetics
of film], ed. B. Èjxenbaum (Moscow, 1927), p. 67.

by the very fact that the space into which the revolver will be aimed and into which it will disgorge its bullet is at the moment of the projection of this close-up merely an intuitive space-meaning, concealing just these "thousand possibilities."

Because of its semantic character, film space is much closer to space in literature than to theatrical space. In literature, too, space is meaning. What else could it be if it is rendered by the word? Many narrative sentences can be transcribed into filmic space without a change in their structure. Let us take this one as an example: "They embrace slowly, then abruptly break apart, savagely snatch up their knives and throw themselves forward, weapons raised." This is a sentence which, even with its grammatical present tense, could serve as an expression of a tense plot-moment in a novel; in reality, however, it is excerpted from Delluc's screenplay *Fête espagnole* and is broken down into shots as follows:

> shot 175—That's it. They embrace slowly, then abruptly break apart, savagely snatch up
> shot 176—their knives
> shot 177—and throw themselves forward, weapons raised . . . .[5]

We must also remember that the narrative has at its disposal, and has had for a long time, some means of presenting space similar to those of film, especially the close-up and the panorama (a smooth transition from shot to shot). As proof let me cite a few traditional stylistic clichés: "I lowered my gaze toward . . . ," "his eyes were riveted upon . . ."—close-ups; "X. looked around the room: On the right side of the door stood an étagère, next to it a closet . . ." —panorama; "here two people were standing in animated conversation, over there a whole group of people who . . . , elsewhere a small crowd was hurrying somewhere . . ."—sudden change in shot.

The resemblance between film and illustration is instructive for the closeness of the filmic and the literary treatment of space. I shall mention only one instance. Certain movements in the art of illustration which specialize in marginalia to the text frequently work with the close-up. There is, for example, Čech's illustrator, Oliva; when Čech's text speaks about Mr. Brouček lighting one match after another, there is a marginal illustration next to the type—a half-open box from which a few matches have fallen out.

5. L. Delluc, *Drames de cinéma* (Paris, 1923), p. 14.

This is a close-up; however, it is not quite the same as in film, because the standard frame is not maintained; that is, the real film close-up takes in the same expanse of screen as, for example, the full shot. Therefore we could speak about the equivalence of illustration and film (except for movement) only if all the illustrations in a given work, close-ups as well as full shots, took up whole pages. However, Oliva consistently avoids any scale in his illustrations, letting the pictures without a frame diffuse themselves in projections over the plane of the pages. Therefore his technique is precisely a reflection of literary space, which is meaning to the extent that it does not have scope; this is because the sign of literary space is the word, whereas the sign of film space is the shot. Film space thus has scope, at least in its signs (proper filmic space-meaning does not, of course, have scope, as we saw when we dealt with the close-up). A higher degree of sheer semantic quality thus distinguishes literary from filmic space, despite their considerable similarities. This has a bearing upon the fact that we can abstract ourselves from space in literature, whereas space is always inevitably present in film. Moreover, literary space has all the summarizing power of the word. Hence the impossibility of a mechanical transposition of a literary description into film. Bofa has vividly illustrated this fact: "The poet wrote that a cab galloped by. The director will show it to us; it is an authentic cab, decked with a coachman in a white hat, whose horse is galloping during a few meters of film. There is no possibility left for you to imagine it; this is the premium for the viewer's laziness."

So far we have spoken as if the total space provided gradually by the context were unique and unchangeable in every film. We must also take into account, however, the fact that space can change in the course of the same film; it can even do so several times. Considering the semantic character of this space, such a change involves a transition from one semantic context to another. A change in scene is something quite different from the transition from shot to shot in the same space. Even if there is a large span between shots, this transition is not an interruption of the continuous succession, whereas a change in scene (a change in the total space) constitutes such an interruption. We must therefore devote our attention to this.

These changes in scene can occur in several ways: by means of a jump, by means of a gradual shift, or by means of bridging. In the first case (a jump), the last shot of the preceding scene and the first one following it are simply juxtaposed. This is a considerable interruption of the spatial context, the extreme boundary of complete disorientation. It is natural that this kind of transition is charged with meaning (is semanticized); for example, it can mean a condensed summation of the action. In the second case (a shift) a sudden fade-out and fade-in are inserted between the two scenes, or the initial shot of the second scene is dissolved into the last shot of the first scene. Each of these devices has its specific meanings. The fade-out can signify, for example, the temporal distancing of scenes following one another; the dissolve, for example, a dream, a vision, a memory; in both cases, of course, many other meanings are possible. In the third case (bridging), the transition is accomplished through a purely semantic process, for instance a filmic metaphor (a motion occurring in one scene is repeated with a different meaning in the following one: we see boys tossing up their leader whom they like—then a change in scene—and a quite analogous motion which is, however, shoveling up broken soil), or anacoluthon ("a shift in construction": the policeman's gesture meaning "the way is clear"—then a change in scene—we see how the iron grating of a shop flies up as if at the sign given by the policeman).

We must add that sound-track film has mulitplied the possibilities of transition. On the one hand, it has made possible new variations in transition by bridging (a sound occurring in one scene is repeated in another with a different meaning); on the other, it has provided the possibility of linking by means of speech (in one scene it is hinted that people will go to the theater; then in the following scene, presented without optical transition, we see a theatrical hall). Each of the methods of transition that we have enumerated has its specific character which in individual cases is exploited according to the structure of the given film. In general we can say only that the more that film is reaching its very essence, the more the gradual shift or bridging is becoming its basic mode of transition. The coming of sound-track film in particular has begun a new stage. As long as film worked with captions, the transition between them was always possible with a simple jump, and thus it was not felt as something exceptional, even in places where there were no captions. Since captions have disappeared, the feeling of the continuity of space has become increasingly stronger. And thus even the transition from scene to scene is not exempt from the general character of filmic space: its successive unfolding is oriented toward continuity.

The successiveness of film space, whether it concerns a change in shot or a change in scene, does not, of course, entail an automatically smooth flow; on the contrary, the tension arising from these changes creates the dynamics of this unfolding of space. It is precisely at these places in a film that the viewer must make a certain effort to understand the spatially semantic relation between contiguous pictures. The degree of this tension varies, but it can be heightened to such an intensity that it alone suffices to carry the dynamics of the whole film, especially if frequent transitions from scene to scene are used, since they are more dynamic and conspicuous than transitions between shots. As an example of a film constructed solely upon this specifically filmic tension, we mention Vertov's *Čelovek s kinoapparatom* [The man with a movie camera] in which the theme is almost entirely suppressed and can be expressed by a single caption: a day in the city streets.

This case is, of course, exceptional. Usually a film has a plot-theme. If we ask about the essence of this theme, we shall discover that a specific meaning is involved here, just as in the case of filmic space. Despite the fact that the "models" of film are concrete people and objectively real things (the actors and the scenery), the plot itself is nevertheless provided by someone (the author of the screenplay) and is constructed during the shooting and montage (by the director) so that the viewers will understand it, will conceive it in a specific way. These circumstances render the plot meaning. The similarity between filmic plot and filmic space-meaning goes even further, however. Filmic plot (as well as narrative plot) is a successively realized meaning: in other words, plot is provided not only by the quality of motifs but also by their succession; if the succession of motifs is changed, the plot changes too. As evidence let me quote from the daily newspaper:

> It happened some time ago in Sweden. At that time the censor did not pass . . . the Russian movie *Bronenosec Potemkin* [The battleship Potemkin]. As is well known, the film begins with a scene depicting the maltreatment of sailors, after which the dissidents are to be shot; but a revolt and

uprising take place on the ship. There is also fighting in the
city. Odessa in the year 1905! A fleet of battleships appears,
but lets the mutineers sail away. This plot was too revolutionary for the censor. The company distributing the film
presented it to the censor once more. There were no changes
in the pictures and captions. The film was simply "recut" and
the scenes scrambled. The result: the film edited in this way
begins with the middle part. With the mutiny! (thus after the
scene of the interrupted execution). Odessa 1905! The Russian fleet, with which the original version ends, appears, but
the first part of the film follows immediately thereafter. Now
after the mutiny the sailors stand in a row; they are bound and
put in front of the muzzles of guns. The film ends!

If, however, the plot is a meaning and moreover a successively
realized meaning, then in a film having a plot sequence there are
two successive semantic series which run simultaneously, but do
not parallel one another, through the whole film: space and plot.
Their interrelation is felt, whether or not the director takes them
into account. If this relationship is treated as a definite value, its
artistic exploitation is guided in every concrete case by the structure of the given film. In general, we can say only this: the plot
is felt to be the basic semantic series, whereas successively realized
space appears as a differentiating factor. This is because space is,
after all, predetermined by plot. We do not, however, mean to
imply that this hierarchy could not be reversed by subordinating
plot to space but only that its reversal is felt as an intentional
deformation. The absolute realization of such a reversal is quite
possible in film because its specific character is not violated by
this; rather it is better defined by it. Our proof could be *The Man
with a Movie Camera* mentioned above. The opposite extreme is
the suppression of successive space in favor of plot; however, to
achieve this completely would mean the nullification of specifically filmic space by making the camera immobile during shooting.
What would remain would be only pictorial space as a shadow of
real space in which the plot took place during shooting. We could
therefore find cases of such a radical "defilmization" of film in the
initial stage of development of this art.

Between these two extremes there is a wide range of possibilities.
The general rules for the actual selection cannot, of course, be

found theoretically because selection is determined not only by the character of the chosen plot but also by the director's intention. To avoid the risk of dogmatism we can say only that the more weakly the plot is connected through motivation (that is, the more it works with mere temporal and causal continuity), the more easily the dynamics of space can assert itself in the plot. Obviously, this does not mean that we could not attempt to link motivation with the strong dynamism of space. After all, the dynamism of space in film is not a simple concept, as we have seen: shots function in the structure of film in one way; changes in scene in another way. We can therefore distinguish between plots which easily yield to a great span between individual shots— those in which motivation is transferred primarily into the interior of the acting characters so that unusual transitions between shots can be conceived as shifts in the field of vision of the characters themselves—and plots easily reconciled with frequent changes in scene—those based on the external acts of the characters. But not even in this instance are we prescribing; we are merely describing the path of least resistance. There is no doubt that the path of greatest resistance can be taken in a concrete case.

Everything which we have said in this study about the epistemological preconditions of film space does not make a claim for absolute validity. As early as tomorrow a revolutionary change in the machine technology of this art may provide it with new, quite unexpected preconditions.

13

Time in Film

Film is an art with many facets. There are threads connecting it to literature (both the narrative and the lyric), drama, painting, and music. Film has specific formal devices in common with every one of these arts, and every one of them has influenced film in the course of its development. The strongest ties, however, link film to the narrative and the drama; this is patently clear from the number of filmed novels and plays. We can say even more: the epistemological conditions provided by its material place film *between* the narrative and the drama so that it has some basic characteristics in common with each of these arts. All three arts are related by the fact that they are arts of plot, and their theme is a series of facts connected by temporal succession and a causal bond (in the broadest sense of the word). This has its significance both for the practice of these arts and for their theory. In practice this close kinship facilitates the easy transposition of theme from one to another as well as the heightened possibility of mutual influence. At the beginning of its development film was under the influence of the narrative and the drama; now it is beginning to reciprocate by means of a reverse influence (for example, the influence of the filmic techniques of the shot and the panorama on the presentation of space in modern narrative prose). For theory the closeness of film to the narrative and the drama makes possible their comparison. To this closely bound trinity of arts we can appropriately apply the general methodological rule that the comparison of materials which have many common features is theoretically interesting because, on the one hand, latent differences come sharply to the fore against a background of many similarities and because, on the other hand, we can arrive at reliable general conclusions without the danger of precipitous generalizations. In this outline we wish to attempt a comparison of filmic time with

"Čas ve filmu," an article for an unrealized anthology on film, written in the second half of the thirties; published in *Studie z estetiky* (Prague, 1966).

dramatic and narrative time, both in order to elucidate film itself through a comparison with arts which are theoretically better studied and in order to obtain through the help of film more precise characteristics of time in the plot arts in general than has been possible up to now.

We have already said that the most basic common feature of the film, the narrative, and the drama is the plot character of their themes. The plot can be defined in the most elementary way as a series of facts connected by temporal succession; it is thus inevitably connected to time. Time is therefore an important structural component in all three of these arts, though each of them has different temporal possibilities and requirements. In the drama, for example, the possibility of the presentation of simultaneous plots or even the displacement of segments of temporal series (the performance of what happened earlier after what happened later) is very limited, whereas the exploitation of simultaneity and temporal shifts are normal in the narrative. In this respect, as we shall see, film stands between the drama and the narrative as regards temporal possibilities.

If we wish to understand the differences among the temporal structures of the three contiguous arts, we must realize that there are two temporal levels in each of them: one provided by the plot sequence, the other by the time which the perceiving subject (the viewer, the reader) experiences. In the drama these two times elapse parallel to one another. When the curtain is up, the flow of time is the same on stage as in the audience (if we disregard subtle discrepancies which do not disturb the subjective impression of sameness; for example, activities whose course does not have significance for the action, such as writing a letter, are abbreviated on stage; the flow of the audience's real time can also be projected into a much larger scope if the parallelism of temporal proportions is preserved). The time of the perceiving subject and that of the plot thus elapse side by side in the drama; therefore the plot of a drama takes place in the viewer's *present,* even if the theme of the drama is temporally located in the past (a historical drama). Hence the feature of dramatic time that Zich designates as its transitoriness, which consists in the fact that only that section of the plot immediately before our eyes appears to us as present, whereas what has preceded is at the given moment already swallowed up by the past; the present then is in constant movement toward the future.

Let us now juxtapose the narrative to the drama. Here, of course, the plot is also presented as a temporal sequence. The relation of this plot time to the temporal flow which the perceiving subject (the reader) experiences is, however, quite different, or more precisely, there is no relation between them. Whereas the flow of plot time in the drama is connected to the elapsing of the viewer's time to the extent that even the duration of the drama is limited by the normal ability of the viewer's concentrated attention, it does not matter how much time we spend in reading; we can read a novel continuously or intermittently, in a week or in two hours. The time in which the narrative plot takes place is completely detached from the real time in which the reader lives. In the narrative the perceiving subject's temporal localization is felt as an indefinite present without temporal flow reflecting itself against the background of the elapsing past in which the plot takes place. Through the separation of plot time from the reader's real time there is the possibility—theoretically infinite—for the condensation of plot in the narrative. A plot covering many years, which would require an entire evening in a dramatic performance, even with great temporal omissions between single acts, can be summed up in one sentence in a narrative: "A certain rich man married a beautiful young girl who, however, soon died and left him a little daughter, Helen."[1]

If we now put film beside these two types of temporal structure, that is, the drama and the narrative, we see that here again it is a matter of a different exploitation of time. At first glance it might seem that film is temporally so close to the drama that their temporal structures are the same. A more painstaking examination, however, will show that filmic time also has many characteristics which distinguish film from the drama and bring it closer to the narrative. In particular, film has an ability to condense plot quite similar to narrative condensation. Here are a few examples. Consider a long journey by train, which has no significance for the plot since it elapses "without any event." The narrative writer would sum this up in one sentence. The film director shows us a railroad station before the departure of the train, the train going through the countryside, a person sitting in a compartment, and perhaps the arrival of the train at the place of destination; thus in a few meters of film and in a few short minutes he "depicts"

1. J. and K. Čapek, "Mezi dvěma polibky," *Zářivé hlubiny* (Prague, 1924), p. 46.

synecdochically the action of many hours or even days. An even more illustrative example is Šklovskij's film *Zapiski iz mertvogo doma* [Notes from the house of the dead] where the march of a column of convicts from Petersburg to Siberia is presented in the following way: We see the legs of the convicts and their guards tramping over the frozen snow, and at the same time we hear the song that they sing; the song continues, and the shots change; we catch sight of a winter landscape, then the procession itself, again close-ups of legs, and so on; suddenly we realize that the landscape through which the procession is passing is not wintry but spring-like; summer and autumn landscapes flash by in the same manner; the song goes on uninterruptedly, and when it is finished, we see the convicts already at their destination. In this way a journey of many months was summed up in a few minutes. The departure of plot time from the viewer's real time is obvious in these cases. In the same way that a narrative writer could abbreviate the long period of the journey by omitting all the detailed events in a short span of several sentences, the scenarist condenses it into a few shots.

Another characteristic which filmic time shares with narrative time is the possibility of transition from one temporal plane to another, that is, the possibility of the successive presentation of simultaneous actions, on the one hand, and the capability of temporal return, on the other. Here, however, the analogy of film with the narrative is not so unconditional as in the previous case. Jakobson has recently pointed out that simultaneous actions are applicable only to film with captions, in fact to that kind of film with a narrative component (the verbal presentation of action), since a caption of the type "And meanwhile," conjoining simultaneous actions, is a narrative device.[2] Flashback also has more limited possibilities in film than in the narrative, though it is not as impossible as in the drama. As an example let us cite an excerpt from Delluc's screenplay *Le Silence*:

52—Pierre's drawn face; he is remembering.
53—Pierre seen from afar in the middle of the apartment. He is searching his memory. Slowly. But for us the shots follow one another very quickly.

2. *Editors' note.* Mukařovský is referring to Jakobson's article, "Úpadek filmu?" [The decline of film?], *Listy pro umění a kritiku* 1 (1933): 45–49; reprinted in Roman Jakobson, *Studies in Verbal Art* (Ann Arbor, 1971), pp. 150–56.

54—Aimée, in an evening gown, falls forward in the middle of the drawing room.

55—Smoke.

56—A revolver.

57—Pierre's hand (the same rings) is holding the revolver.

58—Aimée stretched out on the rug.

59—Pierre standing in front of her.
   He throws the revolver down.

60—Pierre is bending over and is going to lift Aimée.

61—The servants are coming. Pierre instinctively steps back.

62—Pierre's face after the murder.

63—Pierre's face now remembering the scene.

64—A shot of Pierre in the past, at his desk. He is writing. Aimée sits on the arm of his easy chair and tenderly kisses him. A visitor enters. It is Jean, an elegant young man. Aimée leaves, annoyed. Jean follows her intently with his eyes. Pierre notices this and becomes worried.

65—A dinner. Suzie, next to Pierre, is speaking to him with as much emotion as circumstances permit. Jean, next to Aimée, is passionately courting her. Aimée's embarrassment; she is compelled to remain courteous. Pierre watches them anxiously.

66—The same evening. A corner of the drawing room. Suzie is bothering Pierre (who is no longer thinking about his jealousy). But Pierre is either cautious or faithful. He gracefully slips away from her.

67—Another corner of the drawing room. Jean is harassing Aimée with his amorous insinuations; she doesn't know how to get rid of him.

68—Pierre notices them and again becomes furious. Suzie comes up to him, all smiles, but he coolly spurns her.

69—Suzie's face. She is insulted, and her pride has been terribly wounded.

70—Pierre in his smoking room. One morning. He is opening his mail.

71—An anonymous letter: "If you do not want to be intentionally blind, you will defend your honor. Keep a close eye on your wife."

72—Pierre, nervous and grim. He goes out. He hides behind a door opening onto the street.

73—Jean, very elegant, dressed for a visit, in the street. He goes into Pierre's house. Pierre goes in after him.

74—Jean in the drawing room. Aimée comes in. She reproaches him, begs him to leave her in peace, etc. . . . He laughs, doesn't want to know anything, cries out that he is in love, etc. . . . etc.

75—Pierre behind the door.

76—Jean grabs Aimée. She defends herself. He kisses her against her will. Smoke. Aimée falls. Jean flees.

77—Aimée stretched out on the rug.

78—Pierre standing in front of her, the revolver in his hand.[3]

Here we have an obvious flashback: a murder and only afterwards a depiction of how it took place. The flashback is presented here, of course, in a loose temporal sequence, that is, it is motivated by the free association of a recollecting individual. In the drama such a displacement of plot segments would necessarily be understood as a miracle (the resurrection of a dead person) or as a surrealistic destruction of the unity of theme but never as a return to the past. This is because dramatic time is strictly irreversible due to the close bond between plot time and the perceiving subject's time. In sound-track film as well, we could hardly imagine such a transition from a closer temporal plane to a more remote one, even though it is motivated by recollection, for sound (in the above case, a shot and the characters' conversations), added to the optical impression, would make the break between temporal planes impossible. It would not be very plausible, for example, for the person whom we see as dead to appear and even speak in the following scene. In the progression from silent film with captions to silent film without captions to sound-track film the possibility of a temporal shift thus decreases. Nevertheless, the possibility of such a shift is not totally suppressed even in sound-track film. For instance, a flashback motivated by a recollection can be presented in such a way that the recalled scene is rendered only acoustically (a reproduction of a past conversation which the viewer has already heard) while the recollecting person is shown on the screen.

How can we explain these characteristics of temporal structure in film? Let us first note the relationship between the time of the perceiving subject and the time of the picture projected on the

3. L. Delluc, *Drames de cinéma* (Paris, 1923), pp. 24–27.

screen. It is obvious that the temporal flow which the viewer experiences is deautomatized in film similar to the way that it is in
the drama: the "pictorial" time flows parallel to the viewer's time.
This is the resemblance of film to the drama. It is precisely this
similarity that explains why film stood so close to the drama in its
beginnings and again upon the introduction of sound-track. We
must, however, consider another question. Is what we see in front
of us on the screen actually the plot itself? Can we identify the
time of the filmic picture with the time of the filmic plot? The
above examples provide the answer. If a march of many months
from Petersburg to Siberia can be presented in a film without interruption and without any obvious temporal jumps in a few
minutes, it is apparent that the presupposed plot (which, of course,
does not actually have to be performed continuously) elapses in a
different time than the picture. Its temporal localization is also
different. We are aware that the action itself belongs to the past,
whereas what we see in front of us on the screen we interpret as
an optical (in some cases, an optical-acoustic) message about this
past action. Only this message takes place in our present.

Thus filmic time is a more complex structure than narrative and
dramatic time. In narrative time we must take into account only
one temporal flow (the elapsing of the plot), and in dramatic time
a dual flow (the plot sequence and the elapsing of the viewer's
time, the two lines necessarily parallel); in film there is a triple
temporal flow: the plot elapsing in the past, "pictorial" time
flowing in the present, and the perceiving subject's time parallel to
the preceding temporal flow. Film gains ample possibilities of
temporal differentiation through this complex structure. The
exploitation of the viewer's own experience of temporal flow
provides film with a versimilitude similar to the versimilitude of
dramatic plot (rendering it present); but at the same time the
sequence of "pictorial" time inserted between plot and viewer
prevents the automatic linking of the plot flow with the real time
in which the viewer lives. This makes possible the free play of plot
time in a way similar to that in the narrative. We have already
cited examples. Now we shall add one more concerning the interruption of plot flow in film. It is well known that there are static
clustered groups of motifs in the narrative as well as dynamically
ordered motifs (those bound by temporal succession), that is, that
the narrative has the possibility of temporally static description as

well as that of temporally progressive narration. Tynjanov has shown that descriptions cut off from the temporal sequence of the plot also occur in film. He attributes descriptive power to detail, citing a scene in which the robbers, who are leaving a burglarized house, are described. The description is achieved by means of details concerning their weapons, and so forth. At this moment time has stopped. Tynjanov extends this discovery to detail in general and declares that it is excluded from the temporal flow.[4] We could, of course, cite examples of details strikingly incorporated into the temporal sequence. The fallacy of this generalization does not, however, mean that Tynjanov's observation about the case in point is unimportant. Here it is indeed a matter of the suspension of the temporal flow of filmic description made possible only by the fact that the flow of pictorial time mediates between the viewer's time and that of the plot. Plot time can stop because even at the moment of its suspension "pictorial" time flows parallel to the viewer's time (which here, in contrast to the case of the narrative, is deautomatized).

There are other possibilities for playing with time in film at the boundary between "pictorial" time, which corresponds in its course to the viewer's time, and plot time, which is separate. These are slow-motion and fast-motion film, as well as "reversed" film. In fast- or slow-motion film the ratio of the speed of plot time to "pictorial" time is deformed. A much larger (or much smaller) segment of plot time than we are accustomed to is appropriated to a specific segment of pictorial time. In reversed film the plot sequence elapses regressively, whereas the flow of "pictorial" time bound to the viewer's real time is naturally felt as progressive.

In conclusion let us return to the problem of time in plot arts in general in order to attempt a more precise solution than we could suggest at the beginning of this article. In analyzing film, we have detected three kinds of temporal sequences: the first created by the flow of the plot, the second by the movement of pictures (objectively we could say: by the movement of the film strip in the projector), and the third based on the deautomatization of the real time experienced by the viewer. However, traces of this triple temporal stratification can also be detected in the narrative

---

4. J. Tynjanov, "Ob osnovax kino" [On the principles of film], in *Poètika kino* [The poetics of film], ed. B. Èjxenbaum (Moscow, 1927), p. 66.

and the drama. As far as drama is concerned, the existence of two extreme temporal streams—plot time and the perceiving subject's time—is not in doubt. As for the narrative, there is, to be sure, only one distinctive temporal flow, that of the plot, but, as we have already remarked, the viewer's time occurs here at least as a static present. In both cases the existence of two temporal strata is thus discernible. What is seemingly missing is the third stratum, which mediates between these two extremes in film; it is what we have called pictorial time with respect to the material of film. What, in fact, constitutes this time? It is the temporal extent of the very work of art as a sign, whereas the other two times are defined with respect to things which are outside of the work itself. Plot time is related to the flow of a "real" event which is the content (plot) of the work; the perceiving subject's time is, as we have remarked, merely a projection of the viewer's (or reader's) real time into the temporal structure of the work. If, however, "pictorial" time, which we could perhaps designate more generally as "semiotic" time, corresponds to the temporal extent of the work, it is obvious that its preconditions are also present in the narrative and the drama whose works also unfold in time.

If we now look at the narrative and the drama, we discover that even here the duration of the work itself is reflected in its temporal structure through the so-called *tempo,* a term meaning the rhythm of the narration in the individual parts of narrative prose and the overall pace of the stage work (determined by the director). In both cases the tempo appears to us much more as a quality than as a measurable temporal quantity; however, in film, where the temporal extent of the work is based on the mechanically regular motion of film machinery, a quantity also manifests itself in semiotic time, and this time comes to the fore as a distinct component of the temporal structure. If we thus accept as a necessary epistemological precondition *three kinds* of temporal strata in all plot arts, we can say that film is the art where all three strata obtain equally, whereas in the narrative the stratum of plot time comes to the fore, and in the drama it is the stratum of the perceiving subject's time (while the stratum of plot time is passively bound to this).

If we ask—and not only for the sake of symmetry—whether there is an art in which semiotic time prevails, we must turn to the lyric where we can see a complete suppression of the perceiving subject's time (the present without signs of temporal flow) and of plot time (motifs are not connected through temporal succession). Proof of the full significance of semiotic time in the lyric is the importance for it of rhythm, a phenomenon linked to semiotic time, which, with the help of rhythm, becomes a measurable quantity.

14

On the Current State of the Theory of Theater

One of the important problems which the contemporary theater has been trying to solve in various ways is how to establish active contact between the spectator and the stage. Certainly, the theater itself is primarily responsible for the solution of this problem. Indeed, its directors and actors have attempted more than once to "pull" the spectator into the play in some fashion. They have achieved interesting and artistically valuable results, but for the most part these have not been very effective as far as their desired goal has been concerned. There is, however, yet another party in the theater: the auditorium and the spectators sitting in it, hence those who are to be aroused to activity. They have also been considered, however, for the most part not as a concrete community of people frequenting such and such a theater but as representatives of a social whole. The problem has accordingly been shifted to that of the relationship between the theater and society. We know well enough the profound but practically unproductive deliberations about the fact that the necessary precondition of intensive contact and full understanding between the theater and society is a spontaneous unity of a *Weltanschauung* and of a religious and ethical feeling. Examples are ancient Greece, the Middle Ages, and so forth.

But it is not the entire society of this or that time, this or that people, which frequents the theater, especially the contemporary theater; rather it is an audience, that is, a community, often socially heterogeneous (let us not consider social strata alone but also status, age, etc.) but tied together by a bond of receptivity for the art of the theater. The audience is always the mediator between art and society as a whole: literature, painting, music, and the other arts also require an audience, that is, a set of individuals with an inherited or acquired ability to adopt an aesthetic attitude

"K dnešnímu stavu teorie divadla," a lecture at the Circle of Friends of D^{41}, published in *Program D*^{41}, no. 7 (1941).

toward the material with which a given art works.[1] The "theater audience" in general is, however, still too broad and relatively abstract a notion. Every theater, especially a theater of a pronounced artistic movement, has its own audience which knows the artistic stamp of this theater, accompanies an actor from play to play, from role to role, and so on. And this fact is an important precondition of the audience's active attitude toward the theater. This attitude leads to one of the most passable roads toward "pulling the spectator into the play." It depends on the director's artistic intentions whether he wishes to remove the boundary between the stage and the auditorium. Even when this boundary is preserved, however, the relationship between the theater and the audience is bilaterally active if the audience spontaneously and fully accepts the artistic conventions upon which the theater, and precisely this theater, builds its performance. Only in such a case can we expect the audience's reaction to the stage action to become itself an active force which is tacitly but effectively incorporated into the actual theatrical performance. It is sufficiently known how sensitively the stage reacts to the understanding and mood hovering over the quiet auditorium.

The attempt of the Circle of Friends of D^{41}[2] to bring the tenets of the theater closer to the audience through a series of lectures, most of which will be delivered by artists active in D^{41}, therefore seems to be a good beginning for the audience's road to the theater. On the stage, artistic intention can only be embodied, not explicitly explained. The entire work at its origin remains hidden from the spectator; yet awareness of it could substantially facilitate his understanding. A performance itself is already too homogeneous a whole, and it is not easy to penetrate its structure, to see it from within. During a performance it seems quite natural that such and such a word of the text is pronounced in a certain way or is accompanied by a certain gesture, that its effect manifests itself in a particular manner in the facial expressions, gestures, and

1. The feeling for a certain material is not at all general, and rarely has there been an individual, no matter how strong his aesthetic sensibility, capable of belonging to the audience of all the arts. A sense for the aesthetic effect of a word is not necessarily connected with a sense for the artistic effect of a color, a tone, and so forth.

2. *Editors' note.* D^{41} was an avant-garde theater founded by E. F. Burian in 1933. The "D" stands for the Czech word *divadlo* (theater). The index refers to the year of the second half of a particular theatrical season, in this case 1940–1941.

movements of the other actors, and so on. But during rehearsals the spectator would see that the connection of a word with a gesture, and so forth, is the result of an intentional selection from many possibilities, that no component of theater follows automatically from another, and that a theatrical performance is a very complex and dangerously fluid structure. If the spectator is enlightened about the origin of a theatrical performance by those who actively participate in theatrical work every day, he will be able to find a place for himself in the performance which is only seemingly limited to the stage by its course—in reality it always pervades the entire theater.

The organizers of this lecture series have deemed it appropriate that a few words be devoted to the theory of theater as well. By no means, of course, can a systematic exposition of all its problems be presented here, nor is there any need.

We have only a single theoretical task: to show through a few remarks and examples that despite all the material tangibility of its means (the building, machines, sets, props, a multitude of personnel), the theater is only the basis of an immaterial interplay of forces moving through time and space and pulling the spectator into its changeable tension, into the interplay which we call a stage production, a performance. The theoretical preconditions for such a view are provided in the contemporary theory of theater and especially in the Czech theory of theater. The Czech theory of theater has frequently been the object of much criticism, justified, to be sure, as far as an enumeration of the tasks which should be fulfilled is concerned; but it would not be fair to criticize its past as well. I have in mind primarily one of the works of recent years, Otakar Zich's *Aesthetics of Dramatic Art.*[3] In this work the theater has been conceived in its entire breadth and complexity as a dynamic interplay of all its components, as a unity of forces internally differentiated by intertensions and as a set of signs and meanings. The theoretical works of Bogatyrëv, Honzl, E. F. Burian, and of several younger specialists proceed from the same conception of the theater.

But even the generation before Zich made a valid contribution to our knowledge of the essence of the theater. It suffices to mention two recently deceased theater critics, Jindřich Vodák and

3. *Estetika dramatického umění* (Prague, 1931).

Václav Tille. In their formative years they experienced the powerful—from close at hand, almost chaotic—surge of rebirth through
which the European theater has passed since the final decades of
the last century, and which, in fact, has still not ended. In our
country the agitation for theatrical development was even stronger,
because influences from several countries—especially Germany,
France, and Russia—penetrated and intermingled at once. It is
certain that this haste also had its negative consequences. Unelab-
orated and not fully digested conceptions were abandoned for
other newer ones; various conceptions were blended in an artistically "impure" manner; sometimes only the external symptoms of
a particular conception of the theater were adopted rather than its
very essence, and so forth. On the other hand, however, this situation had its positive aspect. Receptivity for the multiple complexity of the theater and the mutual counterbalancing of its components was heightened. If we read Tille's *Memories of the Theater*,[4] we encounter a critic at ease with any theatrical expression,
whether he is reviewing the French, Russian, German, or Japanese
theater or confronting a form in which the actor predominates or
another in which the focal point of the play lies in the stage set or
finally a third, the vehicle of which is the director. He knows how
to distinguish exactly between a system of acting working mainly
with the gesture and one dependent on declamation. He grasps
the almost imperceptible boundary at which gestures turn into
facial expressions, and so on.

This cultivated receptivity had already paved the way for the
thinker who was to give Czech theory of theater its first example
of a systematic and philosophically consistent elaboration of the
tenets of the theater, namely Otakar Zich. It is important to
realize that this way was paved by the local development of
artistic practice and theory, by a development which had not only
the disadvantages of the fact that it occurred in a small nation
inundated by the influences of large nations but also its advantages. The excessively large number of influences ultimately
counterbalanced one another, and practice and theory were consequently liberated from a one-sided indebtedness. If, as the pro-
verb says, a man generally has all the vices belonging to the
virtues with which he is endowed, the opposite is often true of a

4. *Divadelní vzpomínky* (Prague, 1917).

Czech man: he knows how to find the advantages belonging to the disadvantages with which he is afflicted.

But let us now turn to our theme proper. We have spoken about the complexity of the theater. We must therefore show first in what it consists. We shall proceed from a commonly held assertion. Since Richard Wagner's time it has been said that the theater is, in fact, an entire set of arts. This was the first formulation of the complexity of the theater; it has the merit of primacy, but it does not grasp the essence of the matter. For Wagner the theater was the sum of several independent arts. Today, however, it is clear that upon entering the theater, the individual arts renounce their independence, penetrate one another, contradict one another, substitute for one another—in brief "dissolve," merging into a new, fully unified art.

Let us take a look at music, for example. It is not only present in the theater when it directly sounds or even when—in opera—it usurps the stage word. The properties which music shares with theatrical activity (the intonation of the voice in relation to musical melody; the rhythm and agogics of movement; gesture, facial expressions, and voice) cause every theatrical event to be projected against the background of music and formed according to its model. E. F. Burian, a musician and director, has shown to what extent stage time can become rhythmically measurable according to the pattern of music, even if there is no music on stage; and he has shown how akin the role of a linguistic intonational motif in the overall structure of a performance is to the function of a melodic motif in a musical composition.[5] Not only the musical drama has its melodic "leitmotifs"; the spoken drama has them as well.

We encounter a similar situation with sculpture in the theater. If a statue is part of the set, sculpture is present on stage. Even in such a case, however, the function of the statue is different from what it is off stage. Off stage, for instance, right in the lobby of a theater, a statue is merely a thing, a depiction, whereas on stage it is a motionless actor, a contrast to a live actor. Proof of this may be found in the numerous theatrical themes which let a statue

---

5. *Editors' note.* Mukařovský is referring to Burian's article "Příspěvek k problému jevištní mluvy" [A contribution to the problem of stage language], *Slovo a slovesnost* 5 (1939): 24-32.

come to life on stage.[6] Unlike an actor, a statue is constantly present on stage, even if its presence is not materialized. The immobility of a statue and the mobility of a live person is a constant antinomy between the poles of which the dramatic figure oscillates on stage. And when Craig posited his famous requirement of the actor-"über-marionette" whose predecessors were, as he explicitly stated, the statues of gods in temples, he did nothing more than to draw attention to this hidden but always present antinomy of the art of acting. What is usually called a "pose" is clearly a sculptural effect. In the medieval theater "slow and measured movements occur in the pauses of the delivery, whereas the actor stands motionless during the delivery itself."[7] The sculptural mask of classical times, of Japan, and of other times and places also links the actor directly to a statue, and the transition between the immobility of a solid mask and the make-up of a modern actor is quite continuous, as is well known.

The other arts, whether literature, painting, architecture, dance, or film, have a status in the theater similar to that of music and sculpture. Each of them is always potentially present in the theater, but at the same time each of them, when it comes into contact with the theater, loses its intrinsic character, and its essence changes. Moreover, there are two other arts which are inevitably bound to the theater: acting and directing. This last is an activity of artistic nature that struggles for the unity of all the components of theater. The presence of these two artistic components most distinctly characterizes the theater as an independent and unified artistic form.

The complexity of the theater is by no means exhausted by an enumeration of the arts which participate in the structure of a stage production. Each of these components breaks down into secondary components, which again are internally differentiated into other constituents. For example, the components of the dramatic figure are: voice, facial expressions, gestures, movement, costume, and so on. Each of them, moreover, is complex in itself.

6. *Editors' note.* For a more detailed discussion of this phenomenon see R. Jakobson, "Socha v symbolice Puškinově," *Slovo a slovesnost* 3 (1937): 2–24. An English translation of this article, "The Statue in Puškin's Poetic Mythology," appears in Roman Jakobson, *Puškin and His Sculptural Myth,* trans. and ed. John Burbank (The Hague, 1975), pp. 1–44.

7. W. Golther, "Der Schauspieler im Mittelalter" in E. Geissler's anthology *Der Schauspieler* (Berlin, 1926), p. 97.

Thus the voice components are the articulation of speech sound elements, the pitch of the voice and its changes, its tone, the intensity of expiration, and tempo. But we have still not come to the end. The individual vocal components can be broken down further. Take, for example, tone of voice: every person has a particular voice coloration comprising part of his physical personality. A speaker can be recognized by the coloration of his voice even if the listener does not see him. There are, however, also tones of voice corresponding to individual mental dispositions ("angrily," "joyfully," "ironically," etc.), and their meaning is independent of the individual's personal vocal coloration. Both of these kinds of tone of voice can be exploited artistically. The individual vocal coloration of a particular actor employed in a certain play can become a significant factor in the director's "instrumentation" of a stage performance. Temporary tone of voice caused by a mental state is usually accounted for artistically either in the dramatic text itself (the author's stage directions, an abundance of emotional changes and oppositions in the dialogue) or in the actor's performance (cf. the rich scale of tones of voice which—according to Tille—Vojan developed in a writer's neutral text).

The theater therefore has not only a great number of components but also a rich gradation of them. Can any one of them, however, be declared fundamental, absolutely necessary for the theater? The answer is "no" if we regard the theater not only from the standpoint of a certain artistic movement but as a constantly developing and changing phenomenon. Individual developmental stages of the theater and of particular theatrical movements have, of course, their prevailing components. The dominant component of the theater is at one time the dramatic text, at another time the actor, at another time the director or even the stage set; and there are more complicated cases—for example, a theater where the director prevails but where he makes the actor prominent (Stanislavsky). It is just the same in more detailed matters: sometimes components of facial expression, sometimes vocal components, and so on, prevail in the actor's preformance (according to the period, the school, etc.). Even in the voice itself, sometimes articulation prevails, whereas at other times intonation prevails. All of this is extremely changeable, and all components assume the leading role during the course of development without any of them attaining permanent dominance. And this changeability is made possible only because, as we have said, none of the components is absolutely necessary and fundamental for the theater. A written text is not necessary, for there are theatrical forms with dialogue improvised to a considerable extent (e.g., commedia dell'arte and some kinds of folk theater) or even without words at all (pantomime). Even the actor himself, the vehicle of dramatic action, can be missing from the stage—at least temporarily. His role is assumed by another component, for example, by light (in Burian's staging of *The Barber of Seville* the flickering of the light and changes in its color connected with the howling of the storm expressed the people's revolt which was supposed to be taking place off stage—the stage itself was empty) or even by an empty, immovable stage which precisely on account of its emptiness can express a decisive plot reversal (the Moscow Art Theater group, for example, liked to use such "stage pauses"). Cases of this sort are, of course, rare, but they suffice to prove that the theater is not inevitably bound to any of its components and that therefore the freedom of regrouping in it is inexhaustible.

Nor are the individual components of the theater bound by anticipated and unchangeable relations, as it might often appear from the standpoint of rigid convention. There is not a pair of components, no matter how related they may be, whose relation cannot be set into motion. It seems to us, for example, that gestures, facial expressions and speech are necessarily parallel, but the Moscow Art Theater group has shown that their very nonparallelness can be artistically exploited in the theater. Let us read what Tille says about this in his article on their production of *Uncle Vanya*: "The Russian director drew on his experience that in life gestures, facial expressions, and people's actions are not the logical result of the spoken word, just as words are not the result of external movements, but that both spring—sometimes proportionately, sometimes disproportionately—from inner life, that both are caused by a hidden motive force which consists, on the one hand, in the characters of people in action, either through their will or through their uncontrolled energy, and, on the other hand, in those external influences which determine people's behavior without their volition and often even without their awareness."[8] Voice

8. *Divadelní vzpomínky*, p. 199.

and gesture were therefore separated for the purpose of artistic effect. By separating them—in contrast to the former convention, the Moscow Art Theater group influenced not only the further development of the theater but also the extratheatrical life of their audience. The viewer who had experienced the Russians' stage system thereafter perceived himself and his fellow men with more differentiation; for him the gesture was no longer merely a passive companion of the voice but an independent symptom of a mental state, often a more immediate symptom than a vocal expression. In its most diverse variations the theater always affects the spectator in the same direction: it reveals to him again and again the multiple correlation of visible expressions of behavior from new aspects.

An important requirement for the theory of theater follows from this: to make the concept of the theater as a set of immaterial relations the method and goal of its study. An enumeration of the components in itself is a static list. An intrinsic (internal) history of the theater is also nothing but a study of the changes in the interrelations among its components. None of the developmental stages of the theater can be accepted (theoretically) as a perfect realization of its very essence, nor can any of the individual theoretical forms such as the theater of this or that nation, the primitive folk theater, children's theatrical expressions, and so on. The richer and more varied is the material at the scholar's disposal, the more easily he can distinguish individual components and their relations in the total structure of a stage work. But it is not always easy to distinguish individual components from one another, precisely because of the closeness of the relations which can be established among them. For example, it is sometimes almost impossible to distinguish an actor's movement from a gesture (his walk is at the same time a movement and a gesture), or a costume from the actor's physical appearance.

Components also substitute for one another, however. Thus in Shakespeare a richly developed verbal depiction substitutes for the set which the Shakespearean theater lacked. Or light can appear to be part of the actor's costume (if it colors the costume). Directors often exploit the substitution of one component for another as a technical device. In My Life in Art Stanislavsky says that the director can "relieve" the actor by means of the set, for example, by having a striking stage set compensate for weak acting.

The essence of the theater is therefore a changing flux of immaterial relations which constantly regroup. Not only is development from period to period, from director to director, from one histrionic school to another based upon this flux, but so is every individual stage performance. Within a stage performance components also confront and counterbalance one another in the constant tension borne by stage time. Everything, not just moving action but also an apparently motionless pause, is incorporated into the flow of this time. There are even systems of directing and acting based on the exploitation of pauses as a dynamic element. The biographer of the German actor Bassermann says: "In the fourth act [of Schiller's *Wallenstein*] Bassermann plays only the scene of the entry into Egger. And here he wonderfully expresses the destruction of a strong spirit, the dissipation of a great power. He speaks with the mayor and still maintains the attitude of the prince, the friendly attentive sovereign, but he is disturbingly absentminded. His attentiveness suddenly comes and goes. Long pauses punctuate his speech. (For this artistic effect he makes radical deletions in Schiller's text.)"[9] The purpose of Bassermann's method was obviously the heightening of dramatic tension; his means were pauses, hence pure flowing time: immaterial time as the riverbed of immaterial action. Everything on stage is only the material basis of stage activity, the real heroes of which are constantly alternating and interpenetrating actions and reactions. Every shift in the relations of the components is at the same time both a reaction with respect to what has preceded it and an action with respect to what will follow it. Not only the actors but the stage as a whole are the vehicles of the actions and reactions. Like everything in the theater, the stage is in constant movement between an actor and an inanimate object. In a moment of acute tension the revolver which a character aims at his adversary is much more the "agent" than the actor who is playing the character. Even sets can become actors and, vice versa, an actor a set.[10] The sequence of actions and reactions causes a constantly renewed and always resumed tension which is not identical with the con-

9. Julius Bab, *Albert Bassermann: Weg und Werk* (Leipzig, 1929), p. 330.
10. See J. Veltruský, "Člověk a předmět na divadle," *Slovo a slovesnost* 6 (1940): 153–59. *Editors' note.* An English translation of this article, "Man and Object in the Theater," can be found in *A Prague School Reader on Esthetics, Literary Structure, and Style*, ed. Paul L. Garvin (Washington, D.C., 1964), pp. 83–91.

stantly rising plot tension (collision, crisis, peripety, catastrophe) that obtains only in certain genres and developmental stages of the theater. Plot tension presupposes a plot, and even a unified plot; but there are numerous dramatic forms which do not recognize plot unity (e.g., the medieval drama, the revue) or even a plot in the proper sense of the word (e.g., the separate scenes whose *subsequent* connection gave rise to the classical mimos or the medieval spiritual drama).

Having become aware of the essence of the theater, we shall now attempt to verify and illustrate this assertion by analyzing several of its components. Let us first look at the dramatic text. There have been periods which have believed that the sole purpose of the theater is to reproduce the work of a dramatic author (e.g., the French theater of the nineteenth century in which the author usually staged his work himself). At other times, on the contrary, there has been a prevalent opinion that a drama is merely the text of a theatrical performance and not an independent literary work (e.g., Zich's view in his *Aesthetics of Dramatic Art*). Both of these conceptions are, however, only expressions of contemporary views of the theater limited to a particular artistic system. If we look at the drama without the bias of any period, we necessarily find that it is at the same time a homogeneous literary genre, equal to the lyric and the narrative, and one of the components of the theater. In its artistic orientation it can, of course, incline sometimes toward this pole, at other times toward that pole. The development of literature would be as unthinkable without the drama, the dialogic literary genre, as the development of the drama without literature. The drama has constantly drawn from the sources of the lyric and the narrative, and, on the other hand, it has influenced these contiguous genres. As far as the relation of the drama to the theater is concerned, we must keep in mind that in requiring the word for its purposes, the theater can resort to any of the basic literary genres and does so. The medieval *planctus* (the Virgin Mary's laments), though lyrical expressions, were intended to be performed; the narrative enters into contact with the theater, for example, through the dramatization of novels. If the theater nevertheless resorts to the drama more often than to the lyric and the narrative, it is only because the drama is the poetry of dialogue, and dialogue is action expressed in language: the speeches of a dialogue acquire the value of a chain of actions and reactions in the theater.

In becoming a part of the theater, the drama assumes another function and another appearance than that which it has as long as it is conceived as a literary work. One and the same drama by Shakespeare is something different if it is read rather than staged (e.g., the descriptions, which, as we have said, become a word-set on stage, function in reading as lyrical passages of the work). In this respect there are, of course, considerable differences among dramas. There are dramatic works that resist staging to a considerable extent (so-called "closet dramas"), and there are others that have almost no life off stage.[11] In any case, however, there is tension between the dramatic poem and the theater. Only rarely does a drama pass over the stage without dramaturgic adaptation, and the expression "the stage interpretation of a play" is usually just a euphemism which masks the tension between the theater and literature. In "embodying" the drama, the actor and the director of their own free will (and sometimes even against the dramatist's will) emphasize certain aspects of the literary work and de-emphasize others; the actor has the choice of how to treat the "hidden meaning" of the text, the meaning that cannot be explicitly expressed in dialogue but nevertheless belongs to the drama. The writer is the master of the written word alone, but the actor is the master of a rich set of means involving the voice, facial expressions, and so forth. It is even impossible for him to present only what the text contains. We shall always see on stage an entire man, not just what the dramatist shows us of him. Stanislavsky has graphically perceived and rendered the tension between the dramatic work and the stage in a chapter of *My Life in Art* called "When You Play an Evil Man, Find Out Where He Is Good." There he says: "Looking from the auditorium, I clearly perceived the actors' mistakes and began to explain them to my comrades. 'Listen,' I said to one of them, 'you are playing a complainer, you are constantly whining and obviously you care only that your part—God forbid—not come out other than as a complainer. But why should you worry about this, when the author himself has already taken sufficient care of it. As a result you are using only a single color. But black becomes genuine black only

11. Tille says about Rostand's *Cyrano de Bergerac*: "Plays such as Rostand's resemble most the well-constructed texts of operas and spectacle plays in which the author gives only competent artists the opportunity to develop their art" (*Divadelní vzpomínky*, p. 15).

when some white appears for the sake of contrast. So bring into your role a little white in various shades and combinations with other colors of the rainbow. There will be contrast, variety and truth. Therefore, when you are playing a complainer, find out where he is happy and energetic.'"[12]

It is not, of course, always simply a matter of complementing a text with an unequivocal contrast: often there are many semantic possibilities which a text offers an actor. In this respect there is a developmental oscillation in dramatic literature itself. There are periods in which there is an effort to predetermine the theatrical performance as much as possible by means of the text, and there are others in which the text intentionally leaves as much freedom as possible for theatrical realization. Ibsen's dramas, which almost systematically impose upon the text a double meaning, belong to the latter kind. One meaning is expressed explicitly in words, the other is accessible only through the actor's gestures, the intonation and tone of his voice, and the tempo and presentation of the play. This is also the case with Chekhov as well. The charm of Chekhov's plays consists "in what is not conveyed by words but is hidden behind them either in pauses or in the actors' expressions, in the radiation of their inner feeling. This brings alive not only the inanimate objects on stage, the sounds, the sets, and the images created by the actors but also the very mood of the play and of the entire performance. Here everything depends on creative intuition and artistic sensibility."[13] Such, then, is the relationship between the theater and the drama: always tense and for this reason, also subject to change. In essence, however, the theater is not subordinate to literature, nor is literature subordinate to the theater. Each of these extremes can occur only in particular developmental periods, whereas there is equilibrium between the two sides in others.

After looking at the dramatic text, let us now turn to the second of the basic factors of the theater, dramatic space. Dramatic space is not identical with the stage or with three-dimensional space in general, for it originates in time through the gradual changes in the spatial relations between the actor and the stage and among the actors themselves. Every movement on the part of the

12. *Moja žizn' v iskusstve,* 7th ed. (Moscow, 1941), p. 157.
13. *Ibid.,* pp. 285–86.

actor is perceived and evaluated in connection with previous movements and with respect to the anticipated following movement. In the same way, the disposition of the people on stage is understood as a change in their previous disposition and as a transition toward the next disposition. This is why Zich speaks about stage space as a set of forces: "The characters represented by the actors are certain centers of power of various intensity according to the significance of the characters in the given dramatic situation; their dramatic relations provided by this situation are then like lines of force which unite and disunite among the characters. The dramatic stage, filled out by a net of these lines of force and by the motor paths caused by them, is a kind of power field, changeable in its shape and in the force of its individual components."[14]

On account of its energetic nature dramatic space can exceed the stage in all directions. Thus arises the phenomenon called the imaginary stage about which Pražáková and Stiebitz have written (the action behind the stage or, in some cases, even above or below it).[15] Even the main action itself can be temporarily shifted to the imaginary stage, and the different developmental periods of the theater have exploited the multiform possibilities of the imaginary stage in various ways. Sometimes the theater resorts to the imaginary stage for purely technical reasons (actions which would be difficult to realize on stage, e.g., races, large gatherings of people, etc., are placed on the imaginary stage), sometimes convention compels its use (e.g., bloody scenes are transferred to the imaginary stage in French Classicist tragedy); sometimes there are artistic reasons for using it (heightening of tension, etc.). Whether the imaginary stage is used a lot or is avoided is characteristic of the nature of dramatic space for this or that period.

But dramatic space exceeds the stage in another way and more substantially than through just the imaginary stage. It encompasses the stage and the auditorium together. Zich has discerned that "the effects deriving from the dynamic field of dramatic space are transferred to the auditorium, to the audience."[16] The contemporary theory of theater conceives the stage and the auditorium as a

14. *Estetika dramatického umění,* p. 246.
15. K. Pražáková, "Pomyslné jeviště" [The imaginary stage], *Jeviště* 2 (1921), 390–92; F. Stiebitz, "Pomyslné jeviště v antickém a moderním divadle" [The imaginary stage in classical and modern theater], *Věda a život* 3 (1937), 229–42.
16. *Estetika dramatického umění,* p. 246.

single whole from the standpoint of dramatic space.[17] Even if the stage is separated from the auditorium by footlights, however, it does not have an independent existence. The position of an actor at the front of the stage, at the rear, on the left, or on the right holds true from the perspective of the spectator sitting in front of the stage. If the viewers surrounded the stage (as is sometimes the case in folk theater, for example), these coordinates would, as Zich points out, lose their sense. Dramatic space therefore takes over the entire theater and is created in the spectator's consciousness during the production. It is the force which establishes unity among the other components of the theater and at the same time receives concrete meaning from them.

The actor is another important component of the theater which accumulates others around itself. The actor's significance for the structure of a stage production is that he is the most frequent carrier of the action. The fact that the actor is a living human being is also important. Hegel speaks about this in his *Ästhetik*: "The proper sensorily perceptible material of dramatic poetry is, as we have seen, not only the human voice and the spoken word, but an entire man who does not only express feelings, images, and thoughts, but who is engaged in a concrete action and who influences by his total being the images, intentions, acts, and behavior of others and accepts their influences in return or resists them."[18] Thus the actor is the center of stage activity, and everything else that is on stage outside of him is evaluated only in relation to him as a sign of his mental and physical organization. Hence the multitude and complexity of theatrical signs which Zich has revealed in his pioneering book and which Bogatyrëv has since fruitfully elaborated. Other things outside the actor are perceived only through the senses, but the actor and his expressions are accessible to the viewer's direct empathy. The actor therefore appears as the most real of the realities on the stage or rather as the only reality of the stage. The closer to the stage action the actor is, the more immediately experienced are his realities and the many-sidedness of his character and expressions. Hence the difference between the major and minor characters. Because of its participation in the action, even a thing can be experienced by the

17. Viz., M. Kouřil and E. F. Burian, *Divadlo práce* [The theater of work] (Prague, 1936).

18. *Georg Wilhelm Friedrich Hegels Werke* (Berlin, 1843), 10, pt. 3, 512.

spectator as an actor. At this moment it even becomes a reality for the spectator: "A real fountain or an empty Meyerholdian stage where a camping tent, a tripod, and a thermos bottle are the other objects defining the stage. These general and common realities are not on stage either for their beauty or for their 'depiction of the milieu.' They are here for theater, for emotion and fascination; here they are like an actor—they have thousands of meanings according to the relations and the moments in which they inter-vene. . . . They are here for an activity which they do not narrate but which they create in their spatial rhythm or temporal change."[19]

The relationship between an actor and the character that he embodies is of a particular kind. The question of whether the actor creates a character from himself, from his personal emotions and experiences, or apart from his personal life by cold calculation has already been raised many times. Diderot posed it first in his famous *Paradoxe sur le comédien*. The contemporary theory of theater[20] answers it approximately as follows: Both direct ex-periencing of character by the actor and emotionally detached creation of character are always present. In development, however, now this, now that pole is emphasized (e.g., the creation of charac-ter from personal experience prevailed among some great actors in the period of psychological Realism—Hana Kvapilová in our country). After all, let us not forget that the connection between the man and the artist in an actor is reciprocal. An actor not only partially lives a play but also partially plays life. In the lecture *L'Art et le comédien* (1880) Coquelin tells the anecdote about the actor Talme: "It is said that when he learned of the death of his father, he uttered a piercing cry; so piercing, so heartfelt, that the artist always on the alert in the man instantly took note of it, and decided to make use of it upon the stage, later on."[21] There is a tension between the artist's subjectivity and the objectivity of his work in all arts, but it is more intensely experienced in the actor because he is his own material in his entire person, body and soul.

19. J. Honzl, "Vsevolod Meierchold a revoluční oktjabr divadla" [Vsevolod Meyerhold and the revolutionary October of theater], *Moderní ruské divadlo* [The modern Russian theater] (Prague, 1928), p. 72.

20. J. Honzl, "Nad Diderotovým Paradoxem o herci" [On Diderot's *Paradoxe sur le comédien*], *Program D*[40], Feb. 8, 1940, pp. 81–85.

21. *Art and the Actor*, trans. A. L. Alger (New York, 1915), p. 59.

Nevertheless, the connection between an actor's life and his artistic creation is not immediate in a given play. Between them there is a layer comprised of a fixed set of devices which are a permanent feature of a given actor and transfer from role to role. For the audience these fixed devices are inseparably bound to the actor's real person. The audience recognizes an actor in a new role according to these devices; they render him emotionally sympathetic or antipathetic to the audience; the audience evaluates an actor's individual performance against their background. The tension between an individual performance and the fixed set of devices is also, however, a factor of artistic structure in acting. There are periods, kinds of theater, and histrionic personalities in which what is constant in an actor's creation prevails; at other times a striking differentiation of roles is emphasized. The permanent histrionic personality prevails over the differentiation of roles especially often in comedians—for example, Vlasta Burian. After all, comic acting goes even further in stabilizing an acting performance by creating types already independent of a single performer's personality: Pulcinella, Bajazzo, Harlequin, Hanswurst, Kašpárek, and so on. The number of tensions which envelop the actor on stage—like everything else which enters the structure of a stage performance—is by no means exhausted by the contradiction and tension between a histrionic personality and an individual performance. We could enumerate many other antinomies of the histrionic art, especially if we moved from the actor as an individual to the acting company and from a single one of the dramatis personae to the entire set of characters participating in a given stage production.

The audience is another basic factor of the theater. Like dramatic space and the actor, the audience has a summarizing role in the theater in the sense that everything which happens there is addressed in one way or another to the audience. If the actors speak on stage, the difference between their speech and the conversation of everyday life consists in the fact that its effect on the silent partner (and the one only rarely addressed) listening beyond the footlights is taken into account. The reactions of the characters on stage to the speaker's utterances are also calculated for this partner. Frequently the dialogue is conducted in such a way that the audience understands it differently than one of the dramatis personae; the audience can also know more or less about the situation at a given moment than the dramatis personae. All of this tellingly reveals the participation of the audience in the stage action. Not only does the stage action influence the audience, but the audience also influences the stage action, though as a rule only in the sense that in their performance the actors are either supported or restrained by the anticipated perceptiveness of the audience, its mood during the play, and so forth. But there are even cases in which the spectators' participation becomes apparent, as sometimes happens in folk theater (when an actor engages in direct conversation with the audience[22]) or in comic improvisations (e.g., when the actor interprets the audience's laughter as a positive or negative response to his words and appeals to this response in further conversation with his partner: "See what the audience thinks about you," etc.).

The theater also exhibits a constant effort to make the spectator's participation in the stage performance as direct as possible. This is the purpose of placing actors among the spectators, actors' entrances from the auditorium, or the designation of a certain character as a mediator between the stage and the auditorium (the Hobo in the Čapek brothers' play *Ze života hmyzu*). However, even if the theater does not appeal to the spectator in this immediate way, it solicits his participation. Charles Vildrac cites a very instructive example of this from Hilar's staging of Duhamel's play *Lumière*: "We recall the scene where the blind man, Bernard, who is standing at a window opening on a mountain lake at sunset, imagines and poetically describes the beauty of the spectacle which he does not see and has never seen. Well, at the Prague National Theater, when the blind man approaches the window, the beautiful illuminated landscape becomes pitch black, and it is before an absolutely dark background emphasized by the window frame which is strongly lit by an unreal mauve light that the hero utters his description. The spectator is thus invited to take the place of the speaker; in front of this window he, too, becomes a blind man."[23] After all, the roles of the actor and the spectator are much less distinguished than it might seem at first glance. Even the actor to a certain extent is a spectator for his partner at the

22. See P. Bogatyrev, *Lidové divadlo české a slovenské* [The Czech and Slovak folk theater] (Prague, 1940).

23. "Notes sur le théâtre à Prague," *Choses de théâtre* 2 (1923), 12–13.

moment when the partner is playing; in particular, extras who do not intervene actively in the play are distinctly perceived as spectators. The inclusion of actors among the audience becomes quite apparent, for example, when a comedian makes a co-actor laugh by his performance. Even if we are aware that such laughter can be intentional (in order to establish active contact between the stage and the auditorium), we cannot but realize that at such a moment the boundary between the stage and the auditorium runs across the stage itself: the laughing actors are on the audience's side.

The audience is therefore omnipresent in the structure of a stage production. The meaning of not only what is happening on stage but also of things on the stage depends on the audience and its understanding. This is especially true of props which on stage have only that meaning, in some cases only that existence, which the audience attributes to them. An object on stage can strike the audience as something quite different from what it is in reality; indeed, it can be present only in some imaginary way (the imaginary prop in the Chinese theater[24]). In such a case it is enough for the audience to *know* (being instructed by an actor's gestures) that the actor is holding an oar in his hands.[25]

We have reached the end of our outline of the problems of the theory of theater. By no means have we been concerned with a real survey of its problems but rather with a cursory sketch of the perspective from which the contemporary theory of theater views its tasks. We have seen that for the theoretician the organization of the stage work is beginning to acquire more and more distinctly the appearance of a structure, that is, a dynamic organization permeated with and kept in motion by a multitude of always active contradictions among individual components and groups of components—a structure which freely hovers before the spectator's eyes and consciousness without being bound unequivocally to existential reality by any of its components but thereby figuratively signifying all of the reality which surrounds and creates man of a given period and society.

24. Cf. K. Brušák, "Znaky na čínském divadle" [Signs in the Chinese theater], *Slovo a slovesnost* 5 (1939): 91 ff.

25. Cf. E. F. Burian's staging of *Komedie o Františce a Honzíčkovi* in *Druhá lidová suita* which had its premiere at D[39] on May 1, 1939.

15

The Essence of the Visual Arts

The question is: What are the visual arts? At first glance it would seem that the answer should take as its starting point either a definition or an enumeration of these arts—best of all, both a definition and an enumeration. If we attempt to proceed in this way, however, we shall immediately encounter difficulties. In our opinion even the most comprehensive definition, namely, the visual arts are those whose material is inorganic matter, those which work with space and disregard time—a definition clearly delimiting the visual arts with respect to literature and music, theater and dance—can provoke objections. Garden architecture works with organic material. Furthermore, the art of lighting, which claims to be a visual art, is obviously not only a spatial but also a temporal art. Indeed, even a theoretician of the traditional and most intrinsic visual arts could object that the experiencing of time in visual arts occurs wherever a representation of motion is concerned and that even a visual art makes a claim on the viewer's real time itself. This is the case, for example, in architecture when the viewer is compelled by the shape of a structure or that of its surroundings to walk around it in a certain direction before he enters it or to pass through its interior in a certain order. It is by such means that the architect determines the temporal progression and succession in which the viewer is to perceive the separate aspects of a structure or its individual parts. In the same way many objections could arise if we attempted to begin a general characterization of the visual arts by enumerating them. There is very little general agreement not only about what should be considered a visual art (e.g., whether photography is an art) but also about how to classify the accepted traditional arts. There are, for example, those who consider ornamental design an independent art alongside painting and sculpture. As is well known, some movements in architectural theory which are closely linked to practice declare as a principle

"Podstata výtvarných umění," a lecture at the Institute for National Education on January 26, 1944; published in *Studie z estetiky* (Prague, 1966).

that architecture is not an art. Were we to proceed from a definition and an enumeration in our characterization of the visual arts, we could encounter these and similar difficulties. They are in no way, of course, insurmountable obstacles, but their gradual removal would veil and render unclear our proper task: to penetrate to the *essence* of the visual arts.

Let us therefore choose the opposite course. We should presuppose almost nothing, I think, for we are willing to deduce everything that we shall need through our own reflection.

The first stop on our way will be a comparison of a work of visual art with a natural object. Let us imagine a rock and a statue made from the same stone next to one another. There are undoubtedly many similarities, even more than it appears at first glance. The statue was also once a rock, and there are more than a few instances of a sculptor's finding his inspiration in the shape of a rock. Sometimes the shape of an already finished statue shows the contours of the rock from which it has come. If, on the contrary, a statue is made of a soft material (e.g., sandstone) and is exposed to the influence of the weather, it will more and more regain the appearance of a rock in the course of time. Indeed, we can go even further: in its oldest form the most primordial statue— prehistoric, primitive man's statue—was nothing but a mere unshaped, unworked rock. Let us listen to a specialist's words on this point: "The very loosening of a stone from its close contact with the earth's surface represents its first resemblance to man, to human corporeality. If the stone is then erected, the vertical of a human figure together with the point at which this figure is joined to the earth has already been provided."[1]

As is therefore obvious, there are really many similarities between a rock and a statue, and the transition between them is completely indistinguishable. In spite of this, however, the difference between a work of art and a natural object is so considerable that their identification, albeit only in certain extreme cases, strikes us as paradoxical. You will say that this is obvious because a work of art is a product of the human hand and human will, whereas a natural object has a shape which is the product of natural forces: erosion, friction, and so on. But be careful; it is not so simple. Even a natural object can strike a viewer as a work

1. K. H. Busse, 1, 223.

of the human hand. We know of rocks resembling statues whose shapes originated through erosion. Hence the difference between a work of art and a natural object does not lie in how the object has originated, whether the human hand and will have participated in its origin, but in the organization of the object itself. If the organization of the object strikes us in such a way that we presuppose or rather conjecture some subject behind it, it does not appear to us as a natural object. It appears to us as such only if its organization strikes us as a mechanical consequence of natural forces. Thus we sense *someone,* a subject in general, behind a work of art; but a specific person-originator and his intention are inaccessible and frequently even unknown to us. Indeed, as we have already seen, they do not have to exist in the extreme case. Stated clearly: a work of art does not differ from a natural object in that it has an originator who made it but in that it appears as made and in such a way that its organization reveals a specific unified intention. Consequently, we say that a work of art in itself, regardless of whatever is outside it (and thus regardless of anyone's personality) is intentional, or reveals intentionality.

Let us add to this only a minor but important restriction. If a certain object is conceived by a certain perceiver at a certain moment as intentional or unintentional, what is often decisive is not only its organization but also the way in which the perceiver approaches it. Leonardo da Vinci thus advised young painters: "By looking attentively at old and smeared walls, or stones and veined marble of various colors, you may fancy that you see in them several compositions, landscapes, battles, figures in quick motion, strange countenances, and dresses, with an infinity of other objects. By these confused lines the inventive genius is excited to new exertions."[2] In other words, he advised them to conceive accidentally occurring lines and stains on a wall as preliminary sketches for paintings.

In our foregoing comments we separated the work of art from man-the-originator, and now in making this remark, we are suddenly bringing it closer to man-the-perceiver. We have devoted considerable effort to proving that the organization, the shaping, of a work of visual art is not necessarily dependent upon human will, and now it might seem that we are, on the contrary, making

2. *The Art of Painting* (New York, 1957), p. 110.

it dependent upon human will by introducing the perceiver. Let us not, however, forget that there is a fundamental difference between the originator and the perceiver. The originator is a single, unique individual, whereas the perceiver is anyone. The originator determines the organization of the work, whereas the perceiver, confronting a finished work, can interpret it in various ways. This conceptual process on the perceiver's part occurs only in a fleeting moment, whereas the work itself endures. Even after our digression concerning the perceiver we can therefore assert the following with confidence: A work of art in itself is organized intentionally, whereas a natural object lacks intentionality; its organization is accidental. This difference is fundamentally valid and absolutely definite. The transitions and vacillations to which we have referred several times do not invalidate this general principle.

In concluding the first part of our discussion, we have thus arrived at a rather important result. The notion of intentionality, which we have just explained as a matter of the organization of the work itself, will accompany us throughout the remainder of our deliberations.

But in defining the work of art as intentional, in contrast to a natural object, we are still far from finished with the essence of the visual arts, even with art in general. For what we have said about intentionality concerns not only artistic creation but all human creativity. Every object which man creates or recreates for his own purposes bears traces of this intervention forever. Even if its creator has long been forgotten, its organization appears intentional, and this is true even when the purpose it originally served is no longer known. Thus, when an archaeologist, bending over his site, painstakingly searches among fragments of stone for those which bear the slightest traces of intentional organization, he is looking not only for works of art but also for implements of human labor, the objects of everyday life.

Hence we confront the question of whether and how artistic intentionality differs from non-artistic, practical intentionality. We shall start with an illustrative example. We have before us some implement for work or human activity in general, be it a hammer, a plane, or a piece of furniture which has been made with these implements (in the narrow sense of the word). In none of these cases can there be any doubt about intentional organization. Insofar as we view these things as practically designed objects, hence

as tools, we judge their properties with respect to the aim which
the given thing serves. The shape, the material, and every component of the shape and material are evaluated with respect to this
goal. Moreover, we pay attention to them only with respect to it:
what does not serve this aim simply escapes our attention. For
example, in all probability the color of the handle of the hammer
will remain unnoticed. But a moment of decisive reversal can occur
when we start to look at a practically designed object in a different
way, when we observe the object itself and for itself. At that moment a peculiar change will take place—at least in our eyes. Above
all, those properties of the object which have no relation to the
practical aim and were previously overlooked, and which in some
cases were not even perceived (e.g., its color), will come to our
attention. But even those properties which have a practical use
and were formerly the center of attention now appear to us in a
different light. Being deprived of the relation to the aim lying
outside the object, these properties enter into relations with one
another within the object itself, and the object appears to us as if
it were constructed from its own properties bound into a unique
and integral whole. Whereas in the case of a practically conceived
thing a change in any of its properties or parts, undertaken for the
purpose of a better adaptation of the object to its aim, would
change nothing in its essence, now when we evaluate the object
for itself, it appears that the slightest change in any of its properties would touch its very essence and change the thing into something else. Stated concretely, in the case of a chair conceived as an
instrument for sitting, a change in the shape of its back would only
be a stage in a gradual adaptation toward the aforementioned aim;
in the case of a chair viewed for itself, however, such a modification of its unique set of properties into another equally unique
set of properties would be a change in its very essence. In the first
case we would conceive the chair as an implement that can be
produced in an infinite quantity, in the second as a unique work
of art which can be imitated but not duplicated. An effort to
exclude an object which we have conceived as a work of art from
practical usage, even if it is adapted and suitable for a practical use,
is connected with its uniqueness and, of course, its isolation.

  We have thus succeeded in revealing quite a sharp boundary between a work of art and a practical creation. We have done so on
the basis of objects which can be conceived as one or the other

without any change in their organization. It is not difficult to find such objects, for almost any practical instrument—at least at the moment when we examine it without using it—can be conceived in itself and for itself, regardless of the aim which it usually serves. Certainly every one of us has experienced moments of such artistic involvement with an object of practical use—for example, while standing before a new instrument, a piece of furniture, and so forth—which we have not yet associated with any practical use. Most often, of course, if an instrument of practical use is to attract the perceiver's attention to itself, to its organization, it will be shaped in a special way. We have in mind products of the so-called craft industry which are sometimes designated in advance not to be used but to be works of art "in the guise" of practically usable objects, for instance engraved glass cups, plastically embellished faïence bowls, and so on. If works of art in the proper sense of the word, such as paintings or statues, are concerned, it is quite evident that the attitude toward the object is not left to the viewer's whim but that the work itself in its organization directly induces the viewer to focus his attention on itself, on the set of its properties and on the internal organization of this set, and not to look beyond the work for some external aim which it could serve.

We have thus reached the conclusion that products of human activity which in general bear indications of intentionality divide roughly into two large groups. One of them serves some aim, whereas the objects of the second group are designated, if we may say so, as aims in themselves. The objects of the first group can be called implements in the broad sense of the word, the objects of the second, works of art. Each of these two groups is distinguished by a certain manner of intentional organization. An implement suggests that it is designed to serve some purpose; a work of art compels man to adopt the attitude of a mere perceiver. But we have also seen that the organization of an object does not have to function unequivocally in one of these two directions. There are, on the contrary, many cases in which one and the same object can be evaluated both as an implement and as a work of art. Let us add that one entire important visual art is specifically based upon this ambiguity of organization. This is architecture, the creations of which are simultaneously both an implement (Corbusier even said a machine) and a work of art.

It would seem that everything is now clear, but it is precisely at

this moment that urgent questions begin to arise, such as: If both
a work of art and an implement are intentional, then why is the
work of art oriented toward nothing but itself? The idea of being
oriented toward a point different from that at which we find ourselves follows from the very word *intention*. Would it be possible, however, to have an intention that is directed nowhere else
but back toward its starting point? Another question: It is clear
that an object which serves a purpose is good for something. But
what is a work of art good for, if we say that it does not serve a
purpose?

In order to make clear all those things that intimately concern
the very essence of art, we must first thoroughly re-examine intentionality as it manifests itself in the work of art. Here is what
we see. When consideration for an external aim is suppressed
(which is what happens in a work of art), a subject emerges from
behind the work, that is, someone who has either intentionally created it or who perceives it intentionally. This is natural. Intentionality deprived of a relation to an aim adheres more closely to
its human source. In the case of an instrument of practical activity
we do not care either about its originator or its user. What difference does it make who has produced the hammer or who understands what this instrument is for and who uses it? What is important is how well and how reliably it is possible to work with
this hammer. Yet in the case of a painting or a statue, the question
of use does not arise at all, and attention is necessarily directed
toward man. Might the definition of art lie in this fact? There are
some theoreticians of this view, and they claim that the work of
art is simply an expression of a personality and therefore necessary
for man. We know, however, that the intentionality contained in
human creation, and hence in a work of art, does not need to
correspond directly to the originator's individual will and personality; the originator can even be lacking in the extreme case (eroded
rocks in the shape of statues). Furthermore, if the work of art were
exclusively, or even only predominantly, to be an expression of its
originator's personality, what significance would it have for other
people, other perceivers? Another view, much more widespread in
its many variations than the preceding, sees the definition of the
work of art in its effect upon the *perceiver*. The purpose of the
work of art is to arouse the perceiver's pleasure, a special kind of
pleasure which is not diverted by any external interest—because

there is no external aim in art—but which is satisfied only by the observation of the work, by the relation between it and the perceiver. This is so-called aesthetic pleasure. We cannot assume as negative an attitude toward this view as toward the preceding. The work of art no longer appears as a matter of individual but of universal import. An indirect proof of the basic acceptability of this view is the fact that beginning with Kant, who first gave full expression to the idea of the *interesseloses Wohlgefallen* provided by the work of art, the majority of aesthetic theories have proceeded from this premise.

Nevertheless, we do not intend to accept this view passively. We cannot, of course, doubt the existence of aesthetic pleasure: every one of us knows it from personal experience. It is, however, debatable whether aesthetic pleasure is the very kernel of our relation to art, only a mere part of it, or simply an external indication of some more profound relation. After all, the mere fact that the powerful effect of a work of art is usually accompanied not only by pure pleasure but also by its very opposite, displeasure, calls for caution. Indeed, nothing is more subjective and changeable than an emotional relation to things. A work of art, and especially a visual work because matter is its material, is something extremely objective, existing independently of changeable emotions. It does not call upon the perceiver primarily to adopt an emotional attitude toward it but rather to understand it. It is not directed toward one side of man but to man in his entirety, to all his capabilities. Furthermore, it appeals not only to an individual but to everyone. It has been created with a necessary consideration for an audience, hence for a multitude, and a necessary desire on the artist's part was that the work establish an understanding between other people and himself. It has been created with the requisite that all understand it *equally,* that all comprehend it *equally.* Although this requirement is, strictly speaking, only an ideal and practically unrealizable, it is an intrinsic property of art and an essential motivation of artistic creation.

The work of art is therefore a *sign* which is supposed to mediate some suprapersonal *meaning.* But as soon as we utter the words *sign* and *meaning,* the most common and best known signs— the word, language—come to mind. And this is not at all unwarranted. Nevertheless, precisely because of this, we must have a very clear awareness of the *difference* between the artistic sign and such

signs as linguistic ones. The word—in its normal, non-poetic usage—
serves communication. It has an external aim: to depict some
event, to describe some thing, to express some emotion, to stimulate some behavior in the listener, and so on. All of this, however,
goes beyond the word itself; all of this is somewhere outside linguistic expression. Language is therefore a sign-*instrument* serving
an external aim. A product of visual art—for example, a painting—
can also, of course, tend to communicate something and hence be
a sign-instrument. Thus a picture in an illustrated commercial
catalogue serves the purpose of providing information about goods
which cannot be depicted in words, and it is a companion and
equally important complement of the verbal message. Indeed, even
a picture intended as a work of art usually communicates something—and often in a very precise way: for instance, a portrait of a
person or of a landscape (the so-called *veduta*).

Nevertheless, the significance of a work of art as a work of art
per se does not lie in communication. The work of art, as we have
already said, is not oriented toward anything that is outside itself,
toward any external aim. But only something which is outside the
sign itself can be communicated. The artistic sign, unlike the communicative sign, is non-serving, that is, it is not an instrument. The
understanding which the artistic sign establishes among people
does not pertain to *things,* even when they are represented in the
work, but to a certain *attitude* toward *things,* a certain attitude on
the part of man toward the *entire* reality which surrounds him, not
only toward that reality which is directly represented in the given
case. The work does not, however, communicate this attitude—
hence the intrinsic artistic "content" of the work is also inexpres-
sible in words—but *evokes* it directly in the perceiver. We call this
attitude the "meaning" of the work only because it is rendered in
the work objectively by its organization and is thereby accessible
to everyone and always repeatable.

But by what is this attitude rendered in the work? Reference to
a direct analysis of a work gives us the best answer to this question. Let us imagine a painting representing anything (we are not
interested in the theme at the moment). First of all, we shall see a
plane delimited by a frame and on this plane color-patches and
lines. How very simple these elements appear to be, but how complex the interplay of meaning in reality! Each of these elements in
itself and in its connection with the others is in several respects a

vehicle of meaning and a meaning-creating factor, regardless of what is represented by it and the others. Here we cannot carry out a complete, detailed semantic analysis of the elements of the painting, nor do we have to. A brief demonstration will suffice. Let us look at a color-patch and for the time being only one of those which are in the painting. This color-patch is primarily a vehicle of meaning in itself: the color red affects the perceiver differently from, for example, blue or green. It evokes different associated images, stimulates different emotions, different motor reactions, and so forth. This intrinsic meaning of color which is not borrowed from any outside source can sometimes be so strong that it almost becomes reified. The color blue can evoke a distinct image of sky or water even when it is used as a pure color quality rather than for the representation of these objects. Besides this "intrinsic" meaning, however, color is also a semantic factor in relation to the plane of the picture. For the perceiver the same color-patch placed in the middle of this plane will be accompanied by a different semantic nuance than if it were shifted, for example, in a direction diagonal to some corner or perpendicular to some side of the pictorial rectangle—upward, downward, to the right, or to the left. It is only with difficulty and imprecision, of course, that we may express in words these different semantic nuances which, on the one hand, influence the meaning of the color itself in the various placements of a color-patch on the pictorial plane and which, on the other hand, have an effect upon the "sense" of the pictorial plane. Depending on circumstances a color-patch in the middle of the pictorial plane could mean something like calm, balance, or even fixation, immobility, and so on; shifted upward perpendicularly, it could evoke an image of exaltation, calm hovering; shifted diagonally to a corner, it might mean a sudden movement, an impact, a disturbance of equilibrium, an explosion, and so on. We mention all of these possibilities only with the following important reservations. First, words express only awkwardly the meanings which concern us; second, under different circumstances one and the same position of a color-patch on the delimited plane can change its meaning even to the extent of becoming an absolute contradiction. Thus a color-patch placed perpendicularly above the center of the picture but protruding downward into a point will probably be much more likely to evoke an image of collapsing than of hovering.

But we have not yet exhausted the meanings of which a color-patch can be the vehicle. There is still its relation to the other color-patches of the painting and to the color of the surrounding plane in general. If, for example, a red patch is placed on a blue background, it will appear not only optically but also semantically different from the same patch on a green background. The semantic nuances which arise in this way cannot, of course, be expressed in words but can only be felt. We should, however, be aware that a red patch on green, for example, can evoke the image of a flower in a meadow even if its shape has not been elaborated. Of course, this is an extreme case of the reification of a meaning which originally was completely non-objective.

Moreover, if a color-patch is viewed in relation to what is represented, it can acquire still other semantic nuances. Let me mention only the well-known phenomenon that the qualities of the colors themselves can create a certain foreground and background in a painting. The colors that we call "warm," such as red, tend to come to the fore, closer to the spectator, whereas the "cold" colors (e.g., blue) retreat to the background. The painter can exploit this property of colors in the semantic structure of a picture in various ways. Finally, there is the relation of a color to the objectivity of the things represented. If the same color, for example, takes up a substantial part of the contour of a thing, it acquires a close connection with the object quality of the thing, it becomes one of its properties, the local color. The *smaller* the part of the contour of the represented thing that it occupies, the more easily it acquires the quality of *light,* of color value. Very complex semantic plays, the investigation of which would lead us too far afield, are also possible. Nor shall we attempt an analysis of the other components of a painting and an enumeration of their semantic variations and nuances. Our concern has been to suggest how complex a semantic structure a painting is if it is viewed as a work of art, as an artistic sign, not as a communicative sign. From mere means of representation devoid of their own meaning all the individual components of a painting become independent meanings co-determining the meaning of the painting as a whole. And this total meaning of the painting, which arises from the complex interplay of these components, is capable of directly evoking in the perceiver a certain attitude applicable to every reality with which he will come in contact.

Thus it is not only by means of its theme but precisely by means of its artistic, verbally non-communicable meaning that a work of art influences the way in which a perceiver who has really experienced it thereafter views reality and behaves toward reality. And this is precisely the most intrinsic designation of art, of *all* the visual arts—and not only of these but of all the arts in general. We have demonstrated and justified our claim on the basis of painting alone, but it would not be difficult to prove it on the basis of other visual arts as well. Let me mention only in passing a very characteristic circumstance in architecture, an art that oscillates between service to an external aim and artistic semioticity. Buildings in which semantic components (like grandeur, prestige, religious meanings, etc.) come to the fore—hence palaces, public buildings, churches, and the like—acquire an artistic character more easily and more directly than buildings in which the semantic aspect moves into the background in the face of service to an external aim—purely utilitarian structures like factories, commercial buildings, and so on.

Now let us proceed to a summary of the second section of our paper. Whereas the first section showed us the difference between a work of visual art and a natural object, this second part has concerned the difference between a work of visual art and other products of human activity. We have come to the understanding that a work of visual art differs from other products of human activity essentially in the fact that whereas intentionality makes the latter serve a particular purpose, the same intentionality renders the work of art a *sign,* not subordinated to any external purpose but self-sufficient and evoking in man a certain attitude toward all of reality.

Our progression from the broadest comparisons to narrower ones, however, has not yet reached an end. The narrowest comparison, namely, that of works of visual art with those of other arts, still remains. Only after this comparison with the environment closest to the visual arts has been carried out will our paper be complete and the answer to the question "What are the visual arts?" be sufficient. Well, then, how do the visual arts differ from the others? What joins them together? Above all we must be aware of the fact that the interconnection of *all* the arts, not only of that branch which we call visual, is very close. It is not the same as when we compared a work of art with a natural thing and then with a practical product. In those cases the differences between art and what was compared with it lay in the very essence; in this case it is a matter of an intrinsic identity of designations, since every work of art in general is an aesthetic (artistic) sign—a sign whose properties and essence we have attempted to ascertain in the course of our paper. And this common designation, already emphasized by the old saying that art is unique and simply has a multitude of kinds (*ars una, species mille,* it reads in Latin)—this common designation results on the one hand in the fact that one and the same artist very often creates simultaneously in several arts and on the other hand in the fact that perceivers specialize in one or another art according to their inclinations and abilities without feeling this limitation as an impoverishing one-sidedness. A further consequence of the common designation of all the arts is the fact that themes migrate freely from art to art, as well as that the most varied arts are connected to one another (e.g., in the illustration of a literary work) or combined with one another. There is even an art which in its very nature is a combination of several arts. This is theater.

Nevertheless, each art has something which distinctly separates it from the others, and this is its *material.* In this respect the visual arts are separated from the others by a sharp boundary and, again, are very closely connected to one another. Their material—and only theirs—is inorganic, immobile, and relatively unchangeable matter. The tangibility of the material of the visual arts becomes readily apparent in comparison with music, its inorganic nature in comparison with dance, its unchangeability in comparison with literature, the material of which—the word—not only changes relatively quickly through development but can also be subject to subtle semantic shifts in passing from perceiver to perceiver.

We shall not digress by enumerating and explaining the minute deviations from the above properties of material that can be found in individual peripheral cases; rather we shall attempt to show how this tangible, inorganic and unchangeable material affects the arts of which it is the basis. This is an old problem. The most famous treatise on it, Lessing's *Laocoön,* bears the date 1766. Lessing, a rationalist who together with his age understood matters of art from the viewpoint of a norm, albeit not a rigid rule, also conceived this question as something which should be, rather than as a pure assertion of the state of affairs. In his treatise, therefore, he showed that graphic and plastic arts—the visual arts—must adopt a different attitude toward their themes and handle them differently than literature, an art inspired by the Muses. Thus a painting can present the entire appearance of a thing in front of a viewer's eyes at once, whereas literature must depict the same thing in parts, gradually, in time: for literature, a state changes into events. Conversely, graphic arts cannot, of course, present events otherwise than as a state. For Lessing these are not only assertions but also requirements. He believes that the arts, limited by the nature of their materials, must not attempt to overstep the boundaries thus provided.

Although Lessing's treatise contains a great deal of knowledge which has remained a lasting contribution to the study of art up to the present, this basic idea of his has obviously been superseded today. History of art, which in fact developed only after Lessing, instructs us that art, every art, constantly strives to break through the limitation provided by its material, inclining toward different arts at different times. It is, of course, another question whether such a liberation from the preconditions arising from the properties of material can succeed at all. Here it is obvious. In reality even the greatest effort at slipping out of the bonds of material cannot annul the very essence of this material. For this reason everything that a certain art undertakes according to the model of another art necessarily changes its original meaning when expressed by means of a different material. Thus if literature attempts to depict according to the model of graphic art, it cannot compel words to have an effect upon vision; an attempt at coloration in literature will therefore have quite a different result than in graphic art. A noticeable shift in vocabulary will occur: adjectives, nouns, and also verbs capable of *signifying,* not directly presenting, a color will increase excessively in the given writer's vocabulary and will provide it with a special character. Still another verbal differentiation of coloration is possible. If primarily adjectives are used for the expression of colors, the colors will appear as fixed properties of things. If nouns signifying individual color shades are used, the color as a non-objective optical quality (blue, red, etc.) will obtain. Finally, if mainly verbs are used (to redden, to blush, etc.), the meanings of the colors will gain dynamicity. These individual verbal techniques can, of course, correspond to various manners of painting, but even in that case they will not be their equals but will be only their verbal equivalents. So much for literature striving for the nature of visual arts.

Conversely, the visual arts can, and frequently do, strive to overstep the boundaries separating them from the other arts. Thus, just as we have seen literature attempting to compete directly with painting, painting can try to compete with literature. This will happen, for example, when painting attempts the narration of anecdotal themes, as it did before the advent of Realism in about the middle of the last century. It will also happen if painting is seized with the desire to depict figurative designations (metaphors, metonymies, synecdoches) which are the privilege of the poetic word. Not too many years ago we saw in Prague an exhibition of paintings, characteristically called "Poetry," that contained pictures of this kind. After all, even today such a sober relative of painting as photography commonly uses synecdoches in showing us a part of an object instead of the whole. Painting can, however, even experience the lure of non-objective (or rather non-thematic) music and be inspired by its rhythm. We have examples of non-thematic painting which have openly revealed this ambition.

Hence the purpose of material in art—and in the visual arts as well—is not to keep a close watch on the boundaries between individual arts but to provoke by means of these limiting and regulating properties the artist's fantasy to fruitful resistance and, of course, agreement. There are countless cases—and very illustrative ones in the visual arts—in which the material meets the artist head on, in which the work grows out of the material. We have already referred to the cases in which the shape of a rock predetermined the shape of the statue that originated from it. However, it is not only the shape of the material that is decisive; so are its other properties. The hardness or softness of stone, the frangibility of stone in comparison with the suppleness of metal, the shining quality of marble, the luster of metal, the pliability of wood—all of these are not only properties of material but also creative possibilities for a sculptor. There are frequent cases in which art historians have been able to say definitely that some old statue is a copy of a lost original executed in a material different from that of the copy. The influence of the material on the original organization of the work was so considerable that the later transference into a different material was not sufficient to conceal it.

Hence it is obvious that the material by which particular arts differ from one another, and by which, of course, the visual arts as a whole differ from the others, is not a merely passive basis of artistic activity but is an almost active factor that directs the activity and constantly intervenes—whether positively or negatively—in it. In entering the sphere of artistic creation, its individual properties are transferred into the elementary artistic meanings about which we spoke above; they then offer themselves to the artist so that he can knead from them the total complex meaning by which the work affects the perceiver. If we say, therefore, that the visual arts differ from the others in their material, we do not only provide a distinctive feature, as was so in the previous cases, but we get right to the very focal point of artistic creation.

We have come to the end of the road. If there remains more to discuss, it is the place of the visual arts in man's life, and this requires only a few words. In fact, we have already said or at least suggested the most essential thing about it. The visual arts can and do serve to please the eye and the feelings. In addition, they can be of great value for national self-esteem and prestige. They can and often are—especially in certain periods and in certain places—a very important economic factor, whether on the domestic market, in foreign trade, or in stimulating tourism. Furthermore, they can serve for the propagation of ideas or principles, and they can perform other tasks as well. In spite of all this, however, their most essential function, without which all the other tasks remain mere shadows or are not even realized, lies in their influence upon man's attitude toward reality. Works of art are above all non-serving, self-sufficient signs in the sense about which we have spoken in the course of our deliberations. Yet despite their material nature, which at first glance renders them mere things, works of the visual arts are also such signs. Even more: the visual arts are the most effective of all in performing this basic task of art in general. We have to open a book of poetry, we have to enter a theater or concert hall, but we encounter works of visual art on the street, we see them if we look at walls, and even the instruments that we use for the most common daily tasks are for the most part under their influence—either direct or indirect. Such a great influence, of course, calls for caution in selection and evaluation, but this is the beginning of another chapter to which we shall devote a separate lecture in this series.

16

On the Problem of Functions in Architecture

The question of function in architecture is inseparable from the question of function in contemporary thought, cultural creation, and everyday life. The functional view permits us to conceive things as events without denying their materiality. It shows the world simultaneously as motion and as a fixed basis of human activity. The notion of function, the basic working hypothesis of modern culture, is in the process of evolution and internal differentiation. We must therefore always have its characteristics in mind, and we must constantly review them. What are they? What do we want to express when we speak about the function of a certain thing?

First of all, the notion of function means that we commonly use the object which is its vehicle for such and such a purpose. Custom, repeated usage, is a necessary precondition of a function. This term is not appropriate for a single and unique use of a thing. But not even the subjective customariness of a certain usage of a given object, a customariness limited to an individual, comprises a function in the proper sense of the word. Furthermore, there must be social consensus on the purpose which the object serves. A particular mode of using a given object must be spontaneously comprehensible to every member of a given collective. The affinity—though *not* the identity—of the problem of function with the problems of the sign follows from this: The object not only performs but also signifies its function. If we are concerned, for example, with a thing perceivable by the senses, its sensory perception is predetermined by our awareness of what it is used for; both the shape and the incorporation into space of the perceived object often depend on this awareness. Thus if we are aware of what the purpose of the handle of a tool is, we shall interpret it during the process of perception—regardless of its actual position at a given moment—as that part of the object which is usually the

"K problému funkcí v architektuře," *Stavba* 19 (1937–38).

closest to us and the one from which we begin to apprehend the shape. If we cannot, however, identify the handle in the process of perception, it will appear to us as an accidental protrusion illogically disturbing the unity of the shape, and the shape itself will be unsatisfactorily ambiguous for us.

A thing is not, however, inevitably connected with a single function; indeed, there is almost no object that does not serve a whole set of functions. Every act in which an object is used can simultaneously pursue more than one purpose. It is also possible to use a thing for another purpose and with another function than its usual one or even than the one for which its producer designed it. Finally, an object can change its conventional function in the course of time. All of this depends, on the one hand, upon the collective that conventionally associates certain functions with a particular object and, on the other hand, upon the individual who uses the object for his personal aims and largely determines this usage.

Therefore the bond of a thing with a function does not depend only on the thing itself but also on who uses it, on man as a member of a collective and as an individual. The awareness of the collective is not, of course, limited to establishing isolated functions but sets individual functions into complex interrelations, the regularity of which governs the collective's entire active attitude toward reality. The individual as a member of a collective has at his disposal a generally accepted group of functions as well as functions conventionally attributed to the world of phenomena. But in his actions he can deviate from this regualrity by using things in functions that are not connected with them by common consensus, or by reversing—in the multiplicity of functions which have often accumulated around each of these things—their customary hierarchy and rendering a normally secondary function dominant. As is evident, we must distinguish (a) the reality to which the functions are applied, (b) the set of functions lodged in the awareness of the collective and bound by internal interrelations into a structure, and (c) the individual who introduces a constantly renewed accidentality into the functional process and thus sets the structure of functions into motion. None of these three series is unequivocally linked to any of the others nor is passively predetermined by it; their interrelations are changeable, and they undergo development.

Hence we have arrived at a view of functions as a historically changeable structure of forces governing man's entire attitude toward reality. We have now left far behind the notion that function is a unique relationship between a concrete object and a concrete aim. We must still, however, make a further generalization. Both human acts and even the subfunctions that immediately govern these acts can be reduced to certain basic tendencies—the primary functions rooted in the anthropological organization of man. We can presuppose that no matter how much the attitudes which man adopts toward reality in different periods, places, and social conditions change, there is something common to all of them. Several basic tendencies, caused by the fact that man's psychological organization is more or less constant, become evident in one form or another in the manner in which man reacts to reality and reshapes it, affirming it or negating it in his struggle for existence.

We must not, of course, deceive ourselves by supposing that these primary functions can be easily enumerated and catalogued because of their anthropological basis and their apparent small number. Even in the present state of the maximal autonomy of functions it is often difficult to demarcate and delimit precisely the participation of individual functions in a particular act or type of act. It would be even more difficult to estimate precisely which of the discernible functions are primary, that is, not reducible to other functions or historically unconditioned, and which, on the contrary, are derived and have originated by the differentiation of the primary functions. The maximal autonomy of functions that we are prone to consider normal is, however, the result of a long development. Until the nineteenth century—and it is still true today in folkloric cultures insofar as they have been preserved— the structural bond of functions was so close that they acted as whole bundles in which individual functions stood out as nuances, transitory and inseparable from the entire group. For example, it is almost impossible to distinguish the aesthetic function from the magico-religious (cf. tattooing or intentional body scars among some primitive peoples) or erotic functions. Because of the dominance of the structural bond among functions over individual functions it is sometimes possible to identify one and the same function in two different historical or social contexts only with great difficulty. There have been cases, for example, in medieval literature in which the aesthetic function—one of the most distinctly discernible—had to be identified by complex scholarly analysis.

For these reasons an effort at enumerating the basic functions would necessarily be futile. On the other hand, however, there are enough reasons for us to presume that the functions as a whole are rooted in the anthropological organization of man and therefore that in every act, the agent of which is man, all the functions are potentially present, insofar, of course, as they can be related to this act at all. As a rule, the concrete aim of an action implies a whole series of functions, one of which is usually dominant, while the others are concomitant. It is characteristic of the integrity of a set of functions that an agent can alter the functions of a thing according to the situations in which he uses it, or he can even erroneously interpret the function of his own creation. Thus we know of cases in which a painter or other visual artist has involuntarily given a false verbal interpretation of his own subconscious creative intention. It can also happen that the individuals to whom the agent's action is addressed will attribute to this action functions other than those which he has attributed to it and for which he has adapted it, and that they will react to it in accordance with their own conception. Therefore if we presume that a certain product of human activity is designated for fulfilling this or that function, and if we deal with this product accordingly, our presumption has in no way proved that the function (or functions) which we attribute to this product comprises a part of the producer's intention. For example, if a creation that comes from a foreign milieu appears to us as a work of art, we need not presume that the aesthetic function was willed by the originator of the creation or even that this function was distinctly dominant for him. All of this proves that there are potentially present in every act and its result functions other than those which the act obviously fulfills. Indeed, because man is the agent of the act, all the primary functions rooted in his anthropological organization are potentially present, unless, of course, some of them are incompatible with the thing or act.

Having made these general remarks, let us proceed to the question of functions in architecture. We can refer directly to what we have just said, for architecture is a typical example of polyfunctional production. Modern theoreticians of architecture rightly understand a building as a set of life processes for which it is the setting. An architectural creation differs from any genuine instrument of human activity and from an instrument as complex as a

machine by being unconnected to any specific activity and
designed to serve as a spatial milieu for the most varied activities.
The comparison of an architectural creation with a machine
(Corbusier) is an extreme expression of the tendency of a period
toward the least ambiguous functionality in architecture, but in
no way is it a supratemporal characteristic.

Architecture organizes the space surrounding man. It organizes
this space as a whole and with respect to man in his entirety, that
is, with respect to all the physical or psychic actions of which man
is capable and of which a building can become the setting. When
we say that architecture organizes this *space as a whole,* we mean
that none of the parts of architecture has functional independence
but that each of them is evaluated only according to how it forms
—motorically or optically—the space into which it is incorporated
and which it delimits. As an example let us take a machine (e.g., a
sewing machine or a mechanical musical instrument such as a
piano) placed in a dwelling space. Every machine has its specific
function; as an architectural component (a part of a dwelling
space), however, it is not evaluated according to this specific function but according to how it forms space for man's eye and his
movement. Its own function is considered only insofar as it manifests itself in this organization. For example, the specific function
of a sewing machine comes into consideration only to the extent
that its placement allows its operator to sit comfortably without
obstructing the movement of the other inhabitants of the room,
to have enough light, and so on. The specific function of a piano
makes the same demands with respect to architectural space as
well as some others, for example, the requirement for the
optimum acoustical placement. Nevertheless, whether or not the
given machine (instrument) is capable of fulfilling its own task
will remain completely outside the realm of architecture and the
range of its interests. Similarly in the case of sculptures and paintings forming a part of architectural space, the question of architectural value will primarily concern the way in which these works
contribute to the formation of this space. We have said above that
architecture organizes space with respect to man in his entirety,
that is, with respect to all the physical or mental actions of which
he is capable. As a matter of fact, this assertion follows from the
sentence that in essence all the functions are potentially present in
every human act insofar as they are at all compatible with the

given act. In architecture, however, the more heterogeneous the set of activities which an architectural creation has to serve, the more emphatically the omnipresence of all the functions comes to the fore.

Not every building, of course, is designed for all activities; there is a set of architectural types, each of which indicates a certain limitation and delimitation of functionality. But the individual types do not lack interrelations and mutual influences, and only the sum of *all* the architectural types of a certain period and milieu characterizes the entire exploitation of the functional realm by architecture at a given time and in a given milieu. The proof of the close interconnection of the architectural types lies in the fact that every period in architecture has a dominant type with regard to which it solves its basic constructive problems. In Gothic architecture it was the cathedral, in the Renaissance and Baroque periods it was the palace—half-public and half-private, and today it is the private home. And thus, in spite of the differentiation of types, it is valid that architecture relates to man in his entirety, to the sum of his physical and mental needs. In mentioning mental as well as physical needs, we have in mind above all the psychological effects of an architectural creation which we usually describe by such unspecific terms as coziness, monumentality, and so on. The potential relation of architecture to *all* man's needs and aims is vividly illustrated by the possibility of a shift in the dominant function of an architectural creation (cf. the use of a palace as an official building or a stock exchange as a university building) and by the possibility of a shift in the dominant function of an entire architectural *type* (cf. the evolution of a type of basilica from a commercial into a religious building).

Hence the functionality of architecture is a very complex matter. It is not only a question, as the pioneer of the functional view once believed, of a simple relationship between the individual who establishes the purpose and the purpose which necessarily and directly determines the forms and the organization of a building. What we have are *four functional horizons,* and none of these need or do coincide with the others. First, the functions of a building are determined by an immediate purpose; second, they are determined by a historical purpose. Even if, for example, it is a question of a purpose as individual as the building of a family residence, the organization and the lay-out of the building, and hence its functionality, are governed not only by an immediate practical consideration but also by a fixed canon (a set of norms) for this kind of structure and its previous development; the two aspects of purposefulness, the immediate and the historical, can clash in the solution of the given problem. The third functional horizon is created by the organization of the collective to which the client and the architect belong. Even the most utilitarian functions of a building appear and relate to one another in accordance with the organization of society, the available economic and material possibilities, and so forth. Various nuances of the symbolic function are also incorporated into this functional horizon.[1] This social functional horizon also has its own specific requirements that do not necessarily coincide with the requirements of the previously mentioned horizons. Finally, there is the individual functional horizon: An individual can obviously deviate from everything which has been set as a norm by the preceding horizons; he can combine their diverging requirements in various ways; and so on. Nor must we forget that in addition to the effort to adhere to a strict functionality there can occur in any functional scheme a tendency toward a more or less radical violation of it and that the violation of previous functional norms can indicate the beginning of a new functional development and hence the development of architecture itself. Such a violation of functionality as a rule derives from the decision of an individual, whether the individual as client or the individual as architect.

The four functional horizons that we have just enumerated are obviously not identical to one another, nor are they necessarily parallel—quite the contrary. They are, however, in a state of constant hierarchical interrelation; this means that as a rule one of them prevails, although the dominant horizon, of course, keeps changing in the process of development. Thus in modern architecture, immediate purpose received the greatest emphasis at the beginning, but in recent years social functionality has also been stressed. The eclectic architecture of the eighties and nineties put the main emphasis on architectural purpose as a historical fact, that is, on the architectural type. Evidence of this may be found in the fact that very often an architectural type feigned another type:

1. See J. Kroha's article "Dnešní problémy sovětské architektury" [Contemporary problems of Soviet architecture], *Praha – Moskva* 1 (1936): 126–35, 165–66.

for example, an apartment building simulated a palace through the articulation of its façade. The period immediately following, the Art Nouveau architecture, stressed individual functionality. The requirement was to comply with the demands made by the individual, even to adapt a building to fictitious functions which the individual attributed to it, albeit to the detriment of its real task. Hence the exuberant lyricism of architecture in this period.

Therefore, an analysis of the functions in architecture has led us to the conclusion that architecture always appeals to man in his entirety, to all the components of his existence, from his general, common anthropological basis to his social and unique determination. Moreover, architecture in its functionality is predetermined by its immanent history. There is no unambiguous functionality here. The individual functions and their interrelations appear different when projected onto different horizons. The task of an architectural study, therefore, is not only the diagnosis of individual functions but also the conscious control of the individual horizons in which these functions are reflected. In using the word *conscious,* we by no means want to exclude the moment of the irrational, intuitive, and active apprehension, or the constant pressure of unexpectedness coming from individual functionality. Disregard and suppression of the requirements of this horizon could in practice lead to a petrification of development. Every use of a human creation, whether a material or an immaterial thing, is to a certain extent its "misuse," an alteration of its function. Thus in the case of architecture as well, the question of how and to what extent it is possible, and even necessary, to go beyond the given designation of a building, or to shift the participation of the individual functional horizons, is a necessary one, despite its seeming troublesomeness. The question of the subsidiary and often only potential functional possibilities of an architectural creation is also related to this. These are the functions which are not part of the given practical intention but which are perceived as overtones in the psychological effect of the building—sometimes even in its active use. Even these functions cannot be overlooked or suppressed without detriment if they are not to become latently harmful.

Let us now shift to the complex and troublesome problem of the *aesthetic function* in architecture. In this connection we shall have to say something about the relationship between architecture and art. In regard to the position of the aesthetic function among the others, we should at least mention that this function is the dialectic negation of functionality, no matter where and in what environment it occurs. After all, any function besides the aesthetic can manifest itself only where a thing is used for some purpose. No matter where and when it occurs, however, the aesthetic function becomes stronger, the more it renders the thing itself as the purpose, that is, the more it hinders its practical use. If we are to look for an illustration in architecture itself, we can cite the fact that interiors with a hypertrophied aesthetic function inhibit their own usage by attracting too much attention to themselves. Even a modification of an interior resulting from a change or a mere rearrangement of the furniture is temporarily capable of causing an undesired (for the inhabitants) revival of the aesthetic function of individual pieces of furniture, as well as that of the whole interior, thus decreasing the practical usability of the rooms.

This example, however, leads us to a further general thesis. The aesthetic function does not emerge suddenly, without transition, as something added and supplementary but is always potentially present, waiting for the least opportunity for revival. This follows from the thesis which we introduced at the beginning of this paper about the potential omnipresence of all the functions. But the omnipresence of the aesthetic function is especially conspicuous and unlimited. The aesthetic function as the dialectic negation of functionality in general contradicts each function and every set of functions. Therefore its position among the functions is similar to a flow of air among objects or, even better, to a blend of darkness and light. The aesthetic function clings closely to and follows the other functions just as space fills up with air everywhere that an object has withdrawn, or just as darkness penetrates a fold of space from which light has retreated. The aesthetic function immediately penetrates and enlarges proportionately wherever the other functions have weakened, withdrawn, or shifted. Moreover, there is not an object which cannot become its vehicle or, conversely, an object which necessarily has to be its vehicle. If certain objects are produced with the direct intention of aesthetic effectiveness and are adapted formally to this intention, it by no means follows necessarily that they cannot lose this function partially or entirely, for example, because of a change in time, space, or milieu. Hence the aesthetic function emerges and vanishes without being unalterably bound to any object. Because it prefers to occupy a place vacated by all the other functions, it frequently occurs wherever a thing, even an immaterial thing, such as a certain system, has lost its practical function (cf. the beauty of ruins, etc.).[2] But because it is equally related to all the functions by being their contradiction, it is suited for bridging the past and future stratification of functions in developmental shifts and thus, in contrast to the preceding case, is often a factor of development and a herald of change. Even when there is a restratification, the final aim of which is the supremacy of practical functions, the aesthetic function sometimes temporarily takes charge to facilitate the shift. For example, the first symptoms of functionalism, but with aesthetic coloration, appear in van de Velde, the most significant representative of Art Nouveau architecture. He speaks about the *beauty* of a machine as a supremely purposeful creation, about the beauty of a dynamic line, and so on. The two effects of the aesthetic function, the one conserving and the other facilitating change, necessarily follow from its essence. Finally, we must mention that there is a realm of phenomena in which the aesthetic function prevails over the others or at least tends to do so: this is art. No art is separated from the rest of the world of phenomena in a hermetically sealed compartment. There are unnoticeable transitions and a constant fluctuation between art and the extra-artistic, even the extra-aesthetic, sphere.

Having made these few general remarks, limited to the most basic and necessary thesis, let us turn our attention to the special

2. The capacity of substituting for vanished functions belongs to a certain extent to *all semiotic functions,* that is, those which render a thing a sign; cf., the symbolic function which takes over—often concurrently with the aesthetic function—things (institutions) excluded from practical usage. The aesthetic function is one of the semiotic functions, for the object that is its vehicle becomes *ipso facto* a sign, although a special kind of sign. Art, which is supposed to mediate between two parties, the artist and the perceiver, on the basis of a convention created by the immediately preceding state of the artistic structure, reveals the semiotic character of the aesthetic function. The capacity of substituting for a vanished function is, however, stronger in the aesthetic function than in other semiotic functions, for the aesthetic function is the dialectic negation of semioticity itself (cf. the transformation of the communicative function in a literary work or in a painting). Therefore the aesthetic function can even substitute for another semiotic function that has become extinct. For example, it alone is capable of keeping alive a certain ritual whose intrinsic meaning has fallen into oblivion; cf. such relics of folklore as the "burning" of witches in our land. Finally, a thing can permanently lose all its functions, even the semiotic, the aesthetic included; then, of course, it is doomed to destruction.

question of the aesthetic function in architecture. Its position here is peculiar and can be expressed most appropriately in a few contradictions: (1) The aesthetic function can manifest itself in any architectural type beginning with such practical buildings as the granary, the warehouse or the factory. In some architectural types it is even a necessary component of the total effect, for example in monumental structures. Architecture is closely connected in its development to those arts which are called visual; it has in common with them, for example, the problems of space. On the other hand, there is by no means an unambiguous boundary between structures with an aesthetic function and those without it; there are direct links from architecture to crafts, even those which lack aesthetic intention, and to industrial production. In architecture it is impossible for the aesthetic function to prevail— as in the other arts—or at least to reach the extreme limit of possibility in this direction. Here practical functions can never be fully subordinated to the aesthetic function so that a building becomes an aesthetically autonomous creation. If this happened, then—according to Karel Teige's correct formulation—architecture *ipso facto* would turn into sculpture; it would begin to be perceived and evaluated as sculpture. (2) The aesthetic function appears in architecture as something added, something coming from outside. It tends to be found on the surface of a building (cf. the ornament; it even used to be proclaimed that architecture begins where construction ends). It often manifests itself in components less charged with practical functions (as, for example, color[3]). It often appears as something which *exceeds* a required function (a more defined and more regular shape than that which would be necessary for the perfect fulfillment of a practical function, etc.). On the other hand, it is true that the aesthetic function does not come from the outside but is absolutely immanent in architecture. Evidence of this lies in the fact that the aesthetic function merges

---

3. In this connection we can note that the following classification is sometimes suggested: optical effect—aesthetic function; motor effect—practical function. It is true that the aesthetic function is mainly concentrated around visual perception, whereas practical functions are connected especially with the possibilities of movement that a building offers man. Nevertheless, it is impossible to completely exclude the optical factor from the realm of practical functions (cf. the practical significance of the color of a wall in a room of a dwelling, e.g., a study) or the motor factor from the range of the aesthetic functions (cf. the perfect accessibility of the individual parts of a space as an aesthetic requirement).

with practical functions into indiscernible clusters. For example, it is impossible to define precisely the share which the aesthetic has in the functional category of monumentality (with which, of course, it is not identical); likewise the participation of the aesthetic function—despite its obvious presence—is indefinable in the functional effect of dwelling "comfort" or dwelling "coziness." In the course of the historical development of architecture the aesthetic function has gradually blended with other functions: thus with the religious function in the Gothic period, with the prestige function in the Renaissance, with both the ecclesiastic-religious and prestige functions in the Baroque.

If we are to attempt to solve, though only sketchily, these seeming contradictions, we must above all make precise the relationship between architecture and art. As we know, the contemporary theory of architecture radically excludes architecture from art, even though it in no way denies the importance of the aesthetic function for it. A sharp demarcation of art and the extra-artistic sphere accompanies this exclusion. Only the realm of free lyricism unlimited by an extra-aesthetic consideration—in other words, the realm of the predominant aesthetic function—is regarded as art. Since architecture cannot achieve dominance of the aesthetic function without losing its essence, its exclusion from the arts is a logical consequence of the above view of the essence of art. The source of this notion is not a supratemporal principle but a tendency which temporarily dominated artistic theory and practice around the beginning of the last decade (the tendency toward so-called pure art). Of course, we cannot deny that there is a breach between architecture and the other arts in the sense that the other arts function only in the sphere of spiritual culture, whereas architecture functions simultaneously in spiritual and material culture. But, on the other hand, we cannot overlook the circumstances that reconcile it with the other arts. If we view art in all its temporal, spatial, and social breadth, it appears that the tendency toward the domination of the aesthetic function over the others is in no art any more than just a tendency that remains not completely realized, even in the most extreme cases. Furthermore, it will be apparent that without a violent break, every art merges with the sphere uncontestably dominated by extra-aesthetic functions, hence with the extra-aesthetic sphere. There is no sharp division between a literary work and a communicative utterance which is aesthetically colored. The same holds true for painting (e.g., a poster), indeed, even for music where we can find an obvious competition between the aesthetic and extra-aesthetic functions, such as marching music, dance music, and music intended to stir the emotions. The historical development of every art is accompanied by a constant alternation of ebbs and flows of extra-aesthetic functions, and even in the purest artistic creation these functions are not eliminated but are only reorganized, losing their practical impact and entering contact with everyday life only through the mediation of an artistic structure as a whole. Because of its constant contact with the extra-aesthetic sphere, indeed its direct merging with it, art influences the nature and changes of functions and values in everyday life. This fact alone can explain how art, generally limited to a narrow circle of consumers, affects the very heart of everyday life.

In architecture as well as in the other arts there is a constant struggle between the subordination and superordination of aesthetic value, but with the sole difference that in architecture the aesthetic function cannot achieve complete dominance. Yet, the contact of architecture with the extra-aesthetic realm is unusually close not only because within architecture itself creations lacking aesthetic intentionality are in contact with creations having a strong aesthetic function, but also because there is a direct link from architecture to crafts and factory production. The differentiation of architecture from the other arts is therefore at the same time a bond which ties it to them. Architecture, so firmly rooted in material culture, unlike the other arts, is the first to become a bridge over which the conquests of art cross directly into everyday life. Architecture does not mediate only its own conquests but also those of other arts, especially those of the closest ones, painting and sculpture, with which it shares some common or at least similar formal problems, such as the problems of space, light, and color.[4] Despite its exceptional position, therefore, architecture is inevitably linked to art. Its basic dialectic antinomy is in essence valid for every art. We can formulate this antinomy as a constant struggle—always resolved in a new way—between the tendency toward the dominance of the aesthetic function over the others

4. It is interesting that Hegel assigns architecture to the "lowest" place among the arts: in Hegel architecture dominates in the first of the three epochs of artistic development, the symbolic period.

and the tendency toward the dominance of the other functions over the aesthetic. If it is impossible for architecture to achieve an actual dominance of the aesthetic function, it is also true that each of the other arts has a different limit that it can reach in this respect: in music the aesthetic function can very easily and almost completely achieve dominance, in literature less easily and less completely, in drama even less (cf. the difference between the strictness of censorship with regard to literature and to drama). We have already said above that the aesthetic function in architecture appears both as something superficial and as something immanent; this contradiction is only an aspect of the basic antinomy that we have just mentioned. In other words, it is in effect a clash between internal and external form, which is after all manifested in every art, only more visibly in architecture, for the stronger the tension is between the two poles, the less the aesthetic function has the possibility of acquiring absolute dominance over the extra-aesthetic functions. If we look at the position of architecture with regard to art from the viewpoint just described, the quarrel about whether it is or is not an art will appear as a matter of terminology.

Finally, we must say a few words about the way in which the aesthetic function originates in architecture and generates aesthetic value. The theory of functionalism expressed the view that the aesthetic function is a consequence of the undisturbed operation and perfect coordination of the other functions. A compelling aspect of this thesis was that it viewed the work of art as a sum of extra-aesthetic functions and their values. This axiom is also valid for other arts and for the aesthetic function in general wherever it appears. As the dialectic contradiction of all the other functions, the aesthetic function appears as a consequence of their particular interrelation or, in some cases, of a shift in this relation. It is, however, a question whether in architecture as well as elsewhere the perfect agreement of all extra-aesthetic functions and the pleasure deriving from it are the indispensable preconditions of the origin of the aesthetic function. The development of art, including architecture, does not lack examples of a new work, even a valuable one, meeting with a storm of protest. The reception of Adolf Loos' Viennese house on Michaelerplatz is an illustrative case. But, besides this, it is still doubtful whether it is at all possible that the coordination of the extra-aesthetic functions can be perfect, that is, the only possible coordination. The harmonization of the four functional horizons through which every extra-aesthetic function passes, acquiring in each of them a different appearance and a different relation to the others, would belong to such a coordination. The perfect coordination of the functions from the standpoint of one horizon necessarily entails a stronger or weaker violation of the coordination from the standpoint of the other horizons. Rather than the possibility of attaining a total harmony we find here a choice among several ways of violating it. At most we can speak here—as everywhere else in art—about the need for the balancing of functional, and thus structural, consonances with dissonances. In contrast to the stasis of a mere harmony such a balancing is, of course, always labile, dynamic, subject to changes deriving from shifts in the total functional hierarchy which is valid for a given collective. It is, of course, true that architecture can anticipate these transformations of the functional system and tend toward a renewal of functions and their interrelations, but even this, and precisely this, effort will appear from a contemporary viewpoint as a violation resulting in the revival of aesthetic effect. And thus even in this respect architecture belongs among the arts.

Selected Bibliography
of Jan Mukařovský's Writings

This selected bibliography was composed by F. W. Galan from a variety of published and unpublished sources. It lists only Mukařovský's structuralist writings, omitting such minor items as answers to opinion polls, second editions, and Slovak translations. The items are arranged in chronological order.

1. "P. Bujnák a J. Menšík: *Slovenská poetika*" [Slovak poetics]. *Střední škola* 29 (1921–22): 83–85. Review.

2. *Příspěvek k estetice českého verše* [A contribution to the esthetics of Czech verse], 64 pp. Prague: Filosofická fakulta University Karlovy, 1923.

3. "Odpověď na recenzi p. dr. J. V. Sedláka" [A reply to J. V. Sedlák's review]. *Časopis pro moderní filologii* 10 (1923–24): 312–17.

4. "Vyučování jazyku mateřskému na školách francouzských a o potřebě jeho reformy na školách našich" [The teaching of the mother tongue in French schools and on the need for a teaching reform in Czech schools]. *Střední škola* 32 (1924–25): 17–23, 49–60, 129–37, 219–25, 262–65.

5. "Poznámky ke Králově *Prozodii české*" [Notes on Král's Czech prosody]. *Časopis pro moderní filologii* 11 (1924–25): 7–13, 118–24.

6. "Pokus o slohový rozbor *Babičky* Boženy Němcové" [An attempt at a stylistic analysis of Božena Němcová's *Babička*]. *Sborník prací věnovaných prof. dr. Janu Máchalovi k sedmdesátým narozeninám*, edited by Jiří Horák and Miloslav Hýsek, pp. 130–39. Prague: Klub moderních filologů, 1925.

7. "O volném verši českém" [On Czech free verse]. *Časopis Českého muzea* 99 (1925): 97–124.

8. "R. Jakobson: *Základy českého verše*" [Foundations of Czech verse]. *Naše řeč* 10 (1926): 174–80, 212–21. Review.

9. "F. Trávníček: *Příspěvky k nauce o českém přízvuku*" [Contributions to the study of Czech stress]. *Naše věda* 9 (1927–28): 4–11. Review.

10. *Máchův Máj. Estetická studie* [Mácha's *Máj*: An aesthetic study], 166 pp. Prague: Filosofická fakulta University Karlovy, 1928.

11. "Metafora" [Metaphor]. *Masarykův Slovník naučný*, vol. 4, p. 896. Prague: Čs. kompas, 1929. Encyclopedia entry.

12. "Metonymie" [Metonymy]. *Ibid.*, vol. 4, p. 905.

13. "Metrika" [Metrics]. Ibid., vol. 4, p. 907.

14. "Poetika a stylistika a jejich vztahy k dějinám literárním" [Poetics and stylistics and their relations to literary history]. I. sjezd slovanských filologů v Praze 1929. A Contribution to the 1st Congress of Slavicists— a separate preprint.

15. "Rapport de la ligne phonique avec l'ordre des mots dans les vers tchèques," *Travaux du Cercle linguistique de Prague,* vol. 1, *Mélanges linguistiques dédiés au Premier Congrès des philologues slaves,* pp. 121–39. Prague: Jednota českých matematiků a fyziků, 1929.

16. "Boris Tomaševskij: Nová ruská škola v bádání literárněhistorickém" [A new Russian school in the study of literary history]. *Časopis pro moderní filologii* 15 (1928–29): 12–15. Translation from French.

17. "O současné poetice" [On contemporary poetics]. *Plán* 1 (1929–30): 387–97.

18. "J. V. Sedlák: *K problémům rytmu básnického*" [On the problems of poetic rhythm]. *Listy filologické* 56 (1929): 378–84. Review.

19. "Varianty a stylistika" [Variants and stylistics]. *Studie a vzpomínky: Prof. dr. Arne Novákovi k padesátým narozeninám,* edited by Benjamin Jedlička, pp. 52–55. Vyškov: F. Obzina, 1930.

20. "Karel Čapek: *Povídky z jedné kapsy.*" *Nové Čechy* 13 (1930–31): 126–28. Review.

21. "Novela" [Short story]. *Masarykův Slovník naučný,* vol. 5, p. 230. Prague: Čs. kompas, 1931. Encyclopedia entry.

22. "Óda" [Ode]. Ibid., vol. 5, p. 297–98.

23. "La phonologie et la poétique." *Travaux du Cercle linguistique de Prague,* vol. 4, *Réunion phonologique internationale tenue à Prague,* pp. 278–88. Prague: Jednota českých matematiků a fyziků, 1931.

24. "Eufonie Theerových *Výprav k Já*" [Euphony in Theer's *Výpravy k Já*]. *Listy filologické* 58 (1931): 167–86, 326–28.

25. "Karel Čapek: *Povídky z jedné kapsy.*" *Nové Čechy* 14 (1931): 128–30. Review.

26. "Chaplin ve *Světlech velkoměsta.* (Pokus o strukturní rozbor hereckého zjevu)" [Chaplin in City Lights: An attempt at a structural analysis of a dramatic figure]. *Literární noviny* 5 (1930–31): 2–3.

27. "Umělcova osobnost v zrcadle díla. (Několik kritických poznámek k uměnovědné teorii a praxi)" [The artist's personality in the mirror of the work: Some critical remarks on the theory and practice of the study of art]. *Akord* 4 (1931): 253–63. Review.

28. "Básnické dílo jako soubor hodnot" [The poetic work as a set of

values]. *Jarní almanach Kmene. Jízdní řád literatury a poesie,* edited by Adolf Hoffmeister, pp. 118–26. Prague: Kmen, 1932.

29. "Jazyk spisovný a jazyk básnický" [Standard language and poetic language]. *Spisovná čestina a jazyková kultura,* edited by Bohuslav Havránek and Miloš Weingart, pp. 123–56. Prague: Melantrich, 1932.

30. "K problémům českého symbolismu. Poesie Karla Hlaváčka" [On the problems of Czech Symbolism: The poetry of Karel Hlaváček]. *Charisteria Guilelmo Mathesio quinquagenario a discipulis et Circuli linguistici Pragensis sodalibus oblata,* pp. 118–25. Prague: Pražský linguistický kroužek, 1932.

31. "Masaryk jako stylista" [Masaryk as stylist]. *Vůdce generací,* vol. 1, edited by Vasil Škrach, pp. 373–95. Prague: Čin, 1932.

32. "F. X. Šalda a teorie literatury" [F. X. Šalda and the theory of literature]. *F. X. Šaldovi k 22. prosinci 1932,* edited by Josef Hora, pp. 101–07. Prague: O. Girgal, 1932.

33. "Eufonie" [Euphony]. *Ottův Slovník naučný nové doby,* vol. 2/1, p. 471. Prague: J. Otto, 1931–32. Encyclopedia entry.

34. "Rozhovor s Janem Mukařovským. Rozmlouval Bohumil Novák" [An interview with Jan Mukařovský]. *Rozpravy Aventina* 7 (1931–32): 225–26.

35. "Padesátka prof. Viléma Mathesia" [Vilém Mathesius at fifty]. *Národní osvobození,* 3 August 1932, p. 3.

36. "Intonation comme facteur du rythme poétique." *Archives néerlandaises de phonétique expérimentale,* vol. 8–9, edited by F. J. J. Buytendijk et al, pp. 153–65. The Hague: M. Nijhoff, 1933.

37. "Poznámka o próze" [A note on prose]. *Mahenovi. Sborník k padesátinám,* edited by František Halas and Jiří Žantovský, pp. 125–27. Prague: Družstevní práce, 1933.

38. "K estetice filmu" [A note on the aesthetics of film]. *Listy pro umění a kritiku* 1 (1933): 172–78.

39. "Odpověď J. Mukařovského" [Jan Mukařovský's answer]. *Rozhledy po literatuře* 2 (1933): 25.

40. "O. Zich: *Estetika dramatického umění*" [The aesthetics of dramatic art]. *Časopis pro moderní filologii* 19 (1932–33): 318–26. Review.

41. "Obecné zásady a vývoj novočeského verše" [The general principles and development of modern Czech verse]. *Československá vlastivěda,* vol. 3, *Jazyk,* edited by Oldřich Hujer, pp. 376–429. Prague: Sfinx, 1934.

42. "Úvod" [Preface]. *Výbor z prózy Karla Čapka* [An anthology of Karel

Čapek's prose], edited by Jan Mukařovský, pp. 5–37. Prague: Státní nakladatelství, 1934.

43. "Hlaváčkovy *Žalmy*" [Hlaváček's *Žalmy*]. Karel Hlaváček: *Žalmy*, pp. 219–34. Prague: Melantrich, 1934. Preface.

44. "K českému překladu Šklovského *Teorie prózy*" [A note on the Czech translation of Šklovskij's Theory of Prose]. *Čin* 6 (1934): 123–30. Review.

45. "Několik poznámek k novému románu V. Vančury" [Some remarks on the latest novel by Vladislav Vančura]. *Listy pro umění a kritiku* 2 (1934): 297–303.

46. "Komično" [The comic]. *Ottův Slovník naučný nové doby*, vol. 3/1, p. 661. Prague: J. Otto, 1933–34. Encyclopedia entry.

47. "Několik poznámek k nové Nezvalově sbírce" [Some remarks on the latest collection of verse by Nezval]. *Panorama* 12 (1934): 70–72.

48. "O rytmu v moderním českém básnictví a o českém volném verši" [On rhythm in modern Czech poetry and on Czech free verse]. *Čin* 6 (1934): 531–38.

49. "Polákova *Vznešenost přírody*. Pokus o rozbor a vývojové zařadění básnické struktury" [Polák's *Vznešenost přírody:* An attempt at an analysis and historical classification of a poetic structure]. *Sborník filologický* 10 (1934–35): 1–68.

50. "Krása" [Beauty]. *Ottův Slovník naučný nové doby*, vol. 3/2, p. 825. Prague: J. Otto, 1934–35. Encyclopedia entry.

51. "Filosofie a životní praxe" [Philosophy and everyday life]. *Radiojournal*, 25 July 1934, p. 1.

52. "Prof. dr. Otakar Zich." *Universita Karlova v roce 1933–34*, pp. 107–10. Prague: Akademický senát University Karlovy, 1935. Obituary.

53. "Estetická funkce a estetická norma jako sociální fakty" [Aesthetic function and aesthetic norm as social facts]. *Sociální problémy* 4 (1935): 89–104, 197–213, 284–94.

54. "Dialektické rozpory v moderním umění" [Dialectic contradictions in modern art]. *Listy pro umění a kritiku* 3 (1935): 344–57.

55. "Úvodem" [By way of introduction]. With Bohuslav Havránek, Roman Jakobson, Vilém Mathesius and Bohumil Trnka. *Slovo a slovesnost* 1 (1935): 1–7. Programmatic statement introducing the journal of the Prague Linguistic Circle.

56. "Poznámky k sociologii básnického jazyka" [Notes on the sociology of poetic language]. *Slovo a slovesnost* 1 (1935): 29–38.

57. "V sekci literárněhistorické" [In the section on literary history]. *Slovo*

a slovesnost 1 (1935): 68–70. Report on the 2nd International Congress of Slavicists.

58. "Vztah mezi sovětskou a československou literární vědou" [The relation between Soviet and Czechoslovakian literary theory]. *Země Sovětů* 4 (1935–36): 10–15.

59. "Lyrika" [The lyric]. *Ottův slovník naučný nové doby*, vol. 3/2, pp. 1333–34. Prague: J. Otto, 1934–35. Encyclopedia entry.

60. "Může býti dvouslabičné slovo veršem? – Může býti básní rozčleněná próza" [Can a two-syllable word be a line of verse? Can rhythmic prose become poetry?]. *Studentský časopis*, 10 May 1935, pp. 229–30.

61. "Vítězslav Hálek." *Slovo a slovesnost* 1 (1935): 73–87.

62. "Die Phonologie im Vordergrund. Vom II. internationalen Kongress der Lautwissenschaft." *Prager Presse*, 13 August 1935, p. 5.

63. "Replika J. Mukařovského" [Jan Mukařovský's reply]. *Slovo a slovesnost* 1 (1935): 190–92.

64. "Roztříštěný Bezručův verš" [The fractured verse of Bezruč]. *Slovo a slovesnost* 1 (1935): 234–38. Review.

65. "Odborné mezinárodní sjezdy v létě 1935" [International scholarly congresses in the summer of 1935]. *Slovo a slovesnost* 1 (1935): 247–48.

66. "Postavy a díla" [Personalities and works]. *Slovo a slovesnost* 1 (1935): 251–52. Book report.

67. *Estetická funkce, norma a hodnota jako sociální fakty* [Aesthetic function, norm and value as social facts], 88 pp. Prague: F. Borový, 1936. Expanded version of no. 53.

68. "L'art comme fait sémiologique." *Actes du Huitième Congrès international de philosophie à Prague 2–7 septembre 1934*, edited by Emanuel Rádl and Zdeněk Smetáček, pp. 1065–72. Prague: Organizační komitét kongresu, 1936.

69. "Příspěvek k dnešní problematice básnického zjevu Máchova" [A contribution to the current discussion of Mácha's poetic personality]. *Listy pro umění a kritiku* 4 (1936): 25–33, 62–73.

70. "Diskuse o studiu básnického jazyka" [Debate on the study of poetic language]. *Časopis pro moderní filologii* 22 (1935–36): 203–07. Polemical exchange.

71. "Protichůdci. Několik poznámek o vztahu Erbenova básnického díla k Máchovu" [Antipodes: Some remarks on the relationship of Erben's poetic works to Mácha's]. *Slovo a slovesnost* 2 (1936): 33–43.

72. "K. H. Máchas Werk als Torso und Geheimnis." *Slavische Rundschau* 8 (1936): 213–20.

73. "Linguistický sjezd v Kodani" [The linguistic congress in Copenhagen]. *České slovo*, 18 September 1936, p. 8.

74. "Prameny poesie" [The sources of poetry]. *Listy pro umění a kritiku* 4 (1936): 404–06.

75. "K novému vydání *Francouzské poesie* Karla Čapka" [On the new edition of Karel Čapek's French Poetry]. *Slovo a slovesnost* 2 (1936): 253–55.

76. "K problému funkcí v architektuře" [On the problem of functions in architecture]. *Stavba* 14 (1936–37): 5–12. Lecture.

77. "L'individu dans l'art." *Deuxième Congrès international d'esthétique et de la science de l'art*, vol. 1, pp. 349–54. Paris: F. Alcan, 1937.

78. "Je již osud věd . . ." [It is the fate of the sciences]. *A. S. Mágrovi k padesátým narozeninám 6. dubna 1937*, edited by Antonín Hartl, pp. 23–24. Prague: Kruh přátel, 1937.

79. "La norme esthétique." *Travaux du IXe Congrès international de philosophie*, vol. 12/3, edited by Raymond Bayer, pp. 72–79. Paris: Hermann, 1937.

80. "Mánes mládeži" [Mánes for young people]. *Řeči účastníků slavnostního projevu o výtvarném umění pro mládež . . . 9. dubna 1937*, pp. 4–5. Prague: Spolek výtvarných umělců Mánes, 1937. Speech.

81. "Poetika" [Poetics]. *Ottův Slovník naučný nové doby*, vol. 4/2, pp. 1181–83, Prague: Novina, 1936–37. Encyclopedia entry.

82. "O jevištním dialogu" [On stage dialogue]. *Program D*^{37}, 31 March 1937, pp. 232–34.

83. "F. X. Šalda." *Slovo a slovesnost* 3 (1937): 65–78. Obituary.

84. "F. X. Šalda." *Čin* 9 (1937): 53. Obituary.

85. "Stav naší dnešní estetiky" [The state of our current aesthetics]. *Čin* 9 (1937): 70–71. Interview.

86. "Šaldova dramatičnost" [Šalda's sense of the dramatic]. *Listy pro umění a kritiku* 5 (1937): 193–96.

87. "IX. filosofický sjezd v Paříži" [The 9th Philosophical Congress in Paris]. *Slovo a slovesnost* 3 (1937): 172–79.

88. "Kongres pro estetiku a vědu o umění" [The Congress on Aesthetics and Theory of Art]. *Slovo a slovesnost* 3 (1937): 187.

89. "Estetička funkcija kao socijalna činjenica." *Ars*, 1937, pp. 79–86. Croatian translation of the first chapter of no. 67.

90. "Dénomination poétique et la fonction esthétique de la langue." *Actes du Quatrième Congrès international des linguistes tenu à Copenhague du 27 août au 1er septembre 1936*, edited by Louis Hjelmslev et al, pp. 98–104. Copenhagen: E. Munksgaard, 1938.

91. "Genetika smyslu v Máchově poesii" [The genesis of meaning in Mácha's poetry]. *Torso a tajemství Máchova díla. Sborník pojednání Pražského linguistického kroužku* [The torso and the mystery of Mácha's work: A collection of studies of the Prague Linguistic Circle], edited by Jan Mukařovský, pp. 13–110. Prague: F. Borový, 1938.

92. "F. X. Šalda." *Universita Karlova v roce 1936–37*, pp. 53–60. Prague: Akademický senát University Karlovy, 1938. Obituary.

93. "F. Žákavec jako generační typ" [F. Žákavec as a representative of a generation]. *Chodsko. Věstník Baarovy společnosti* 2 (1938): 6–7.

94. "Trojí podoba T. G. Masaryka. (Několik poznámek k problematice plastického portrétu)" [The threefold image of T. G. Masaryk: Some remarks on the problems of vivid portraiture]. *Lidové noviny*, 27 February 1938, supplement, pp. 56–60.

95. "Sémantický rozbor básnického díla: Nezvalův *Absolutní hrobař*" [The semantic analysis of a poetic work: Nezval's *Absolutní hrobař*]. *Slovo a slovesnost* 4 (1938): 1–15.

96. "Situace moderního umění" [The situation in modern art]. *Právo lidu*, 5 June 1938, supplement, pp. 266–68.

97. "K noetice a poetice surrealismu v malířství" [On the epistemology and poetics of Surrealism in painting]. *Slovenské smery umelecké a kritické* 5 (1937–38): 226–30.

98. "Nezval německy" [Nezval in German]. *Slovo a slovesnost* 4 (1938): 245–49.

99. "La langue poétique." *Rapports du Vme Congrès international des linguistes, Bruxelles 28 aôut – 2 septembre 1939*, pp. 94–102. Bruges, 1939.

100. "Srovnávací slovanská metrika orientovaná fonologicky" [Comparative Slavic metrics on a phonological basis]. *Zbirka odgovora na pitanja – Réponses aux questions. 18. – 25. IX. 1939. IIIème Congrès international des slavistes*, pp. 161–63. Belgrade: Publications du comité d'organisation.

101. "La valeur esthétique dans l'art peut-elle être universelle?" *Les conceptions modernes de la raison*, vol. 3, *Raison et valeur*. Publications de l'Institut international de collaboration philosophique, vol. 3, pp. 17–29. Paris: Institut international de collaboration philosophique, 1939.

102. "Karel Čapek. Ein Exotiker aus dem Geiste der tschechischen Sprache." *Slavische Rundschau* 11 (1939): 3–6.

103. "Karel Čapek – spisovatel" [Karel Čapek: Writer]. *Přítomnost*, 8 March 1939, pp. 156–57.

104. "Próza Karla Čapka jako lyrická melodie a dialog" [Karel Čapek's prose as lyrical melody and as dialogue]. *Slovo a slovesnost* 5 (1939): 1–12.

105. "Dvě knihy pamětí z českého obrození" [Two memoirs from the Czech National Revival]. *Slovo a slovesnost* 5 (1939): 58–59. Book report.

106. "Významová výstavba a kompoziční osnova epiky Karla Čapka" [The semantic structure and compositional scheme of Karel Čapek's narrative]. *Slovo a slovesnost* 5 (1939): 113–31.

107. "Josef Král a dnešní stav české metriky i prosodie. Několik poznámek na okraj Rybova vydání II. části spisu *O prosodii české*" [Josef Král and Czech metrics and prosody today: Some marginal notes on Ryba's edition of the 2nd part of On Czech Prosody]. *Slavia* 17 (1939–40): 282–93.

108. "Arne Novák, literární historik a kritik" [Arne Novák: Literary historian and critic]. *Lidové noviny*, 28 November 1939, p. 7. Obituary.

109. "Arne Novák zemřel. Věnováno návštěvníkům tryzny dne 8. ledna 1940" [Arne Novák is dead]. Published privately, pp. 9–17. Prague: Kmen, 1940.

110. "Nové německé dílo o základech literární vědy. (Marginálie ke knize J. Petersena *Die Wissenschaft von der Dichtung*)" [A new German work on the principles of literary study: Marginal notes on Julius Petersen's Die Wissenschaft von der Dichtung]. *Slovo a slovesnost* 5 (1939): 210–16.

111. "Upravovat staré texty?" [Should we reedit old texts?]. *Hovory o knihách*, 21 December 1939, pp. 6–7. Answer to a poll.

112. "Tradice tvaru" [The tradition of form]. *Strážce tradice. Arne Novákovi na památku*, edited by Jiří Horák, Albert Pražák and Julius Heidenreich, pp. 265–77. Prague-Olomouc: F. Borový-R. Promberger, 1940.

113. "Perský básník v češtine" [A Persian poet in Czech]. *Literární noviny*, February 1940, pp. 40–41.

114. "Estetika jazyka" [The aesthetics of language]. *Slovo a slovesnost* 6 (1940): 1–27.

115. "Dialog a monolog" [Dialogue and monologue]. *Listy filologické (Oldřichu Hujerovi k šedesátým narozeninám)* 76 (1940): 139–60.

116. "Strukturální estetika" [Structural aesthetics]. *Ottův Slovník naučný nové doby*, vol. 6/1, pp. 452–55. Prague: Novina, 1939–40. Encyclopedia entry.

117. "Strukturální věda o literatuře" [The structural study of literature]. Ibid., pp. 457–59.

118. "Profesor Albert Pražák šedesátiletý" [Professor Albert Pražák at sixty]. *Čteme* 2 (1939–40): 183–84.

119. "Kniha o básnickém řemesle" [A book on poetic craft]. *Lidové noviny*, 17 September 1940, p. 7. Review.

120. "O jazyce básnickém" [On poetic language]. *Slovo a slovesnost* 6 (1940): 113-45.

121. "Šklovskij, Viktor Borisovič." *Ottův Slovník naučný nové doby*, vol. 6/2, pp. 744-45. Prague: Novina, 1940-43. Encyclopedia entry.

122. *Kapitoly z české poetiky*. Díl I. *Obecné věci básnictví* [Chapters in Czech poetics, vol. 1, General topics of poetry]. Contains author's preface (pp. 9-12) and nos. 15, 19, 28, 36, 44, 56, 82, 83, 90, 107, 109, 112, 114, 115, 116, 117 and 120, all in Czech. 332 pp. Prague: Melantrich, 1941.

123. *Kapitoly z české poetiky*. Díl II. *K vývoji české poesie a prózy* [Chapters in Czech poetics, vol. 2, Toward the development of Czech poetry and prose]. Contains nos. 6, 24, 30 (revised), 41 (rev.), 42, 43 (rev.), 48, 49, 54, 61, 69, 72, 75, 95, 104 and 106. 524 pp. Prague: Melantrich, 1941.

124. "Poesie v malířském díle Jana Zrzavého" [Poetry in the work of the painter Jan Zrzavý]. *Dílo Jana Zrzavého 1906-1940*, edited by Karel Šroubek, pp. 66-74. Prague: Umělecká beseda-Družstevní práce, 1941.

125. "K dnešnímu stavu teorie divadla" [On the current state of the theory of theater]. *Program D*^{41}, 28 January 1941, pp. 229-42.

126. "Mezi poesií a výtvarnictvím" [Between literature and visual arts]. *Slovo a slovesnost* 7 (1941): 253-74.

127. "Tendenční umění" [Tendentious art]. *Ottův Slovník naučný nové doby*, vol. 6/2, pp. 1048-49. Prague: Novina, 1940-43. Encyclopedia entry.

128. "Od básníka k dílu. V. Vančura" [From the poet to his work: Vladislav Vančura]. *Panorama* 19 (1941): 87-89.

129. "O několika českých prací z poetiky" [On several Czech studies in poetics]. *Slovo a slovesnost* 7 (1941): 156-61. Review.

130. "Jak užívat slov?" [How should one use words?]. *Eva*, 1 November 1941, p. 7. Radio lecture.

131. "Předmluva" [Introduction]. *Čtení o jazyce a poesii* [Readings on language and literature], edited by Bohuslav Havránek and Jan Mukařovský, pp. 7-9 (with Bohuslav Havránek). Prague: Družstevní práce, 1942.

132. "Strukturalismus pro každého" [Structuralism for everyone]. *Čteme* 4 (1942): 55-58. Interview.

133. "Nová kniha studií o Janu Nerudovi" [A new book of essays on Jan Neruda]. *Slovo a slovesnost* 8 (1942): 152-60.

134. "O několika českých pracích z poetiky" [On several Czech studies in poetics]. *Slovo a slovesnost* 8 (1942): 165–66. Polemical exchange.

135. "Poetika jako základ literární výchovy na střední škole" [Poetics as the basis of literary education in high school]. *Střední škola* 50 (1942–43): 205–15.

136. "Dvě knihy o básnících" [Two books about poets]. *Slovo a slovesnost* 9 (1943): 145–51. Review.

137. "K teorii recitace" [On the theory of recitation]. *Slovo a slovesnost* 9 (1943): 163–64. Review.

138. "K literárnímu odkazu Věry Liškové" [On the literary legacy of Věra Lišková]. *Posmrtný odlitek z prací Věry Liškové*, edited by Bohuslav Havránek, pp. 5–8. Prague: Melantrich, 1945. Introduction.

139. "O Vladislavu Vančurovi. (Přednáška proslovená při tryzně v domě Vladislava Vančury dne 12. června 1945.)" [Vladislav Vančura: A commemorative speech delivered at Vladislav Vančura's house on 12 June 1945]. *Tvorba*, 2 August 1945, pp. 42–44.

140. "O Vladislavu Vančurovi, básníku a člověku" [Vladislav Vančura, poet and man]. *Panorama*, 25 October 1945, pp. 35–38.

141. "K premiéře Koptovy hry *Blázen Kabrnos*" [The opening of Kopta's play *Blázen Kabrnos*]. *Rudé právo*, 30 October 1945, p. 3.

142. "Poetic Nomenclature and the Aesthetic Function of Language." *Review*, Winter 1945, pp. 152–57. Translation of no. 90.

143. "Předmluva" [Preface]. Karel Honzík: *Tvorba životního slohu. Stati o architektuře a užitkové tvorbě vůbec* [The creation of a life style. Articles on architecture and functional design in general], pp. 7–19. Prague: V. Petr, 1946.

144. "Jindřich Štýrský." *Jindřich Štýrský. 364. výstava Spolku výtvarných umělců Mánes 4. – 25. dubna 1946*, pp. 4–8. Prague: Spolek výtvarných umělců Mánes, 1946. Introduction to exhibition catalogue.

145. "Vladislav Vančura, écrivain et résistant." *Tchéchoslovaquie* 1 (1946–47): 15–18.

146. "Postavení a úkoly inteligence v národním životě" [The place and tasks of the intelligentsia in national life]. *Rudé právo*, 9 January 1946, p. 1.

147. "K umělecké situaci dnešního českého divadla" [On the artistic state of contemporary Czech theater]. *Otázky divadla a filmu* 1 (1945–46): 61–65.

148. "*Pražský žid*. Na okraj premiéry" [*Pražský žid:* The opening night]. *Program Národního divadla* 1945–46, pp. 2–3.

149. "K otázce takzvané orientace" [On the question of so-called orientation]. *Tvorba*, 6 March 1946, pp. 148–49.

150. "V. Vančura – mrtvý čtyři roky" [Vladislav Vančura: Four years since his death]. *Mladá fronta*, 30 May 1946, p. 4.

151. "V. Vančura, hrdina a básník" [Vladislav Vančura: Hero and poet]. *Rudé právo*, 1 June 1946, p. 4.

152. "Dnešný stav slovenskej poézie" [The current state of Slovak poetry]. *Kultúrny život* 1 (1946): 3-7.

153. "Zúčtování a výhledy" [Retrospect and prospects]. *Tvorba*, 26 June 1946, pp. 408-11.

154. "Toyen za války" [Toyen during the war]. *Doba* 1 (1946-47): 46-48. Speech at exhibition opening.

155. "Francie vzdala hold V. Vančurovi" [France has honored Vladislav Vančura]. *Rudé právo*, 24 July 1946, p. 4. Excerpt from a speech delivered at the Sorbonne.

156. "K sémantice básnického obrazu" [A note on the semantics of the poetic image]. *Kvart* 5 (1946-49): 19-24.

157. "Ce qu'on appelle orientation." *Europe* 24 (1946): 133-38. Translation of no. 149.

158. "O recitačním umění" [On the art of recitation]. *Program D^{47}*, 21 December 1946, pp. 107-13.

159. "Básnické slovo a skutečnost" [The poetic word and reality]. *Čeština v životě a ve škole. Cyklus rozhlasových přednášek*, edited by Jaroslav Zima and Alois Jedlička, pp. 36-40. Prague: Zemská školní rada, 1947. Radio lecture.

160. "Předmluva" [Introduction]. Bohuslav Havránek – Jan Mukařovský – Felix Vodička: *O básnickém jazyce. Cyklus rozhlasových přednášek* [On poetic language: A series of radio broadcasts]. Prague: Svoboda, pp. 5-6.

161. "Jazyk, který básní" [Language which makes poetry]. *Ibid.*, pp. 7-17.

162. "Básnický jazyk a společnost" [Poetic language and society]. *Ibid.*, pp. 42-51.

163. "Šalda stále živý" [Šalda is still alive]. *F. X. Š. Soubor díla F. X. Šaldy*, pp. 3-6. Prague: Melantrich, 1947.

164. "F. X. Šalda, kritik národního života" [F. X. Šalda: A critic of national life]. *Tvorba*, 2 April 1947, pp. 233-37.

165. "F. X. Šalda, zakladatel české literární kritiky" [F. X. Šalda: The founder of Czech literary criticism]. *Rudé právo*, 4 April 1947, p. 2.

166. "Země česká poctívá umělce" [Bohemia honors its artists]. *Tvorba*, 14 May 1947, pp. 357-58. Speech.

167. "K desátému výroči úmrtí F. X. Šaldy. Proslov při premiéře Racinovy *Faidry* ve Stavovském divadle"[On the 10th anniversary of F. X. Šalda's

death: A speech at the opening night of Racine's *Phèdre* in the Stavovský Theater]. *Otázky divadla a filmu* 2 (1947): 181–89.

168. "Za Vilémem Mathesiem" [Vilém Mathesius in memoriam]. *Slovo a slovesnost* 10 (1947–48): 1–4.

169. "Nizámího *Sedm princezen.* Referát a několik poznámek k otázkám básnické translatury" [Nizámi's *Sedm princezen:* A report and some remarks on the problems of literary translation]. *Slovo a slovesnost* 10 (1947–48): 42–50.

170. "O ideologii czechoslowackiej teorii sztuki" [On the conceptual basis of the Czechoslovakian theory of art]. *Myśl współczesna* 2 (1947): 342–51. In Polish.

171. "Umění a světový názor" [Art and world view]. *Slovo a slovesnost* 10 (1947–48): 65–72.

172. *Kapitoly z české poetiky.* Díl I. *Obecné věci básnictví* [Chapters in Czech poetics, vol. 1, General topics of poetry]. 2d ed. of no. 122. Expanded by nos. 126, 149, 153, 156, 158, and 170. 352 pp. Prague: Svoboda, 1948.

173. *Kapitoly z české poetiky.* Díl II. *K vývoji české poesie a prózy* [Chapters in Czech poetics, vol. 2, Toward the development of Czech poetry and prose]. 2d ed. of no. 123. Expanded by nos. 31, 139, and 140; nos. 69 and 72 transferred to no. 174. 448 pp. Prague: Svoboda, 1948.

174. *Kapitoly z české poetiky.* Díl III. *Máchovské studie* [Chapters in Czech poetics, vol. 3, Studies on Mácha]. Contains author's afterword (p. 327), bibliography (pp. 311–25), and nos. 10, 69, 72, and 91. 322 pp. Prague: Svoboda, 1948.

175. "Předmluva" [Preface]. Boris Mejlach: *Lenin a kultura. Lenin a problémy ruské literatury konce 19. a začátku 20. století* [Lenin and culture: Lenin and problems in Russian literature of the end of the nineteenth century and the beginning of the twentieth century], pp. 9–14. Prague: Mladá fronta, 1948.

176. "Poznámky vydavatelovy" [Editor's notes]. F. X. Salda: *Boje o zítřek. Meditace a rapsódie,* edited by Jan Mukařovský, pp. 195–96. Prague: Melantrich, 1948.

177. "Vztah mezi individuem a kolektivem . . ." [The relationship between the individual and the collective]. *Účtování a výhledy. Sborník Prvního sjezdu českých spisovatelů,* edited by Jan Kopecký, pp. 81–82. Prague: Syndikát českých spisovatelů, 1948. Speech.

178. "Ke Sjezdu národní kultury" [The Congress of National Culture]. *Rudé právo,* 10 April 1948, p. 1.

179. "K třetímu dílu Vančurových *Obrazů*" [A note on the third volume of Vančura's *Obrazy*]. *Svobodné noviny,* 4 May 1948, p. 5.

180. "Šest let bez Vančury" [Six years without Vančura]. *Tvorba*, 2 June 1948, p. 436.

181. "D^{34} – D^{48} ve vývoji českého divadla" [D^{34} – D^{48} in the development of Czech theater]. *Umělecký měsíčník D*^{48}, 10 June 1948, pp. 326-27.

182. "Několik slov na uvítanou Národní knihovně" [Words to welcome the National Library]. *Rudé právo*, 1 October 1948, p. 4.

183. "Kam směřuje dnešní theorie umění?" [What is the direction of current theory of art?]. *Slovo a slovesnost* 11 (1948-49): 49-59.

184. "Ke kritice strukturalismu v naší literární vědě" [On the criticism of structuralism in our literary studies]. *Tvorba*, 4 October 1951, pp. 964-66.

185. "Standard Language and Poetic Language," "The Aesthetics of Language," "The Connection between the Prosodic Line and Word Order in Czech Verse," "K. Čapek's Prose as Lyrical Melody and as Dialogue." *A Prague School Reader on Aesthetics, Literary Structure, and Style.* Selected and translated by Paul L. Garvin, pp. 17-30, 31-61, 113-32 and 133-49. Washington, D.C.: Georgetown University Press, 1964. Translations of nos. 29, 114, 15, and 104.

186. *Studie z estetiky* [Studies in aesthetics]. Contains author's afterword (p. 337), nos. 26, 28, 38, 45, 52, 54, 67, 68, 74, 77, 79, 90, 92, 95, 96, 97, 101, 124, 125, 128, 143, 144, 147, 154, 156, 170, 171, 181, and previously unpublished studies:
    a. "Význam estetiky" [The significance of aesthetics]. (1942)
    b. "Úkoly obecné estetiky" [The tasks of general aesthetics]. (early 1940s)
    c. "Místo estetické funkce mezi ostatními" [The place of the aesthetic function among the other functions]. (1942)
    d. "Záměrnost a nezáměrnost v umění" [Intentionality and unintentionality in art]. (1943)
    e. "O strukturalismu" [On structuralism]. (1946)
    f. "Umění" [Art]. (1943)
    g. "Básník" [The poet]. (1941)
    h. "Jevištní řeč v avantgardním divadle" [Stage language in avant-garde theater]. (1937)
    i. "Čas ve filmu" [Time in film]. (late 1930s)
    j. "Podstata výtvarných umění" [The essence of the visual arts]. (1944)
    k. "Detail jako základní sémantická jednotka v lidovém umění" [Detail as the basic semantic unit in folk art]. (1942)
    l. "Individuum a literární vývoj" [The individual and literary development]. (1943-45)
    m "Osobnost v umění" [Personality in art]. (1944)
    n. "Josef Šíma." (1936)

o. "Otakar Zich." (1934)
all in Czech. 375 pp. Prague: Odeon, 1966.

187. "Jana Mukařovského cesta k vědě." Zapsal Jaroslav Jirsa" [Jan Mukařovský's path to scholarship]. *Student*, 8 November 1966, p. 3. Interview.

188. "Rozhovor s Janem Mukařovským. Rozmlouval Vítězslav Rzounek" [An interview with Jan Mukařovský]. *Impuls*, 20 November 1966, pp. 814-18.

189. "Chybí vůle něco chtít? Rozmlouvaly Jitka Šestáková and Táňa Štěpánková" [Is the will to accomplish gone?]. *UK* (=Univerzita Karlova), 16 December 1966, p. 2. Interview.

190. "O języku poetyckim." *Prazka szkoła strukturalna w latach 1926-1948* [The Prague school of structuralism: 1926-1948], edited by M. R. Mayenowa, pp. 130-206. Warsaw: Państwowe wydawnictvo naukowe, 1966. Polish translation by W. Gorny of no. 120.

191. "Literaturnyj jazyk i poetičeskij jazyk." *Pražskij lingvistíčeskij kružok* [The Prague Linguistic Circle], edited by N. A. Kondrakov, pp. 406-31. Moscow: Progress, 1967. Russian translation by A. G. Širokova of no. 29.

192. *Kapitel aus der Poetik.* Translated by Walter Schamschula. 160 pp. Frankfurt am Main: Suhrkamp. German translation of nos. 28, 42, 82, 90, 115, 116 and 117.

193. "K metodologii literární vědy" [On the methodology of literary study]. *Orientace* 3 (1968): 29-38. Previously unpublished study of 1944.

194. "Básník a dílo" [The poet and the work]. *Orientace* 3 (1968): 51-57. Previously unpublished study from mid-1940s.

195. "Pojem celku v teorii umění" [The concept of the whole in the theory of art]. *Estetika* 5 (1968): 173-81. Previously unpublished lecture of 1945.

196. "Varianten und Stilistik." *Poetica* 2 (1968): 399-403. German translation by Wolf and Herta Schmid of no. 19.

197. "Formalisme russe et structuralisme tchèque," "Entretien avec Jan Mukařovský," "Plan graphique, phonologie et poétique." *Le Cercle de Prague* (=*Change*, no. 3), edited by J. P. Faye and Léon Robel, pp. 54-59, 65-68, 88-90. Paris: Seuil, 1969. French translation by O. Kulik of no. 63 and reprint of part of no. 23.

198. "Structure, mode, demande." *La mode: l'invention* (=*Change*, no. 4), edited by J. P. Faye et al, pp. 208-22. Paris: Seuil, 1969. French translation by O. Kulik of parts of no. 67.

199. "Trois conférences sur la culture de la manifestation parlée. 1. La

parole, le geste, la mimique. 2. La culture de la voix. 3. L'art de la conversation." *Acta Universitatis Carolinae. Philosophica et historica* 5 (1969): 7–19. Translation by E. Dvořák of radio broadcasts of 1940.

200. *Aesthetic Function, Norm and Value as Social Facts*, Michigan Slavic Contributions, vol. 3. Translated with notes and afterword by Mark E. Suino. 102 pp. Ann Arbor, Mich.: Department of Slavic Languages and Literatures, 1970. Translation of no. 67.

201. *Kapitel aus der Aesthetik*. Translated by Walter Schamschula. 160 pp. Frankfurt am Main: Suhrkamp, 1970. German translation of nos. 67, 68, and 186c.

202. *Wśród znaków i struktur. Wybór szkiców* [Among signs and structures. A selection of articles], edited with an introduction by Janusz Sławiński. 392 pp. Warsaw: Państwowy instytut wydawniczy, 1970. Polish translation by Jacek Baluch, M. R. Mayenowa, Józef Mayen, and Lucylla Pszczołowska of nos. 26, 36, 56, 67, 82, 90, 95, 104, 115, 125, 156, 186e, 186i, and 186l.

203. "Littérature et sémiologie." *Poétique* 1 (1970): 386–98. Reprints of nos. 68 and 90.

204. *Cestami poetiky a estetiky* [On the track of poetics and aesthetics]. Contains author's afterword, nos. 17, 27, 28, 71, 74, 161, 193, 194, 195, and previously unpublished studies:
    a. "Problémy estetické hodnoty" [Problems of aesthetic value]. (1935–36)
    b. "Problémy estetické normy" [Problems of aesthetic norm]. (1935–39)
    c. "Problémy individua v umění" [Problems of the individual in art]. (1946–47)
    d. "Vančurovská prolegomena" [Prolegomena to Vančura]. (I. 1940; II. 1945–49)
    e. "Přísloví jako součást kontextu" [The proverb as a component of context]. (1942–43)
    368 pp. Prague: Československý spisovatel, 1971.

205. *La funzione, la norma e il valore estetico come fatti sociali. Semiologia e sociologia dell' arte*. Translated with introduction and notes by Sergio Corduas. 200 pp. Turin: G. Einaudi, 1971. Italian translation of nos. 67, 68, 186a, and 186e.

206. "Zur tschechischen Übersetzung von Šklovskij's *Theorie der Prosa*." *alternative*, no. 80 (1971), pp. 166–71. German translation by Hans Günther of no. 44.

207. *Arte y semiología*. Translated with an introduction by Simon Marchan Fiz and I. P. Hloznik. Madrid: Alberto Corazón, 1971.

208. "Mer amanite bleue." *Prague Poesie Front Gauche* (=*Change* no. 10), edited by Henri Deluy, Elisabeth Roudinesco et al, pp. 215-16. Paris: Seghers/Laffont, 1972. French translation by Henri Deluy of a part of no. 47.

209. *Il significato dell' estetica.* Translated by Sergio Corduas. 477 pp. Turin: G. Einaudi, 1973. Italian translation of nos. 26, 28, 38, 67, 76, 77, 79, 90, 101, 125, 143, 156, 170, 171, 186a, 186b, 186c, 186d, 186e, 186f, 186g, 186h, 186i, 186j, 186k, 186l, and 186m.

210. "Zur Ästhetik des Films," "Die Zeit im Film." *Poetik des Films.* Edited and translated by Wolfgang Beilenhof, pp. 119-30, 131-38. Munich: Wilhelm Fink, 1974. German translation of nos. 38 and 186i.

211. *Studien zur strukturalistischen Aesthetik und Poetik.* Translated by Herbert Grönebaum and Gisela Riff, with an afterword and notes. 328 pp. Munich: Carl Hanser, 1974. German translation of nos. 17, 54, 95, 155, 120, 126, 139, 156, 170, 195, 186d, and 186m.

212. *Studii de estetică.* Translated with introduction and notes by Corneliu Barborică. 466 pp. Bucarest: Univers, 1974. Rumanian translation of nos. 28, 36, 67, 68, 76, 114, 120, 156, 170, 186c, 186d, 186f, 186j, and 186l.

213. "K češskomu perevodu *Teorii prozy* Šklovskogo," "Prednamerennoe i neprednamerennoe v isskustve." *Strukturalizm: "za" i "protiv."* *Sbornik statej* [Structuralism: "For" and "against": A collection of essays], edited by E. J. Basin and M. J. Poljakov, pp. 27-36 and 164-92. Moscow: Progress, 1975. Russian translation of nos. 44 and 186d.

214. "Estetičeskaja funkcija, norma i cennost' kak social'nye fakty." *Trudy po znakovym sistemam* 7 (1975): 243-95. Russian translation by V. A. Kamenskaja of no. 67.

215. *On Poetic Language.* Translated and edited by John Burbank and Peter Steiner, postscript by Peter and Wendy Steiner. 88 pp. Lisse: The Peter de Ridder Press, 1976. Translation of no. 120.

216. "Art as Semiotic Fact," "Poetic Reference," "The Essence of the Visual Arts." *Semiotics of Art: Prague School Contributions,* edited by Ladislav Matejka and Irwin R. Titunik, pp. 3-9, 155-63, 229-44. Cambridge, Mass., and London, England: The MIT Press, 1976. Translations by I. R. Titunik, S. Janecek, J. Burbank, and P. Steiner of nos. 68, 90, and 126.

217. *The Word and Verbal Art: Selected Essays by Jan Mukařovský,* Yale Russian and East European Studies, 13. Translated and edited by John Burbank and Peter Steiner, with a foreword by René Wellek. 238 pp. New Haven and London: Yale University Press, 1977. Translation of nos. 36, 44, 82, 90, 115, 120, 126, 156, 186g, 186k, and 186l.

Index